D1500021

FEAR OF FRYING

A Sensible Approach to Quick & Easy, Healthy,
Low-Fat Eating for the Busy Family

Virginia N. White

with

Rosa A. Mo, R.D.

C H R O N I M E D
P U B L I S H I N G

Library of Congress Cataloging-in-Publication Data

White, Virginia N.

Fear of frying: a sensible approach to quick and easy, healthy, low-fat eating for the busy family / Virginia N. White with Rosa A. Mo, R.D.

     p   cm.

Includes index

ISBN 1-56561-091-1; $12.95

Edited by: Jolene Steffer and Jeff Braun
Cover Design: Garborg Design Works
Production: Judy Turner and David Enyeart
Art/Production Manager: Claire Lewis
Printed in the United States of America

Published by
Chronimed Publishing
P.O. Box 59032
Minneapolis, MN 55459-9686

10   9   8   7   6   5   4   3   2   1

Notice: Consult Your Health Care Professional

Readers are advised to seek the guidance of a licensed physician or health care professional before making any changes in prescribed diet or health care regimens, as each individual case or need may vary. This book is intended for informational purposes only and is not for use as an alternative to appropriate medical care. While every effort has been made to ensure that the information is the most current available, new research findings, being released with increasing frequency, may invalidate some data.

*This book is dedicated
to the memory of my mother,
who taught me to love the written word,
and in honor of my father,
who taught me to cook with love.*

Acknowledgments

This book is truly a collaborative effort that could not have been completed without the recipes and ideas of my family and friends. I want to thank everybody who donated favorite family recipes, most of which I modified to fit the goals of this book. As a small token of my gratitude, I have named the recipes after the contributors or identified the donor at the beginning of the recipe.

Special thanks go to Lorna Wendt and my husband, who both urged me to write a cookbook that would include quick, easy, and healthy recipes that would appeal to everyone in the family. My daughters, Christy and Julie, were the primary taste testers and deserve recognition and thanks for their willing spirit and sense of adventure.

I would like to thank Vicki Greene and Bob Moehl for helping me to finally put a name on this book.

Once again, it was a pleasure to work with Rosa Mo, whose good humor and vast knowledge about nutrition were very helpful. And thanks to everyone at Chronimed Publishing for helping to take the fear out of frying.

About the Recipes

The nutrition analysis for each recipe was done according to the following guidelines:

> If a recipe offers a choice of ingredient amounts, the recipe was analyzed for the higher amount. If a recipe offers a choice of ingredients, the ingredient with the higher fat or caloric content was used in the analysis. All optional ingredients were included in the analysis.

> Numbers were rounded to the nearest whole or half value.

> Finally, unless indicated, the smaller yield for the recipe was used to calculate the portion size, hence the resulting analysis is for the larger serving.

Nutrient analysis of recipes was performed using Nutritionist IV for Windows, Diet Analysis Module, Version 3.5 (First DataBank, N-Squared Computing, The Hearst Corporation, 1111 Bayhill Drive, San Bruno, CA 94066).

Table of Contents

Fear of Frying

Introduction

Whenever I teach cooking classes or speak to people interested in improving their eating habits, I hear the same lament: "I don't have the time to spend hours in the kitchen and learn about nutrition. Plus, my children won't eat that kind of food anyhow." Believe me, I understand. I, too, am a working mother who never has enough time, and I have a husband and children with selective taste buds and their own definitions of "healthy."

Still, we should not ignore the alarming statistics. More than half of all American adults and as many as one-fourth of our children have elevated cholesterol levels. According to the American Heart Association, one out of four Americans suffer from cardiovascular disease. Many doctors believe this is a direct result of the typical American diet that obtains over 40 percent of its total calories from fat and takes in 400 milligrams or more of cholesterol each day.[1] Despite the headline-making warnings over the past 15 years, coronary heart disease remains the number one cause of death in the United States, killing over half a million people each year.[2]

Yet, this health problem is not found all over the world, or even in all industrialized nations. Overwhelming research shows that our diet is one of the major reasons for this serious health problem. When high-cholesterol and high-fat diets are linked with smoking, obesity, and high stress, cardiovascular disease often results.

Given all this information, why don't we change our eating habits, take in less cholesterol and fat, and live longer and healthier lives? The answer is simple. We don't have time to change our cooking habits, and we don't like the taste of low-fat and low-cholesterol foods. This is complicated by the fact that some of us are scared of the foods we eat (fear of dying from frying) and scared of what we consider healthy but tasteless alternatives (fear of dying from boredom). As a result, many people become confused and give up.

That is why my family and friends urged me to tackle this problem. They wanted a cookbook that would take the fear out of healthy cooking and make it easy.

The need to create a practical, family-oriented low-fat and low-cholesterol cookbook became even clearer when I started teaching cooking classes to mothers of young children. I was amazed by what I learned. It seems that the new four food groups for many children are macaroni and cheese, hot dogs, chicken nuggets, and grilled cheese sandwiches washed down by soda. One mother even said her three year old would only eat hot dogs. So, to avoid a scene at each meal, he got hot dogs twice a day—every day.

It is important for all of us, especially mothers, to understand that arteries do not clog overnight or start clogging when we are adults. It starts when we are very young and gets worse each year we eat foods high in saturated fat and cholesterol.

I soon realized that one of the most important things I could do was to offer people an alternative way of eating that was low in fat and cholesterol, quick and easy to prepare, sensible, and appealing to everyone in the family. Since we are all creatures of habit and want to eat foods we love, I knew this cookbook would only work if it included healthier versions of some of our favorite dishes.

I enlisted the help of my family and friends and asked them for the recipes of their favorite dishes. The only prerequisite was that the dishes had to be quick and easy to prepare and popular with everyone in the family—including the children. I collected those recipes, reduced the amount of fat and cholesterol only to the point that the taste was not jeopardized, and added my own favorite recipes. The result is *Fear of Frying,* a wonderful collection of easy, low-fat and low-cholesterol recipes that are the tried and true favorites of all ages.

If you have youngsters, throw away your box of macaroni and cheese and use my recipe on page 151. I've noted other "kid's favorite" recipes in this book as well. **Look for the *Kids Love This* or *Teens Love This* symbols.** Starting your children on these recipes will help them avoid the build up of fatty deposits inside their young artery walls. If you are older, you will want to use my quick and easy recipes so that you can prevent any further arterial clogging and damage. Keep in mind that these recipes have been made healthier only to the point where the taste was not altered. If you are a working person you will be thrilled to see how quick and easy, as well as healthy and delicious, these recipes really are. After trying these recipes, you will no longer fear healthy cooking.

These recipes are not part of a fad-diet that will leave you hungry, weak, cranky, miserable, and counting the days until you can quit. This is not a diet of deprivation but a way of eating that does not ask you to eat less food. Instead, you will eat less of the wrong kind of food and more of the right kind of food; food that leaves you satisfied and energized instead of hungry and weak. This is a healthy and natural way of eating and living that may add years to your life and may help to cut your risk and your family's risk of contracting many debilitating and life-threatening diseases. Furthermore, this nutritious way of eating is time-tested and proven to work. It does this first by addressing two common dietary problems: cholesterol and fat.

Understanding Cholesterol

Cholesterol is a white, fatty substance produced by the liver and body cells which is used to build cell walls, make hormones, and make bile to aid in digestion. It is found only in animal cells and is essential to human life. Even though you need cholesterol to live, after six months of age, you do not need to eat it. A healthy body produces enough cholesterol to take care of its needs.

Many studies have found that there is very little evidence of premature coronary heart disease in adults who have consistently maintained total blood cholesterol levels below 180 milligrams per tenth of a liter of blood (180 mg/dl). The research has continually shown that the risk of a premature heart attack (before age 50 for women or 55 for men) rises among people whose blood cholesterol levels are above 200 milligrams per deciliter. According to the National Cholesterol Education Program, a cholesterol level of 200 to 239 mg/dl generally places an adult in a borderline high risk category for a premature heart attack, and a reading above 240 mg/dl pushes an adult up to a high risk category. An important statistic to remember is that the cholesterol of the average man who suffers a heart attack is 225 mg/dl, and most heart attacks occur in people with cholesterol levels between 200 and 240 mg/dl.[3] The good news is that if you have elevated blood cholesterol levels, every 1 percent decrease in blood cholesterol can lead to a 2 to 3 percent decrease in heart attack risk.

We now know, though, that the total amount of circulating cholesterol can be less important than the type of molecule carrying the cholesterol around the blood. Cholesterol is carried in the blood by lipoproteins. Low-density lipoproteins (LDLs) are the most abundant and carry about 65 percent of the circulating cholesterol to the body's cells. High density lipoproteins (HDLs) carry about 20 percent of the circulating cholesterol.[4] Low density lipoproteins are considered the bad cholesterol because they carry cholesterol to the cells where it can build up and cause lesions or cholesterol deposits. High density lipoproteins, on the other hand, have the ability to attract cholesterol from nonliver tissues and other lipoproteins. HDLs soak up the unnecessary cholesterol in the bloodstream and transport it back to the liver where it can be excreted as bile.

I find that one of the most common problems people have, is remembering which is the good cholesterol and which is the bad. I, too, had that problem until I discovered a trick that helped me. I think of the "L" in LDL as standing for lumpy. A mental picture of lumpy cholesterol, helped me remember that the LDLs are the type of cholesterol that lump-up in or clog the arteries. On the other hand, if you think of the "H" in HDL as an abbreviation for healthy, you will probably remember that the HDLs are the good cholesterol.

It is important not to confuse blood cholesterol with dietary cholesterol. Dietary cholesterol is found in food whereas blood or serum cholesterol is found in our blood. When people talk about "good" or "bad" cholesterol, they are referring to the HDLs and LDLs found in blood cholesterol not in food. Eating foods high in cholesterol, however, can result in an increase in the production of the LDLs (bad cholesterol) in our body. HDLs (healthy cholesterol), on the other hand, generally do not increase with dietary changes. In most cases, the way to raise the HDL level in the bloodstream is to increase exercise, lose weight, and quit smoking.

Now that we understand what cholesterol is and what purpose it plays in our lives, it is important to know what our cholesterol levels should be. It is recommended that an adult over thirty should have a total cholesterol of below 200 mg/dl, preferably below 180 mg/dl. Of the total cholesterol, the LDL level should not be over 130 and the HDL should be above 40.

In general, a high level of HDL is good because it is thought to be protective against coronary heart disease caused by atherosclerosis. Atherosclerosis is the process where fatty deposits, composed mostly of cholesterol, build up inside the cells of artery walls, narrowing the arteries and eventually interfering with the flow of blood. Over time, these narrowed arteries can cause a stroke or heart attack. HDLs soak up the extra cholesterol and take it out of the body where it can no longer build up in the arterial walls. Even though high levels of HDLs are good, they do not necessarily protect you from elevated levels of LDLs.

Knowing the ratio of your total cholesterol to your HDL is very important in understanding your cholesterol. To find out whether or not you have a healthy ratio, divide your total cholesterol number by your HDL cholesterol number. The resulting number represents the ratio between your total cholesterol and your HDLs. The ratio should not be above 4.5, with some doctors advocating a ratio of 3.5 or lower.

So far all the statistics you have read, have referred to adults. Children also have to be mentioned because the adverse effect of a typical American diet, which is high in cholesterol and fat, starts at a very young age. In fact, autopsies of deceased teenagers have shown that the build up of cholesterol in their arteries can already be detected at that early age. Although the research on children has just begun and the results are not finalized, it is generally agreed by most pediatricians that children before puberty should have a total cholesterol level of 140 mg/dl or less, and teenagers should aim for a number under 170. The American Heart Association sets a more stringent goal for total serum cholesterol values for children and young adults at an average of 140 mg/dl.[5] The current average for this age group is 160 mg/dl.

The last term that is important to know when discussing cholesterol is triglyceride. Triglycerides are fats formed from three fatty acids and a glyceride molecule. Ninety-five percent of dietary fat and ninety percent of body fat is made up of triglycerides. Knowing your triglyceride level can help your doctor understand how your body processes fat, and what kind of diet you should be on. Triglyceride levels should fall below 140 if you are under 30 years old, below 150 if you are 30 to 39, below 160 if you are 40 to 49, and below 190 if you are older than 50.[6]

Fat Facts

In simple terms, the American diet is too fatty. We eat three to four times more fat than protein and derive over 40 percent of our calories from fat. Even though we only need about one tablespoon of polyunsaturated fat in our daily diets, we eat 6 to 8 tablespoons of fat a day. Since each gram of fat contains 9 calories, over twice as much as carbohydrates and proteins, fat is very fattening. The American Heart Association advises people that the single most important dietary change that most Americans should make is to eat less fat and cholesterol.

Although there are many types of fats, polyunsaturated, monounsaturated, and saturated fatty acids are the ones referred to the most when discussing cholesterol. All fats and oils contain different amounts of monounsaturated, polyunsaturated, and saturated fatty acids. Depending on which one predominates, the fats or oils are called saturated, monounsaturated, or polyunsaturated. Saturated fats are loaded with all the hydrogen atoms that can fit in their molecular structure. Unsaturated fats (polyunsaturated and monounsaturated) are not loaded with all the hydrogen atoms they can carry.

After many years of research, we now know that saturated fat plays a major role in atherosclerosis, the build up of fatty deposits inside the cells of artery walls. Most saturated fats are easily identified since they are usually solid at room temperature and generally come from animal by-products, with the exception of palm oil, palm kernel oil, and coconut oil. When highly saturated fats are eaten, they interfere with the removal of cholesterol from the bloodstream and stimulate the production of LDL (bad) cholesterol.

Some research has shown that the effect of saturated fat on blood cholesterol is about three times worse than that of cholesterol derived from food. For this reason all healthy adults, whether young or old, should try to obtain less than 7 to 10 percent of their calories from saturated fat and less than 20 to 30 percent of their calories from any kind of fat. Children under the age of two need to eat more fat than adults, and children over the age of two should consume a fat intake equivalent to about 30 percent of their calories.

Since most Americans obtain 15 percent of their calories from saturated fat, we have to cut down on our consumption of highly saturated foods such as: cheese, ice cream, whole milk, and butter. About half of the fat from beef, lamb, and pork is saturated and poultry with the skin is slightly less saturated. (Removing the skin from chicken and turkey removes a lot of fat). Generally speaking, fats that are more than one-third saturated are likely to raise blood cholesterol levels.

The worst saturated fat offenders are the tropical oils that are used in commercially baked items such as cookies, cakes, and crackers. Palm oil, palm kernel oil, and coconut oil are rich in lauric, myristic, and palmitic acids which are the three saturated fatty acids mostly to blame for raising blood cholesterol. It should be mentioned here that there is absolutely no dietary need to eat saturated fat, since a healthy body can produce all the saturated fat it needs.

On the other hand, we do need to eat a very small amount of polyunsaturated fat in order to obtain the essential fatty acids which cannot be synthesized in our body. Since these fatty acids are easily obtained in a normal diet, it is important to remember that large amounts of polyunsaturated fat do not need to be eaten; about one tablespoon a day is enough, and the typical American eats much more than he or she needs.

Polyunsaturated fats usually come from vegetable products, and are found in most vegetable oils, such as corn oil, sunflower oil, safflower oil, and soybean oil. When saturated fats are replaced with polyunsaturated fats and the total fat intake is reduced, blood levels of cholesterol usually decrease. There has been some research, however, that link polyunsaturated fat with cancer. So, as with all fats, polyunsaturated fats should be limited.

The following oils are listed from least saturated (healthiest) to most saturated (less healthy): canola oil, safflower oil, sunflower oil, corn oil, soybean oil, peanut oil, cottonseed oil, palm kernel oil, coconut oil. Even though 14 percent of the fatty acids in olive oil are saturated, 72 percent are monounsaturated; that makes olive oil one of the healthiest oils.

Monounsaturated fat has received a lot of good press lately. It is generally accepted that this fat, found in olive oil, canola oil, avocado oil, and peanut oil, does not raise blood cholesterol levels. Some research indicates that using monounsaturated fats instead of saturated fats may be beneficial in lowering LDL cholesterol without reducing HDL (healthy) cholesterol. Moreover, we do know that people in countries that consume monounsaturated fat, in the form of olive oil, instead of polyunsaturated fat have considerably lower amounts of heart disease. Olive oil is one of the few fats that has not been linked with cancer. (Canola oil, also known as rapeseed oil, has become popular too recently for the research to be complete, and there are some new concerns about peanut oil.)

The last form of fat that should be mentioned is hydrogenated fat. Hydrogenation is a process in which hydrogen gas is forced into liquid vegetable oil, usually soybean oil, to make it more solid at room temperature. This process takes an unsaturated fat (not saturated with hydrogen molecules) and makes it more saturated. In other words, a relatively good dietary fat is turned into a partially saturated fat. Hard shortenings, hard margarines, and processed peanut butter use this process; therefore our use of them should be limited. (Softer margarines are a little better because they are made up of more water and less oil, and are usually less hydrogenated). Hydrogenated coconut oil or palm oil are particularly bad since these oils are highly saturated to start with and made even worse after the hydrogenation process.

New research on margarines, which often contain partially hydrogenated vegetable oil, indicates that they may not be as safe as originally believed. The culprit in margarine is trans fatty acids. These acids are formed when liquid vegetable oil is partially hydrogenated to make it more solid. The trans fatty acids that are formed are unsaturated fats that can raise cholesterol possibly as much as saturated fats. The good news is that many of the diet margarines or spreads are less hydrogenated and therefore contain less trans fat. The bad news is that some diet margarines do not melt well and have a different taste.

The bottom line is that we eat too much fat and we are getting fatter. This increases our risk of heart disease, obesity, some forms of cancer, and gallbladder disease. Most health experts recommend that we limit our intake of fat to less than 30 percent of our diet and increase our exercise according to our physical limitations.

The chart below indicates how many grams of fat are allowed for various diets. Those of you who want to restrict your fat intake to 30, 25, or 20 percent of your diet should identify the number of calories you *should* be eating each day given your level of physical activity and your bone structure, and look under the appropriate column to see how many grams of fat you are allowed to eat. Use the second chart to find the number of calories you *should* be eating daily according to your sex, height, weight, and physical activity. If you are overweight you should eat fewer calories, less fat, and increase you level of physical activity according to your physical limitations.

Maximum Amount of Fat Permitted Daily

Total Daily Calories	Grams of Total Fat Daily			Saturated Fat Daily
	30%,	25%,	20% of calories	10% of calories
1,200	40,	33,	27 grams	13 grams
1,500	50,	42,	33 grams	17 grams
2,000	67,	56,	44 grams	22 grams
2,500	83,	69,	56 grams	28 grams
3,000	100,	83,	67 grams	33 grams
3,500	117,	97,	78 grams	39 grams
3,850	128,	107,	86 grams	43 grams

Table calculated by multiplying the calories by .10, .20, .25, or .30, and dividing the resulting number by 9.

Fear of Frying

Recommended Calorie Consumption Based on Physical Activity for an Adult Female With a Medium-Sized Frame

(If you have a small frame, you should weigh 5 to 10 pounds less and eat about 100 fewer calories for each level of activity. If you have a large frame, you can weigh 9 to 12 pounds more and eat about 200 more calories for each level of activity.)

Height	Weight	Light Activity	Moderate	Heavy
5'0"	107-119	1,700 calories	1,900	2,250
5'2"	113-126	1,800 calories	2,000	2,400
5'4"	120-135	1,900 calories	2,150	2,550
5'6"	128-143	2,050 calories	2,300	2,700
5'8"	136-151	2,150 calories	2,450	2,850
5'10"	144-159	2,250 calories	2,550	3,000

Recommended Calorie Consumption Based on Physical Activity for an Adult Male With a Medium-Sized Frame

Height	Weight	Light Activity	Moderate	Heavy
5'5"	130-143	2,050 calories	2,350	2,750
5'7"	138-152	2,200 calories	2,450	2,900
5'9"	146-160	2,300 calories	2,600	3,050
5'11"	154-170	2,450 calories	2,750	3,250
6'1"	162-180	2,550 calories	2,900	3,400
6'3"	172-190	2,700 calories	3,300	3,850[7]

Currently, most of our packaged and canned foods are required to indicate the grams of total and saturated fat per serving, identify the percentage of the total calories that comes from fat, and list the nutritional content in a uniform manner. At last, those of us who are interested in what we are eating can read and understand food labels. As a result, most of us are discovering that processed and packaged foods contain a large amount of hidden fat in the form of tropical oils or hydrogenated oil.

What to Eat

Knowing what to eat is equally as important as knowing what not to eat. In fact, many scientists now believe that 40 percent of all cancer incidence in men, and 60 percent in women, is related to diet.[8] These are new statistics because we have not always eaten the diet we have now which is so high in fat and cholesterol. In fact, according to the Washington DC Center for Science in the Public Interest, we have increased our consumption of fat by 34 percent, from 32 percent of the calories in 1910 to 43 percent by 1981; increased our consumption of sugar and other natural sweeteners by 100 percent in the same period, from 12 to 24 percent of calories; and decreased our consumption of complex carbohydrates from 37 to 22 percent of calories.[9] The facts are that in most cases our grandparents did not eat as much fat as we do now; and even if they ate a lot of cholesterol, its adverse effect was not compounded by fast-paced, highly stressful lives and the consumption of great quantities of saturated fat.

Complex Carbohydrates

The consumption of complex carbohydrates has decreased dramatically in the past few decades, and this decrease is very alarming. Carbohydrates, which are found in plants (beans, legumes, nuts, grains, vegetables, and fruits) and milk and milk products (sugar lactose), are the body's main source of energy. Food carbohydrates are made up of complex polysaccharides, starch, glycogen, lactose, and sucrose. Complex carbohydrates are primarily the starches found in grains, beans, and vegetables, while simple carbohydrates are the sugars known as fructose, glucose, maltose, lactose, and sugar alcohols.

Throughout the world complex carbohydrates are a main source of protein, the basic material of life, but on the American table they have been replaced with animal protein. In 1910, flour and cereal products used to supply most of our protein. Now they provide about 17 percent, while animal flesh provides about 42 percent.[10] This is the root of the problem since animal flesh is filled with saturated fat, cholesterol, and calories while complex carbohydrates from plants and grains are low in fat, do not have cholesterol, and have fewer than half the calories of fat.

Many of our health problems could be alleviated if we would increase our consumption of complex carbohydrates and decrease our consumption of foods that are high in fat and cholesterol. The easiest way to do this is to eat more fruit, vegetables, and beans, and less meat, eggs, and high-fat dairy products. Some nutritionists are even urging us to increase our consumption of fruits and vegetables to 4 to 8 servings a day, and decrease our consumption of fish, poultry, and meat to 0 to 2 servings a day. An easy way to start following these recommendations would be to replace the soda you drink with fruit or vegetable juice.

If you are on a diet or watching your weight, don't be panicked by the amount of fruits and vegetables you are supposed to eat. Decreasing the amount of fat and animal protein you eat, often leads to a healthy weight loss all by itself. This happens because each gram of fat has 9 calories while each gram of fruit and vegetable is equal to four. Furthermore, it appears that fat calories, and especially fat that is eaten with sugar, are more likely to be stored as body fat and carbohydrate calories are more likely to be burned off as body heat.

It is important for dieters to know that fat and fatty foods are fattening. When fat is eaten with sugar it may be even worse. There is growing evidence that promotes the theory that fat and sugar eaten together are more likely to be stored as body fat. So, eating more fruits and vegetables will usually not lead to a weight gain if you decrease your consumption of fat and fatty foods. Combining a low-fat diet with a regular exercise program that fits the physical needs and limitations of the individual, usually results in a healthy long-term weight loss.

Nutritionists are also encouraging us to eat more beans and legumes which are packed with all kinds of health benefits. The most popular fresh beans, or edible pods, are green and yellow snap beans, Italian green beans, and Haricots verts or French beans. Legumes, the close cousins of beans, are the edible seeds enclosed in pods and include: dried beans, chick-peas, lentils, peas, nuts, seeds, and soybeans. Beans and legumes have been called the perfect food because they are brimming with vitamins, minerals, complex carbohydrates, vegetable protein, and fiber while they are very low in fat and sodium. They are also a great food for people with diabetes because beans are digested slowly and this causes a healthier slow rise in blood sugar.

If you eat a lot of vegetable protein instead of animal protein, keep in mind that vegetable protein is not a complete protein. Vegetables need to be served with grains or dairy products in order to make them complete, and all of us need to eat complete proteins in order to live. (The U.S. Recommended Dietary Allowance for protein is about 50 grams daily for most women between 25 to 50 years of age and 63 grams for most men in that age group.) Combining vegetables, legumes, or beans with wheat, oats, corn, rice, milk, cheese, yogurt, or eggs will usually do the trick. Many indigenous dishes naturally do this, for example: beans and rice, pizza, peanut butter sandwiches, and macaroni and cheese.

Eating more complex carbohydrates, such as vegetables, beans, and legumes, increases our intake of fiber, minerals, and vitamins. Dietary fiber is a carbohydrate which comes from plants, often from their cell walls, and is indigestible. Insoluble fiber, which cannot be broken down in water, helps with digestion by softening the stool, and this helps it move through the dietary tract. By absorbing many times its weight in water, insoluble fiber helps a person feel full when eating, does not contain a lot of calories from fat, helps to prevent constipation, and lowers the risk of colon, rectal, and other cancers. This type of fiber is most often found in whole wheats and wheat bran.

Water-soluble fiber, found in oatmeal, oat bran, barley, and fruit pectin, has received a lot of attention lately. Some research has indicated that eating large amounts of water-soluble fiber can be effective in lowering blood cholesterol levels, especially the bad LDLs. Whether or not that claim has been exaggerated is not completely clear. It is clear, however, that we do not eat enough dietary fiber. The average American eats 15 to 20 grams of fiber a day, and that should be increased to at least 30 grams a day, with some nutritionists recommending a goal of 45 to 60 grams. Any increase in fiber consumption should start slowly, come from a variety of plant sources, and be supplemented with the drinking of plenty of liquids to ensure proper bowel function.

Vitamins, Minerals, and Phytochemicals

Another benefit of complex carbohydrates and high-fiber foods is that they are often rich in vitamins and minerals, especially the antioxidants. The whole question of vitamins and minerals has been researched quite a bit in the past few years. As a result, we are now beginning to understand just how important these nutrients are in ensuring vitality and fighting diseases, perhaps even cancer.

Much of the research has centered around a group of vitamins—C, E, and beta-carotene—that are known as antioxidants. These vitamins can neutralize the damaging effect of cellular renegades known as free radicals. Oxygen-free radicals are the product of normal cellular metabolism and the exposure to carcinogens and pollutants. They damage DNA, corrode cell membranes, damage artery walls which can cause the buildup of cholesterol, kill cells, and play a major role in the development of cancer, heart disease, cataracts, and, perhaps, even aging. Antioxidants collect the harmful free radicals and haul them away. Even though there is a lot of confusing research about taking antioxidant supplements, eating fruits and vegetables rich in antioxidants is still and has always been recommended.

The recent discovery of phytochemicals has received a lot of attention in the press. Simply defined, phytochemicals are the hundreds, and perhaps thousands, of chemicals found in plants. These newly identified chemicals are found in very small amounts in about 40 fruits, vegetables, herbs, and grains. These chemicals help to protect the plant from the ravages of the sun and the environment. Their protective qualities may also hinder the development of cancer in people by interfering with the complex processes that lead to its growth.

It is important to note, that our dietary needs evolved over thousands of years around a diet consisting of fruits, nuts, grains, and vegetables with the occasional piece of meat and very little fat. It makes sense that through the centuries our bodies have become dependent upon these fruits, vegetables, and grains to provide us with the nutrients, vitamins, and chemicals we cannot produce. When we do not eat enough of these foods, our bodies are not getting the diet they have evolved to depend upon, and eventually get clogged up and don't function as well as they should. Deep down in our hearts, most of us know or suspect that eating a multiple vitamin or a handful of other vitamins will never cure the bad effects of poor eating habits. It takes more than a pill to erase thousands of years of evolution!

Certain fruits and vegetables are more packed with vitamins A, C, beta-carotene, and phytochemicals than others. (Beta-carotene is the chemical precursor that the body uses to make vitamin A; but, it does not cause vitamin A toxicity because the body only converts what it needs into vitamin A.) Generally speaking, the color of the fruit or vegetable will help you know which have the most vitamins. For instance, the darker orange fruits or vegetables and the darker green vegetables are often filled with vitamins, especially beta-carotene. I like to think that nature is helping us out by visually indicating some of the healthiest fruits and vegetables.

The information on phytochemicals is not complete since research on their health-promoting powers is fairly new. So far, phytochemicals have been found in over 40 plants, including: broccoli, cauliflower, cabbage, dark green leafy vegetables, onions, garlic, leeks, chives, citrus fruits, strawberries, raspberries, grapes, apples, grains, soybeans, hot chili peppers, turmeric, and cumin. There is no doubt that research will continue and animal studies will be supplemented by human studies. Remember that eating the whole fruit or vegetable is the best way to get these nutrients.

The smallest amount of a mineral or vitamin in its natural form can make a difference. For instance, selenium, a trace mineral and metal in our body, also contains antioxidant properties that can protect our body against cancer and heart disease. It appears that selenium can counteract some of the cancer-causing effects of fat, and may have a special role in fighting breast cancer by retarding tumor development.[11] Selenium-rich foods such as seafood, whole grains grown in selenium-rich soil, asparagus, fresh radishes, carrots, and cabbage should be included in most healthy diets. Supplementation may be dangerous because too much selenium can be harmful.

It appears that another mineral, calcium, is capable of protecting our health in many ways. Recently, we have learned about calcium's ability to prevent and slow osteoporosis, the disease that weakens the bones especially right before and after menopause. Research has shown that people need calcium all their lives, and women need large amounts of it after menopause. As important as calcium is, it is one of the nutrients most likely to be eaten in amounts below the Recommended Dietary Allowance (RDA).[12] New research has shown that proper amounts of calcium consumption can be important in preventing heart disease and developing colon cancer.

The RDA for calcium is 800 milligrams, a little more than three cups of milk a day for men and women. The National Institutes of Health, however, declared this amount to be too low. This group recommends that premenopausal women consume 1,000 milligrams of calcium daily, and postmenopausal women, who are not taking estrogen replacement, consume 1,500 milligrams.[13] It is very important that teenagers consume enough calcium because their calcium requirements are very high at that age.

Calcium obtained from foods is much better absorbed and used by the body than are calcium supplements. Healthy levels of vitamins D and C and lactose (milk sugar) also help in the absorption process. Healthy foods rich in calcium include: low-fat or nonfat yogurt, sardines with bones, red salmon with bones, collard greens, skim milk and low-fat or nonfat milk products.

Cruciferous vegetables, which include cabbage, Brussels sprouts, cauliflower, broccoli, kale, mustard greens, rutabagas, and turnips, are believed to play an important role in fighting disease as well. According to *The Wellness Encyclopedia of Food and Nutrition,* cruciferous vegetables contain nitrogen compounds called indoles that appear to be important in protecting against cancer of the stomach and large intestine. When this anti-cancer agent combines with the antioxidant nutrients these vegetables have in abundance, the production of anti-cancer enzymes seems to be stimulated while the antioxidants carry off the cancer-causing free radicals.

Iron, the last mineral to be discussed, has been in the news quite a bit lately. It has been known for years that many women of childbearing age are iron deficient, but recently the question has been raised whether or not lower levels of iron protect women from heart disease. At this point, many doctors think it is the estrogen and not necessarily lower levels of iron that protect premenopausal women from heart disease. What role iron plays in heart disease is not exactly clear yet, but people who are iron deficient should be careful with their diet. Dieters, strict vegetarians, pregnant women, menstruating women, endurance athletes, teenagers, and children should eat diets that supply enough iron. Consult a doctor, however, before you decide to take iron supplements because too much iron can be dangerous.

Red meats, like lamb and beef, are rich in heme iron, the most easily absorbed type of iron, but they're also high in fat and cholesterol. Beans, legumes, nuts, leafy green vegetables, dried fruits, and grains provide nonheme iron, which is absorbed better when eaten with foods high in vitamin C. Foods high in oxalic acid like spinach, beet greens, and Swiss chard inhibit the absorption of iron, as do eggs, coffee, and tea. Poultry and fish also contain heme iron. It is important that strict vegetarians take special care to get enough iron from their combinations of beans, legumes, nuts, fruits, and grains. Since iron is absorbed when eaten with foods rich in vitamin C, remember to be sure to drink some citrus fruit juices with your meals.

Ending the Fear of Healthy Cooking

How you start depends on what kind of diet you are used to. Some of us will probably just have to make some minor adjustments to our diets. But others who have high-fat diets will have to adjust their thinking and look differently at the portion-sizes of meat and vegetables.

Most people consider the meat on their plate the main course. This is not true in many other countries where meat is looked upon as a flavor or "side dish." It is not difficult to slowly cut down on the size of the portions of meat you serve while increasing the size of side dishes like vegetables, starches, and grains. If you do it slowly enough, your family will probably not even notice. Foods high in complex carbohydrates tend to be bulkier than high-fat foods and therefore more filling.

When you do eat meat, choose select cuts which have less fat. Prime cut has the most fat, choice cut has less, and select has the least. Trim off all visible fat and remember to serve smaller portions of meat and larger portions of the "side-dishes."

Many times I use meat in my cooking only as a flavor. For instance, when I use ground meat in my tomato sauce, I only use about a quarter of a pound. That small amount of meat adds flavor and texture, and, if it is well drained, very little fat. You too can start cutting down on the amount of meat you use in sauces, stir-fries, and chili until it becomes a flavor additive instead of a fat additive.

In addition, try to serve at least one meatless dinner a week. My family loves pasta and homemade soup, so that is not much of a problem for me. Be careful, though, not to substitute cheese for meat because that can be even worse. Eating more fruits, vegetables, beans, legumes, and grains will leave you feeling full and satisfied after you eat and not add a lot of fat with its hard-to-burn calories to your diet.

Do not overcook your vegetables until they are soggy and tasteless. Steam them or cook them in a small amount of boiling water only to the point where they become tender. Overcooking your vegetables not only reduces the taste but boils away the nutrients. Season your vegetables with a natural dehydrated butter such as Butter Buds® or Molly McButter®, mustards, horseradish, and the sauces found in this book. My Orange Sauce (pg. 120) enhances the flavor of peas, broccoli, and asparagus perfectly.

Snacks add an additional challenge because most of our snacks are filled with fat and salt and are eaten in great quantities. Kids and adults love their potato chips, ice cream, and cookies. Try keeping pretzels or light popcorn in the house instead of potato chips. Pretzels are particularly tasty when dipped in your favorite hot and sweet mustard.

Keep the high-fat snacks out of the house and substitute healthier ones. Most people will snack on what's available and easy to get. Very often, kids eat what they can see or easily reach, which one writer termed, see-food. So, make sure they see a bowl of fruit on the counter instead of a box of cookies.

That brings us to a very important point. If you are a parent, practice what you preach. Don't lecture your children about eating too much junk food, while you snack on chips. Letting your children know what is healthy to eat and what is not is a good idea, but lecturing them may turn them off to the idea. Just keep the house filled with a variety of healthy, good-tasting foods and remember that most of us can eat a treat every now and then without worrying.

If you keep a bowl of cut-up vegetables in the refrigerator ready to eat, you will find that they make a delicious snack, especially when dipped in nonfat blue cheese dressing or your favorite gourmet mustard. This snack usually only works if the vegetables are cut-up and ready to be eaten. Most people don't want to bother with peeling vegetables when they want a quick snack; so, prepare a whole bowl and keep it filled.

When my children were very little, I used to give them a bowl of Cheerios® to snack on, and now I find them choosing their favorite cereal to eat as a snack. There are many brands of healthy cereals that are fun to eat right out of the box. Read the labels and find one that suits your tastes and needs.

Now that there is a great variety of delicious low-fat or nonfat frozen yogurts available, it is easier to eat less ice cream. Find the flavor of yogurt that you like the best and keep it in the freezer instead of ice cream.

Our family often eats fruit shakes when we want something cold and creamy to eat. Just plop a banana, some nonfat yogurt, some strawberries, and a touch of honey into the blender for a wonderful fruit shake that will please everyone. The fun thing about fruit shakes is that you can be very creative and use many different combinations of fruits to create different tastes.

Recently, I discovered that fruit shakes are great for breakfast. They are not only healthy and delicious, but easy to make and can be eaten in the car for people on the run. My teenagers are hooked on them.

Bake your own cookies from recipes in my other cookbook, *Let Them Eat Cake,* and start reading the nutritional labels on the packages of the cookies you buy. Choose ones with lower amounts of fat. Don't worry, you don't have to buy the unappealing fat-free brands. There are many popular major brands that obtain less than 30 percent of their calories from fat.

That brings us to label-reading. It is very important that you start reading the nutritional labels so that you can find the hidden dietary offenders that are so abundant in packaged and processed foods. The word "light" or "lite" does not have to mean that the food is low in fat or cholesterol, and "low in cholesterol" on a packaged food does not necessarily mean it is low in fat as well. So read the labels on that nondairy creamer, muffin package, or frozen yogurt, to mention a few, and choose the food that fits into your dietary needs. Do not become a victim of incomplete, misleading, or false advertising.

There are simple things you can do to cut the amount of fat you eat. Serve fresh, crusty breads or bagels with your meals or as snacks. They are low in fat, high in complex carbohydrates, very filling, and taste great with your favorite jams or honey. (You don't need to cover a great-tasting piece of bread with butter; it is wonderful on its own.)

Order salad dressing on the side when you have a salad in a restaurant, and only use as much as you need. At home, start buying light salad dressing and mixing it with fat-free salad dressing. (I do this because I haven't found many fat-free salad dressings that I like; however, I have been pleased with several light varieties.)

Call the butter or margarine on your table what they actually are—fat, and use them sparingly.

Look at cheese as a lump of fat and avoid eating it as much as possible. I have a hard time eating much cheese now because I can't help but think of the amount of fat and calories I am eating and what it is doing to my arteries. If your children insist on grilled cheese sandwiches, use as little cheese as possible and try the reduced-fat varieties. Adding sliced tomatoes or apples to the sandwich can also cut down on the amount of cheese that you need to use.

Encourage the kids to eat turkey, chicken, or water-packed tuna sandwiches more often. Other kinds of processed meats are loaded with fats and preservatives. Vegetable pockets and pizza bagels are popular in my house. (Recipes are included in this book.)

Use a fat-free mayonnaise or some of the great tasting gourmet mustards when you make your sandwich.

In fact, use as many of the fat-reduced dairy items as you can. I have not been too pleased with the nonfat sour creams, but I always use nonfat yogurts, skim milk, and low-fat cottage cheese.

Saute your vegetables in a touch of olive oil, vegetable oil cooking spray, or, better yet, use chicken broth or wine.

Trim all the visible fat off your meat and do not eat the skin on your poultry.

Bake, grill, or roast your foods instead of frying them.

Fear of Frying

If you have enough sun, grow some basil, parsley, and other fresh herbs to have on hand when you need them. They are easy to grow and taste great in many recipes. Fresh herbs provide a lot of flavor to dishes and that usually results in less need for salt and fat.

Use naturally dehydrated butter, such as Butter Buds or Molly McButter, when you want a buttery taste.

Reduce the number of egg yolks you use in baking by increasing the number of egg whites.

Encourage family members who are older than two to drink lower-fat milk. If they are drinking whole milk now, start buying 2% milk, and slowly work your way down to skim (according to their age and dietary needs). Contrary to popular belief, whole milk does not have more calcium, vitamins, or minerals, just more fat.

Avoid soda; it has no nutritional value, is loaded with calories, and can interfere with the absorption of some essential minerals like calcium. Remember, diet soda has its own set of problems. Start buying seltzer and mix it with fruit juices to make your own soda.

Keep a bowl of fresh fruit on the counter where everyone can see it and eat as a snack.

Incidentally, frozen grapes and bananas are very popular with the older kids and fun and easy to eat.

Drink enough water and liquids each day. You will find that fruit juice, vegetable juice, skim milk, and plain water can be filling. Most experts recommend that you drink at least eight glasses of water a day.

Most importantly, start your children off with a healthy diet from the very beginning. After the age of two, you can start reducing the fat they eat. Fruits and vegetables should be part of every meal. Salt, sweeteners, and sweet foods should be consumed sparingly. It is so much easier to start feeding children a healthy diet from birth, than to try to change years of bad, and perhaps deadly, eating habits. (Remember that babies have higher fat requirements than adults. Don't become a fanatic and deprive them of the fat they need to grow.) It really takes no more time to give your child an apple than to give him or her a cookie or potato chips.

If you eat a healthy diet regularly, you do not need to cut all treats from your life or your children's lives forever. If you do that, the children will resent it and may make your life miserable. Everyone wants an ice cream or a hamburger with fries from time to time. If we all eat a healthy diet most of the time, there is no problem with the occasional splurge.

After all is said and done, we alone are responsible for what we feed our children and we alone are responsible for what we eat. This book will help you take back that responsibility. Furthermore, you will not have to deprive yourself of eating great-tasting food, spend hours in the kitchen cooking or shopping in health food stores, or get a degree in nutrition. You now have most of the information you need to know, and a whole collection of quick and easy recipes that are based on some of America's favorite dishes which have been made healthier. Take your first step to ending your fear of healthy cooking right now!

References

1. Sonja L. Connor., M.S., R.D., and William E. Connor, M.D., *The New American Diet* (New York: Simon and Schuster, 1986) page 22.
2. *Ibid.,* page 19.
3. "The HDL/Triglycerides Trap," from "Face the Fats: A collection of articles from Nutrition Action Healthletter," Volume 17, Number 7 (Washington, DC: Center for Science in the Public Interest, September, 1990) page 21.
4. Victor Herbert and Genell J. Subak-Sharpe, *The Mount Sinai School of Medicine Complete Book of Nutrition* (New York: St. Martin's Press, 1990) page 76.
5. *Ibid.,* page 79.
6. Bonnie Liebman, "The Fat Primer," from "Face the Fats: A collection of articles from Nutrition Action Healthletter," page 6.
7. From the 1959 height-weight tables of the Metropolitan Life Insurance Company, New York City.
8. Sheldon Margen, M.D., and the Editors of the University of California at Berkeley "Wellness Letter," *The Wellness Encyclopedia of Food and Nutrition: How to Buy, Store, and Prepare Every Variety of Fresh Food* (New York: Rebus, 1992) page 11.
9. Jane Brody, *Jane Brody's Nutrition Book* (New York: Bantam Books, 1988) page 13.
10. *Ibid.,* page 41.
11. The Preventive Total Health System™, by the Editors of *Prevention Magazine, Understanding Vitamins and Minerals* (Pennsylvania: Rodale Press, 1984) pages 125-125.
12. Patricia Hausman, M.S., *The Right Dose, How to Take Vitamins and Minerals Safely* (New York: Ballantine Books, 1987) page 268.
13. *Ibid.,* page 268.

SUPER

FOODS

In order to help you decide what to eat, I have compiled a list of some of the most nutritious foods. You could call them super foods. Each food included in this list is easily purchased and brimming with heart-healthy nutrients that should be part of everyone's diet. For over 20 years, research has consistently found that people who eat greater amounts of these super foods have lower rates of cancer and less heart disease. In fact, eating a healthy diet may be one of our greatest weapons against cancer. This is true because fruits and vegetables are filled with fiber, carotenoids (relatives of beta-carotene), and phytochemicals (a general term for the hundreds of nutritionally vital chemical substances in many fruits, vegetables, herbs, and grains).

These newly-discovered substances provide disease-preventing nutrients that we are just beginning to understand. The hundreds of interconnected nutrients in most fruits or vegetables make the whole fruit or vegetable a powerful tool in fighting disease and maintaining good health. Taking a handful of vitamin supplements will never replace the benefits of eating the fruit or vegetables from where the vitamins originated.

We may not be able to avoid pesticides, remove all stress in our lives, or pick out healthy genes, but we are able to choose what foods we eat and serve our families. Because certain foods pack a disease-preventing wallop that may extend our lives, we should all make these super foods a regular part of our diet.

Apples

Apples are rich in pectin, a water-soluble fiber that helps keep blood sugar stable and can lower blood cholesterol. Apples have practically no fat, cholesterol, and sodium, but are very filling and make a great snack. They contain carotenoids and phytochemicals, including: octacosanol, ellagic acid, caffeic acid, and ferulic acid. These nutrients may help prevent cancer and other diseases.

Apricots

The yellow-orange color of apricots indicates that they are packed with beta-carotene. A diet rich in beta-carotene may help prevent several forms of cancer and heart disease. Dried apricots are a good source of potassium with little or no fat, cholesterol, or sodium.

Asparagus

Asparagus is filled with the antioxidant selenium. Antioxidants collect free radicals in our blood which cause cell damage. An antioxidant-rich diet may help protect us against cancer and heart disease.

Bananas

Bananas are a great source of potassium, which is important in regulating blood pressure. They are also a good source of vitamin C.

Beans

Dried beans and legumes such as pinto beans, kidney beans, lima beans, navy beans, soybeans, and chick-peas are good sources of water-soluble and insoluble fiber. Dried beans are also filled with several types of phytochemicals and iron, and may help reduce the risk of heart disease, prevent certain types of cancer, relieve constipation, and regulate blood sugar, which can help people with diabetes, in particular.

Berries

Blueberries, blackberries, raspberries, cranberries, and strawberries are full of fiber, pectin, potassium, vitamin C, and phytochemicals. They may help prevent diarrhea, certain types of cancer, and heart disease. Cranberry juice may help reduce urinary tract or bladder infections, but since it contains many calories, try the lower-calorie type.

Carrots and Other Orange Vegetables

Carrots, butternut squash, acorn squash, hubbard squash, and pumpkins are great sources of beta-carotene. Eating a diet filled with orange-yellow vegetables may reduce the risk of lung and ovarian cancer and may help prevent cataracts.

Cherries

Cherries make a great snack because they satisfy that sweet-tooth urge without providing a lot of calories and fat. They are a good source of vitamin A.

Citrus Fruits

Oranges, grapefruits, tangerines, limes, and lemons brim with vitamin C, phyto-chemicals, and fiber. They are an important part of a heart-healthy, anti-cancer diet. Fruits that are high in vitamin C, including kiwifruit, may help prevent cancers of the throat, larynx, mouth, and esophagus.

Cruciferous Vegetables

This category includes broccoli, cauliflower, brussels sprouts, cabbage, and bok choy. These vegetables contain fiber and high levels of indoles which help to block carcinogens from damaging cells and causing cancer. Eating a diet high in cruciferous vegetables may reduce the risk of breast and colon cancer. Many nutritionist believe these vegetables are one of the best anti-carcinogens we can eat.

Figs and Dates

Figs and dates are high in calories but they are loaded with fiber and very filling.

Fish

Fish is a great source of protein and leaner than red meat. The omega-3 fats in fish make the blood less prone to unusual clotting, and thus may help prevent cardio-vascular disease. Fish also provides a good source of potassium which helps regulate blood pressure.

Garlic, Onions, Leeks, and Chives

Garlic, onions, leeks, and chives contain the phytochemicals allyl sulfides and allium compounds which may reduce carcinogens and decrease the reproduction of tumor cells. Eating large amounts of garlic may reduce LDL (bad cholesterol), break up blood clots, and reduce the risk of stomach and colon cancer, but only when eaten in very significant amounts.

Grains, Oats, and Bran

Whole grains, which include amaranth, barley, buckwheat, millet, oats, quinoa, rice, rye, triticale, and wheat, are an important source of fiber. Oatmeal and oat bran provide water-soluble fiber which many believe has the ability to lower cholesterol. Bran is a great source of insoluble fiber with all its digestive benefits.

Grains also provide iron, potassium, thiamine, riboflavin, and magnesium. Adding pastas, brown rice, whole grain breads, and cereals to your diet is a delicious way to get nutrients that are naturally low in fat and calories.

Dark Green Leafy Vegetables

Spinach, chicory greens, swiss chard, kale, mustard, collard, beet, and turnip greens are great sources of vitamin A as carotene, vitamin C, and fiber. They have been linked with reducing the risk of high blood pressure and stomach and breast cancer. Since dark green leafy vegetables have more carotene than lighter vegetables, make sure your salad has a lot of them in it. Remember, though, that salad dressing contains a tremendous amount of fat—11 or more grams per tablespoon—so use a low-fat or nonfat version instead.

Melons and Orange-Colored Fruits

Cantaloupes, apricots, mangoes, and papayas are some of the orange, non-citrus fruits that are brimming with healthy nutrients. Their orange color comes from the antioxidant beta carotene. Honeydew, casaba, and cantaloupe are good sources of vitamins A and C and potassium.

Milk and Dairy Products

The wide variety of nonfat milk and dairy products now available are a great source of calcium and vitamin D without the added fat of whole milk. Drinking milk throughout your life helps develop strong bones and teeth and decreases the risk of osteoporosis. In addition, drinking milk can regulate blood pressure and decrease the risk of colorectal cancer. Acidophilus-rich nonfat yogurt can also help maintain a healthy level of acidophilus, a natural bacteria in the digestive tract. The acidophilus in some yogurts may help prevent yeast infections in women. Some women take acidophilus supplements or eat acidophilus-rich yogurt when they have to take an antibiotic, and this may decrease the possibility of a yeast infection.

Peas

Peas, which are a type of legume, are mentioned separately because they are available in fresh and dried forms. Dried peas are a great source of protein with practically no fat and a good source of fiber.

Pineapple

Pineapples contain vitamin C and manganese, a trace mineral that is necessary for metabolizing protein and carbohydrates. Pineapples are also a good source of the phytochemical bromelain which may help prevent cancer, blood clots, and inflammation.

Peppers

Red peppers are a great source of vitamins A and C. Green peppers provide a good amount of vitamin C, and chili peppers are filled with the phytochemical capsaicin which may help prevent arthritis, asthma, and bronchitis.

Potatoes

Potatoes are a great source of fiber and potassium, making them an important part of a diet that regulates high blood pressure. They also have a good supply of vitamin C, iron, magnesium, and phosphorus. Sweet potatoes have the added benefit of being full of beta carotene. In fact, one cup of mashed sweet potatoes provides more than eight times the recommended dietary allowance of beta carotene. Potatoes have been linked with reducing the risk of lung cancer. Remember, even though potatoes are naturally low in calories, butter, sour cream, and frying add calories and fat.

Tomatoes

If you are a botanist you might call the tomato a fruit; but whatever you call it, tomatoes are a good source of vitamins A and C. Tomatoes also contains the phytochemicals lycopene and gamma amino butyric acid which may help prevent cancer and hypertension.

Information on "Super Foods" was compiled from general sources and information found in "Phytochemicals: Plants Against Cancer," Nutrition Action Healthletter, *Volume 21, Number 3 (Washington DC: Center for the Science in the Public Interest, April, 1994) page 1; "Will 'Designer Foods' Fortified with Phytochemicals Fight Cancer?"* Environmental Nutrition, *Volume 16, Number 3 (New York: Environmental Nutrition, Inc., March, 1993) page 1; Patricia Hausman and Judith Benn Hurley,* The Healing Foods *(New York: Dell Publishing, 1989).*

REDUCING

THE

FEAR of FRYING

Healthy Tips

1. Keep the house stocked with fresh, ready-to-eat fruit. Kids eat "see-food." They eat what they see and what they can get their hands on easily. Buy the fruits and vegetables in amounts that can be eaten before they spoil or start to lose their nutrients.

2. Have a bowl of vegetable sticks or baby carrots in the refrigerator. Use a mixture of a hot and sweet mustard and nonfat yogurt as a dip. Always eat vegetables sticks or fruit with your sandwich.

3. Snack on air-popped corn and low-salt pretzels, using sharp mustard as a dip. Low-fat cereal right out of the box is another good snack, as is fresh, crusty bread or bagels topped with jam.

4. Don't keep a lot of cookies, potato chips, and pre-baked goods in the house. If they are not there, you will not eat them. Replace them with Banana Crunch® or Caramel Corn Rice Cakes® for a sweet taste.

5. Snack on a piece of fruit around 4 p.m. to keep your energy up and satisfy your sweet tooth. You may even want to dip it in a touch of honey.

6. Eat a small bowl of low-fat cereal before a late dinner or party, so you won't be starving and tempted to fill up on hors d'oeuvres, which are usually loaded with fat.

7. Eat a high-fiber, low-fat cereal for breakfast. It will keep you going all morning, and it is much healthier than doughnuts or croissants. (If you don't like high-fiber cereals, mix one with your favorite low-fat cereal.) Fruit shakes are also good for breakfast. Just make sure to eat breakfast!!!

8. Replace your soda with a mixture of seltzer water and fruit juice. Start drinking some vegetable juices with lunch or dinner.

9. Buy or make homemade low-fat soup and eat it for lunch or dinner. Bean soup is very filling and usually quite healthy.

10. Remove the skin from poultry and skim off excess fat from gravies, soups, stews, etc. Fat will stick to ice cubes dropped into or skimmed over soup or stew. Discard the ice cubes before they melt. Another way to remove fat is to refrigerate the item until the fat hardens. Cover the cooled soups or stews with wax paper and the fat will cling to the wax paper. Peel the wax paper and fat off of the soup.

Tricks of the Trade

1. Use generous amounts of Butter Buds and Molly McButter, e.g. when you want a buttery taste. These are great on vegetables and air-popped corn.

2. Reduce or eliminate butter and margarine from your cooking. Use olive oil, canola oil, or a low-in-saturated-fat oil instead. To reduce the oil, substitute honey, corn syrup, and fructose for some of the sugar; or, use apple sauce, fruit purée, nonfat or low-fat yogurt, or nonfat mayonnaise. Sometimes it is best to use some butter or margarine mixed with a little canola oil.

3. Prune purée can be used to replace butter, margarine, and oil in some baked goods. It works well in chocolate cakes, brownies, and fruit cookies. Be aware, though, that using prune purée gives the baked item somewhat of a prune taste. You can buy prune purée where canned Solo pie fillings are sold or you can make your own. To make prune purée, place ⅔ cup or one pound of pitted prunes and ¾ cup water in a food processor. Process on high until completely puréed. You can use the prune purée to replace the fat completely on a one-to-one basis, or you can reduce the amount of fat you use and replace it with the purée. The prune purée will last several months tightly covered and refrigerated.

4. Use egg substitute such as Eggbeaters® or replace most of the whole eggs with egg whites.

5. When cooking with skim milk, add a little nonfat dry milk to make the recipe taste richer and creamier.

6. Skim buttermilk or nonfat yogurt add thickness and richness but not fat to baked goods.

7. Low-fat cottage cheese whipped in the food processor gives a cheese-like flavor to creamy casseroles.

8. Skimmed evaporated milk can be used in place of cream in some sauces or soup recipes, and it can be whipped into a mock whipped cream.

9. A half cup of nonfat yogurt, half cup of low-fat cottage cheese, and two teaspoons of lemon juice pureed in the food processor makes a good sour cream substitute.

10. Mix nonfat yogurt and nonfat dry milk for a creamy, less acidic product.

11. Use Dutch unsweetened cocoa powder instead of chocolate squares.

12. Try using a variety of gourmet mustards, horseradish, salsa, and nonfat mayonnaise in place of regular mayonnaise.

13. Keep fresh basil in the house or chop it and put it in the freezer. I always have some basil growing on the windowsill in my kitchen. Fresh herbs add wonderful flavor and taste to many dishes.

14. When sauteing a dish, use vegetable oil cooking spray and a touch of water, and saute over medium-low heat. If you use nonstick skillets it is easier, but try to buy quality nonstick cookware that is guaranteed not to chip or scratch.

The Fearless Kitchen

The fearless kitchen looks like everyone else's but contains certain essential items that make healthy, quick, and easy cooking a snap.

1. A good quality, large food processor is a must for every cook. A blender is also very convenient and makes great fruit shakes.

2. Good quality, nonstick cookware will cut down the fat you need to use.

3. A broiler or gas grill, good-sized freezer for frozen soups and broths, good-sized refrigerator for fruit and vegetables, sharp cutlery, and a mini-chopper are always helpful.

4. Some kind of fat skimmer or fat mop is helpful for removing excess fat from soups or stews. Fat skimming can be done with a spoon but takes more time. Some people skim a paper towel over the soup to remove the last drops of fat. A baster is good for removing fat while meat is roasting.

5. A microwave is not necessary but makes life easier.

6. A good colander or strainer is important for rinsing beans, and a lettuce spinner will make your salads less soggy.

7. Extra virgin olive oil, canola oil, balsamic vinegar, and a variety of other vinegars (sherry, tarragon, red and white wine vinegar, etc.) will always be found in a fearless kitchen. Vegetable oil cooking spray will be right next to the Worcestershire sauce.

8. Horseradish, anchovy paste, and sun-dried tomato paste are commonly used.

9. A variety of pastas, white and brown rice, and tomato sauces will be found on the shelves.

10. A well-stocked spice cabinet is important. Make sure the dried spices are not too old because they lose their flavor. Quality bread crumbs come in handy. Lower-salt soy sauce is good for stir-frying and hot sauce adds zip to many dishes.

11. Coarse or kosher salt and a pepper mill filled with peppercorns are used often.

12. Fresh baking soda and baking powder are essential. Old baking soda and powder lose their ability to make baked goods rise.

13. Lower-salt and fatless chicken and beef broth will be on the shelf or in the freezer. A variety of canned chopped tomatoes or stewed tomatoes, sun-dried tomatoes, and red and green salsa will be next to them.

14. Baking items will include: unbleached all-purpose flour, whole-wheat flour, Wondra® quick-mixing flour, cornmeal, rolled oats, oat bran, white and brown sugar, confectioner's sugar, honey, molasses, vanilla extract, rum extract, lemon extract, cocoa powder, nonfat dried milk, and jarred or dried mincemeat.

15. Raisins, prunes, dried apricots, and dried or frozen cranberries will be available year round in a fearless kitchen.

16. Fresh basil and parsley will be in the refrigerator or freezer, or growing on the windowsill. Fresh oregano and rosemary are also nice but not essential.

Reducing the Fear of Frying

17. Butter Buds or some other naturally dehydrated butter will have a place of honor.

18. Nonfat yogurt, skim milk, light or nonfat cream cheese, light whipped butter, diet margarine, and freshly grated Parmesan cheese will be in the refrigerator. (You might see low-fat cottage cheese and skim buttermilk there if baking is going on.) Frozen nonfat or low-fat yogurt and sorbets will be in the freezer.

19. Fresh fruits will be on the counter. Fresh vegetables, wrapped in paper bags or slightly dampened cloth towels, will be in the vegetable bins.

20. A variety of dried and canned beans will be found on the pantry shelves.

21. Healthy soups, especially the bean variety, are very popular in this kitchen.

22. A variety of jams and jellies are used on the fresh, crusty bread that will be found there.

23. Orange juice, V-8 juice, tomato juice, and other juices are always handy.

24. Garlic, a variety of onions, and potatoes are usually not far.

25. Low-fat or nonfat salad dressings are often used in a fearless kitchen.

26. A variety of rice cakes (butter, cheddar cheese, caramel corn, and banana) are often found in this kitchen.

27. Pretzels and low-fat microwave popcorn are waiting to be snacked upon.

28. The cookies and cakes in this kitchen are either homemade (using recipes from this book and my other cookbook, *Let Them Eat Cake)* or lower-fat, store bought versions.

29. A wonderful variety of natural, low-fat hot and cold cereals are always on the shelf to be eaten for breakfast or as a snack.

30. A variety of mustards and nonfat or low-fat mayonnaise are essential.

APPETIZERS
AND
SNACKS

Black Bean Dip

———————

Beans are full of flavor, fiber, and nutrients, and they are very versatile. This full-flavored dip has very little fat, no cholesterol, and a wonderful taste. The jalapeño pepper adds a little zip that you can increase or decrease depending on your preference.

1 2/3 cups cooked or canned black beans, rinsed and drained

1 small garlic clove, chopped

1/3 cup chopped green pepper

1 to 1 1/2 teaspoons chopped jalapeño pepper
 (Note: always wear rubber gloves when working with hot peppers)

4 teaspoons red wine vinegar

1 tablespoon fresh lemon juice

1/2 teaspoon salt

Freshly ground pepper to taste

Place all the ingredients in a large food processor or blender. Puree for at least 60 seconds or until smooth and creamy. Cover and refrigerate several hours. This dip lasts several days in the refrigerator. Serve with low-fat crackers, rice cakes, or pita bread.

Preparation time: 10 minutes. Refrigeration time: several hours. Yield: 1 to 1½ cups or 25 hors d'oeuvres.

Nutrition analysis: 13 calories per serving; 1 gm. protein; 2.5 gm. carbohydrate; 0 fat; 0 cholesterol; 0.5 gm. fiber; 112 mg. sodium

Percent of calories from protein: 22%; from carbohydrates: 75%; from fat: 4%

Exchange values: less than ½ bread

Cape Cod Shrimp

Our friends introduced us to this recipe when we visited them in Cape Cod. After tasting it, I knew it was a winner and I decided to create a healthier version. You will be amazed how popular this recipe is and how quickly it disappears.

1 teaspoon sweet and hot prepared mustard
(I use Nance's® Sharp and Creamy Mustard
or Middlesex Farms® Sweet and Hot Mustard)

3 1/2 tablespoons low-fat or fat-free mayonnaise

1 1/2 tablespoons nonfat plain yogurt

1 to 1 1/4 teaspoons curry powder

Dash of soy sauce

16-ounce bag frozen large, cooked shrimp, defrosted
(fresh peeled and cooked shrimp may also be used)

4 to 5 tablespoons Indian chutney

Low-fat water wafers, small croustades (crispy hors d'oeuvres
shells), or Paris Toast Squares®

Mix the mustard, mayonnaise, yogurt, curry powder, and soy sauce together in a small bowl. Spread a small amount of the mayonnaise mixture (about ½ teaspoon) on each cracker, toast square, or croustade. Place one shrimp on each cracker, and top with a small dollop of chutney. Serve immediately.

Preparation time: 15 minutes. Yield: 45 to 55 hors d'oeuvres

Nutrition analysis for 45 servings: 18 calories per serving; 2 gm. protein; 1 gm. carbohydrate; 0.5 gm. fat; 20 mg. cholesterol; 0 fiber; 25 mg. sodium

Percent of calories from protein: 49%; from carbohydrates: 28%; from fat: 22%

Exchange values: ½ meat

Chicken Meatballs

1 tablespoon chopped fresh chives

1 tablespoon chopped fresh parsley

3 small scallions, chopped (use 3 inches of the middle of each, mostly the green tops)

10 fresh rosemary leaves or 1/4 to 1/2 teaspoon dried rosemary

2 medium-sized, whole, skinless, boneless chicken breasts (4 single breasts)

1/4 to 1/2 teaspoon salt

1/4 teaspoon ground pepper

1 large egg white

Vegetable oil cooking spray

Dip
1 tablespoon honey plus 2 tablespoons hot and sweet mustard

Mix the first 4 ingredients in a large food processor until well blended. Add the chicken breasts, salt, pepper, and egg white, and chop using the on/off button until the chicken is mushy but not pureed. Roll the mixture into teaspoon-sized balls. (Any size works but larger balls take longer to cook). Spray a large, heavy skillet very generously with cooking spray. Heat over medium-low heat for 45 seconds. Cook a third of the meatballs at a time in a covered skillet for 2 minutes on each side (about 8 minutes total), or until completely cooked. Drain well, respray the skillet, and repeat until all the meatballs are cooked. Mix the honey and mustard together thoroughly, and heat on the stove or microwave until hot but not boiling. Serve this as a dip or sauce for the meatballs.

Preparation time: 10 minutes. Cooking time: 25 minutes. Yield: 65 to 75 small balls

Nutrition analysis: 10 calories per serving; 1.5 gm. protein; 0.5 gm. carbohydrate; 0 fat; 4 mg. cholesterol; 0 fiber; 24 mg. sodium

Percent of calories from protein: 65%; from carbohydrates: 12%; from fat: 22%

Exchange values: less than ½ meat

Chutney Cheese Spread

This delicious, creamy spread is quick and easy to make. Double or triple the recipe to feed a hungry crowd.

2 tablespoons nonfat plain yogurt

3 tablespoons low-fat or nonfat cream cheese, at room temperature

3 tablespoons mild mango chutney, well chopped

¼ teaspoon curry powder

Mix the yogurt and cream cheese together until smooth and creamy. Stir in the chutney and curry powder, and mix well. If you have time, cover the mixture and refrigerate it for at least 30 minutes. (The spread will keep for several days in the refrigerator.) Serve with low-fat water crackers.

Preparation time: 5 minutes. Refrigeration time: 30 minutes. Yield: ⅔ cup, or 24 single servings, or 6 servings of 4 crackers each

Nutrition analysis for 6 servings (numbers in parentheses indicate nutrition analysis for 24 servings): 29.5 (7.5) calories per serving; 1 (0.5) gm. protein; 6 (1.5) gm. carbohydrate; trace of fat; 0 cholesterol; 0 fiber; 49.5 (12.5) mg. sodium

Percent of calories from protein: 17%; from carbohydrates: 83%; from fat: 1%

Exchange values: ½ (0) fruit

Healthier Hummus

---

2 cups cooked and drained chick-peas or garbanzo beans; reserve the liquid (canned beans can be used)

3 to 6 tablespoons bean liquid (if you have trouble with gas discomfort, use water)

1 tablespoon sesame seeds

3 to 4 tablespoons lemon juice

2 garlic cloves, chopped

2 to 3 green onions, chopped

Salt and freshly ground pepper to taste

Parsley for garnish

Put the chick-peas, bean liquid, sesame seeds, lemon juice, garlic, and green onions in a food processor or large blender. Process on high for 3 minutes, or until creamy and smooth, scraping the sides often. Add more bean liquid if you want a creamier consistency. Season to taste, and refrigerate to let flavors blend for at least 30 minutes.

Serve as a dip with fresh vegetables, as a spread on lightly toasted pita bread, or as a vegetarian roll-up with alfalfa sprouts on lightly toasted flat Mediterranean mountain bread. (I recommend Cedar's® bread.)

Preparation time: 5 minutes. Chilling time: 30 minutes. Yield: 1½ cups (enough for 30 to 40 hors d'oeuvres or 6 flat bread roll-ups)

Nutrition analysis for 30 servings: 14.5 calories per serving; 0.5 gm. protein; 2.5 gm. carbohydrate; 0.5 gm. fat; 0 cholesterol; 0.5 gm. fiber; 48 mg. sodium

Percent of calories from protein: 17%; from carbohydrates: 61%; from fat: 22%

Exchange values: less than ½ bread

Hot Salmon Spread

Appetizers are often filled with fat and hardly any healthy ingredients. This recipe, however, combines calcium-rich salmon with a host of other tasty ingredients to make a delicious and healthy spread.

Vegetable oil cooking spray

7-ounce can salmon, drained, bones removed, and flaked

1 tablespoon lemon juice

2 tablespoons minced fresh chives

2 tablespoons minced onion

1 tablespoon minced fresh dill

1 cup nonfat plain yogurt, drained

1 tablespoon nonfat powdered milk

1 tablespoon cornstarch

1/4 teaspoon garlic powder (optional)

Salt and freshly ground pepper to taste

Preheat oven to 350°. Spray a 3-cup baking dish with cooking spray. Mix the salmon, lemon juice, chives, onion, and dill together in the baking dish. Mix the yogurt, powdered milk, cornstarch, and garlic powder together. Stir this into the salmon mixture. Cover, and bake for 15 minutes, then uncover and bake an additional 15 minutes. Taste, and add salt and pepper if necessary. Serve with low-fat crackers.

Preparation time: 10 minutes. Cooking time: 30 minutes. Yield: about 1½ to 2 cups or 25 hors d'oeuvres

Nutrition analysis: 18.5 calories per serving; 2 gm. protein; 1.5 gm. carbohydrate; 0.5 gm. fat; 4.5 mg. cholesterol; 0 fiber; 52 mg. sodium

Percent of calories from protein: 48%; from carbohydrates: 27%; from fat: 25%

Exchange values: less than ½ milk; less than ½ meat

Jiminy Crab

Idette, Allan, and I invented this recipe one New Year's Eve when we were visiting our friends Dale and Todd. It was gourmet night and my turn to prepare the appetizer. Much to my surprise, I discovered that I left some key ingredients home. We took up the challenge and created an instant hit.

Vegetable oil cooking spray

3 tablespoons light cream cheese, at room temperature

3 tablespoons nonfat plain yogurt

1 teaspoon sweet and hot mustard

1 to 2 dashes Worcestershire sauce

Dash of balsamic vinegar (if you don't have it, omit it from the recipe)

1 teaspoon fresh lemon juice, or to taste

1 teaspoon flour

6-ounce can white crabmeat, squeeze out excess liquid

Dash of horseradish

1 teaspoon chopped chives

Preheat oven to 350°. Spray a small (2 to 3 cup) glass baking dish with cooking spray. Mix all the ingredients thoroughly in the baking dish. Check for taste. You may want to add a dash more lemon juice, balsamic vinegar, Worcestershire sauce, horseradish, or mustard. Cover and bake for 30 minutes. Serve hot with water crackers.

Preparation time: 10 minutes. Cooking time: 30 minutes. Yield: 25 to 30 servings

Nutrition analysis for 25 servings: 10 calories per serving; 1.5 gm. protein; 0.5 gm. carbohydrate; 0.5 gm. fat; 7 mg. cholesterol; 0 fiber; 41 mg. sodium

Percent of calories from protein: 60%; from carbohydrates: 14%; from fat: 27%

Exchange values: less than ½ meat

Martha's Cheese & Onion Spread

My friend Martha served her version of this spread at a party years ago. I was surprised at how tasty the combination of ingredients was and at how easy it was to make.

Vegetable oil cooking spray

16 ounces low-fat (1%) cottage cheese

1 tablespoon flour

2 large egg whites

1/2 garlic clove, minced

1 medium yellow onion, chopped

1/4 cup shredded low-fat cheddar cheese

Preheat oven to 275°. Spray a 3-cup baking dish with cooking spray. Puree the cottage cheese in a food processor for 2 minutes, stopping to scrape the sides once or twice. Add the flour, egg whites, and garlic, and puree for 10 seconds. Add the onion, and puree for 15 seconds. Add the cheddar cheese, and puree for 2 to 3 seconds. Pour into the prepared baking dish, cover, and bake for 20 minutes. Uncover, raise the oven temperature to 300°, and bake for 20 to 30 additional minutes, or until hot and bubbly. Serve with low-fat crackers or toasted pita bread.

Preparation time: 10 minutes. Cooking time: 40 to 50 minutes. Yield: about 2 to 2½ cups or 40 hors d'oeuvres.

Nutrition analysis: 12.5 calories per serving; 2 gm. protein; 0.5 gm. carbohydrate; 0.5 gm. fat; 1 mg. cholesterol; 0 fiber; 50.5 mg. sodium

Percent of calories from protein: 60%; from carbohydrates: 22%; from fat: 18%

Exchange values: ½ meat

Mexican Black Bean Dip

This mildly spicy dip combines the goodness of beans with the flavor of Mexico. What a great way to introduce your family and friends to the world of beans.

1 1/2 teaspoons olive oil

Vegetable oil cooking spray

2 garlic cloves, minced

1 small onion, minced

15-ounce can Goya® black bean soup (don't use condensed soup as a substitute)

16-ounce can low-fat or fat-free refried beans

1 teaspoon dried mustard

2 tablespoons taco seasoning mix

4-ounce can or 6 tablespoons mild taco sauce

2 teaspoons white wine vinegar

Heat the olive oil and a generous spray of cooking spray for 45 seconds in a large, heavy skillet. Stir in the garlic and onion, and sauté over medium-low heat for 3 minutes, stirring frequently. Be careful not to let the mixture burn. Stir in the rest of the ingredients, and bring just to a boil. Simmer uncovered for 15 minutes, stirring occasionally. Serve hot or cold with low-fat tortilla chips or low-fat toasted pita bread.

Preparation time: 10 minutes. Cooking time: 20 minutes. Yield: about 3 cups or 30 servings

Nutrition analysis: 34.5 calories per serving; 2 gm. protein; 5.5 gm. carbohydrate; 0.5 gm. fat; 0 cholesterol; 0.5 gm. fiber; 264 mg. sodium

Percent of calories from protein: 19%; from carbohydrates: 62%; from fat: 18%

Exchange values: ½ bread

Salmon Spread

This is a wonderfully light, easy, and delicious spread to serve at a party.

1 to 1 1/4 cups low-fat (1%) cottage cheese

2 to 3 teaspoons lemon juice

2 to 3 dashes hot sauce (optional)

2 scallions, chopped (use some of the green)

2 ounces smoked salmon or lox

Put the cottage cheese, lemon juice, and hot sauce in a food processor or blender. Process on high for 2 to 3 minutes or until smooth and creamy, scraping the sides occasionally. Add the scallions, and process for 30 seconds more. Add the smoked salmon, and process for 30 additional seconds or until everything is pureed. Cover, and chill for 1 to 2 hours. Serve with thinly sliced toasted bagels or low-fat, light-tasting crackers.

Preparation time: 5 minutes. Chilling time: 1 to 2 hours. Yield: 36 to 40 hors d'oeuvres

Nutrition analysis: 14.5 calories per serving; 1.5 gm. protein; 2 gm. carbohydrate; 0 fat; 0.5 mg. cholesterol; 0.5 gm. fiber; 58.5 mg. sodium

Percent of calories from protein: 38%; from carbohydrates: 52%; from fat: 10%

Exchange values: less than ½ bread; less than ½ meat

Sandy's Mexican Dip

16 ounces low-salt, all-natural salsa

2 to 3 tablespoons low-fat or nonfat sour cream

2 to 4 tablespoons low-fat shredded cheddar cheese

7-ounce bag Guiltless Gourmet™ No Oil Tortilla Chips, low-fat crackers, or toasted pita bread wedges

Mix the salsa, sour cream, and cheddar cheese together. Serve cold, or microwave on high for 1 to 2 minutes. Serve with tortilla chips, crackers, or toasted pita bread wedges.

Preparation time: 5 minutes. Yield: 10 servings

Nutrition analysis: 113 calories per serving; 2 gm. protein; 21.5 gm. carbohydrate; 1 gm. fat; 2 mg. cholesterol; 1.5 gm. fiber; 584 mg. sodium

Percent of calories from protein: 8%; from carbohydrates: 82%; from fat: 10%

Exchange values: 1½ bread

Sandy's Marinated Broccoli

My friend Sandy introduced me to this hors d'oeuvre. I've served it at most of my cocktail parties, and someone always asks me for the recipe. It's hard to believe a bowl of broccoli would be so popular, but the marinade gives it a wonderful taste.

1 1/2 to 2 pounds raw broccoli florets (raw green beans and carrot sticks also are good in this marinade)

1 garlic clove, quartered

1 1/2 cups low-fat Italian dressing

1/3 cup red wine vinegar

1 tablespoon sugar

1 tablespoon dried dill weed

1/2 teaspoon salt

1/2 teaspoon black pepper

1 teaspoon dried basil

Wash and dry the broccoli. Cut the florets into bite-size pieces. Put the florets and garlic in a large bowl with a leak-proof top. Mix the rest of the ingredients together thoroughly, then pour over the broccoli. Stir the broccoli until it is well coated. Cover and refrigerate for 24 hours, stirring or turning the bowl over several times. Drain the broccoli in a colander for at least 10 minutes. Remove the garlic, and serve the broccoli.

Preparation time: 10 minutes. Marinating time: 24 hours. Yield: 25 hors d'oeuvres servings

Nutrition analysis: 16.5 calories per serving; 1 gm. protein; 2.5 gm. carbohydrate; 0.5 gm. fat; 0 cholesterol; 0 fiber; 77 mg. sodium

Percent of calories from protein: 23%; from carbohydrates: 57%; from fat: 21%

Exchange values: ½ vegetable

Tex-Mex Pie

This spread or dip can be made in a variety of ways. Depending upon your dietary needs, low-fat or nonfat sour cream can be used to replace the yogurt/ cottage cheese mixture, and a guacamole layer can be added.

1 pint cold nonfat plain yogurt, well drained

1/2 cup cold low-fat (1%) cottage cheese

1/2 to 1 teaspoon chopped jalapeño pepper (optional)

4-ounce can tiny shrimp, well drained

6 ounces chili sauce

6 scallions, finely chopped (use the white part plus 2 inches of green)

2.25-oz. can sliced black olives, well drained

3/4 cup finely chopped green pepper

2 tablespoons shredded low-fat cheddar cheese

Purée the yogurt, cottage cheese, and jalapeño pepper in a food processor or large blender on high until completely smooth and creamy. Spoon the yogurt/cottage cheese mixture on the bottom of a 9-inch quiche or pie plate. Cover this layer with the shrimp followed by a layer of chili sauce. Sprinkle the scallions, then the olives, then the green pepper, and finely the shredded cheese over the chili sauce layer. Serve cold with low-fat tortilla chips.

Preparation time: 15 minutes. Yield: about 50 single servings

Nutrition analysis: 16.5 calories per serving; 1.5 gm. protein; 2 gm. carbohydrate; 0.5 gm. fat; 4.5 mg. cholesterol; 0 fiber; 73.5 mg. sodium

Percent of calories from protein: 37%; from carbohydrates: 45%; from fat: 18%

Exchange values: less than ½ milk, vegetable, meat, and fat

Tipsy Melon

1 ripe honeydew melon

1 ripe cantaloupe

1/4 cup of your favorite fruit liqueur
  (orange, raspberry, peach, melon, etc.)

2 tablespoons apricot preserves

1 tablespoon fruit liqueur

3 to 4 tablespoons nonfat plain yogurt

This is a refreshing hors d'oeuvre or a low-fat, low-calorie dessert. Buy honeydew melons when they're ripe and have a fragrant scent, slightly sticky, velvety skin, and a buttery color. Cantaloupes are ripe when they've lost their green color, have a fragrant, sweet scent, and can be gently pressed at the base.

Peel both melons, and cut them into bite-size melon balls or cubes. Put them in a large bowl, and pour ¼ cup liqueur over them. Stir well, cover, and refrigerate for 30 minutes, stirring several times. Mix the preserves, 1 tablespoon liqueur, and nonfat yogurt together. Drain the melon thoroughly, and serve with the yogurt dip.

Preparation time: 10 minutes. Marinating time: 30 minutes. Yield: hors d'oeuvres for 25

Nutrition analysis: 38 calories per serving; 0.5 gm. protein; 9 gm. carbohydrate; 0 fat; 0 cholesterol; 0.5 gm. fiber; 9 mg. sodium

Percent of calories from protein: 5%; from carbohydrates: 95%; from fat: 0%

Exchange values: ½ fruit

Tortilla
Chips

Corn or flour tortillas

Vegetable oil cooking spray

Seasoned salt (optional)

Place a cookie sheet in the oven, then preheat the oven to 350° (make sure the oven reaches 350° before baking the tortillas). Spray each side of each tortilla with cooking spray. Lightly salt the tortillas if desired. Place the tortillas in a single layer on the cookie sheet. Bake for 3 to 4 minutes or until just before desired crispness is reached (they will continue to crisp up while cooling). Let cool on the cookie sheet. Break the tortillas into chips when they are cool.

Preparation time: 1 minute. Cooking time: 3 to 4 minutes

Nutrition analysis without added salt: 67 calories per serving; 2 gm. protein; 13 gm. carbohydrate; 1 gm. fat; 0 cholesterol; 1.5 gm. fiber; 53.5 mg. sodium

Percent of calories from protein: 12%; from carbohydrates: 73%; from fat: 15%

Exchange values: 1 bread, less than ½ fat

White Bean Dip

This quick, easy, delicious, and healthy dip can also be used as a spread on pita bread.

1 to 1 1/2 teaspoons chopped jalapeño peppers, depending on how hot you like your food (Note: always wear rubber gloves when working with hot peppers)

1 large garlic clove, chopped

2 scallions, chopped (use some of the green part)

16-ounce can white kidney beans, rinsed and drained

2 tablespoons fresh lemon juice

2 tablespoons chopped fresh parsley

1 teaspoon Dijon mustard

Salt to taste

Place the jalapeño pepper, garlic, and scallions in a food processor or large blender. Blend until well chopped. Add all the other ingredients, except the salt, to the food processor. Puree until very smooth (at least 60 seconds). Place in a serving dish, cover, and chill overnight. Taste after the ingredients have melded together, and add salt if necessary. Serve with low-fat crackers, rice cakes, or pumpernickel squares, or use as a sandwich spread on pita bread.

Preparation time: 10 minutes. Refrigeration time: overnight. Yield: about 1 to 1½ cups or 25 hors d'oeuvres

Nutrition analysis: 17 calories per serving; 1 gm. protein; 3 gm. carbohydrate; 0 fat; 0 cholesterol; 1 gm. fiber; 67 mg. sodium

Percent of calories from protein: 25%; from carbohydrates: 71%; from fat: 4%

Exchange values: ½ bread

Artichoke & Spinach Dip

Spinach dip served in a hollow pumpernickel loaf is a popular hors d'oeuvre. This spinach dip is equally popular, but much healthier.

Vegetable oil cooking spray

2 tablespoons low-fat cottage cheese

2 tablespoons plain nonfat yogurt

2 tablespoons fat-free mayonnaise

1/2 teaspoon dry mustard

3 scallions (use the white part plus 3 inches of the green part), chopped

14-ounce can artichoke hearts, rinsed, drained, and chopped

3 tablespoons shredded part-skim mozzarella cheese

10-ounce package frozen chopped spinach, thawed, with liquid squeezed out

1/4 teaspoon garlic powder

Salt and freshly ground pepper to taste

Preheat oven to 350°. Spray a 2¾-cup glass or ceramic baking dish with cooking spray. Place the cottage cheese, yogurt, mayonnaise, and dry mustard in a food processor. Process on high for 1 minute or until the cottage cheese is creamy. Add the scallions, artichoke hearts, and cheese. Process until the ingredients are chopped but not pureed. Add the spinach, garlic powder, salt, and pepper. Process briefly using the on/off button until everything is mixed together but not pureed. Pour into the prepared baking dish, and cover. Bake for 15 minutes, then uncover, and bake for 15 more minutes or until hot and bubbly. Serve with low-fat crackers or water crackers; or if you prefer, hollow out a small loaf of pumpernickel bread, fill it with the cooked spinach dip, and serve it with chunks of the pumpernickel bread.

Preparation time: 10 minutes. Cooking time: 30 minutes. Yield: about 2 cups or 40 servings

Nutrition analysis: 9 calories per serving; 1 gm. protein; 1 gm. carbohydrate; 0.5 gm. fat; 0.5 mg. cholesterol; 0.5 gm. fiber; 34 mg. sodium

Percent of calories from protein: 35%; from carbohydrates: 43%; from fat: 22%

Exchange values: ½ vegetable

Artichoke Spread

Vegetable oil cooking spray

14-ounce can artichoke hearts, rinsed and drained

1 1/2 teaspoons Dijon mustard

2 tablespoons nonfat plain yogurt

2 tablespoons fat-free mayonnaise

1 tablespoon grated Parmesan cheese

Preheat oven to 350°. Spray a 2¾-cup glass or ceramic baking dish with cooking spray. Place all the ingredients in a food processor or large blender. Using the on/off button, process on high just until all the ingredients are mixed but not puréed. Pour into the prepared baking dish. Bake uncovered for 20 to 30 minutes or until hot and bubbly. Serve with low-fat crackers, water crackers, thin toast, or toasted pita bread. This spread freezes well.

Preparation time: 5 minutes. Cooking time: 20 to 30 minutes. Yield: about 1½ cups or 25 servings

Nutrition analysis: 9 calories per serving; 0.5 gm. protein; 1 gm. carbohydrate; 0.5 gm. fat; 0.5 mg. cholesterol; 0.5 gm. fiber; 48 mg. sodium

Percent of calories from protein: 20%; from carbohydrates: 47%; from fat: 34%

Exchange values: less than ½ vegetable

Fear of Frying

BREAKFAST
AND
LUNCH
ALTERNATIVES

Cranapple Orange Bread

This bread is absolutely delicious and very popular during the holidays, but we enjoy it all year long. The wonderful combination of fresh fruit keeps this bread moist and gives it a great flavor.

Vegetable oil cooking spray

1 cup unsifted but stirred whole-wheat flour
(if you prefer a whiter, lighter bread, omit the
whole-wheat flour and use only all-purpose flour)

1 cup unsifted but stirred unbleached all-purpose flour

1 1/2 teaspoons baking powder

1/2 teaspoon baking soda

1/4 teaspoon salt (optional)

1 teaspoon ground cinnamon

1 medium-small, sweet red apple, peeled, cored, and sliced

1 medium navel orange, peeled, pitted, and quartered

1 cup whole cranberries, washed and dried

1/2 cup granulated sugar (this can be mixed with brown sugar if
you prefer a darker bread)

1 whole large egg

2 large egg whites

2 tablespoons canola oil or low-in-saturated-fat oil

2 tablespoons honey

1 teaspoon vanilla extract

Orange liqueur (optional)

Preheat oven to 350°. Spray an 8½" x 4½" loaf pan with cooking spray. In a large bowl, stir both flours, baking powder, baking soda, salt, and cinnamon together thoroughly. Set aside. In a large food processor, chop (do not puree) the apple, orange, and cranberries. This should make a little more than 1 heaping cup of chopped fruit. Keep 1 level cup plus 1 heaping tablespoon in the food processor, and set the rest aside to use in something else.

Add the sugar, eggs, oil, honey, and vanilla to the fruit in the food processor. Using the on/off button, process just until everything is mixed together; do not puree. Stir this mixture into the flour mixture just until everything is moistened. Do not over-mix. Pour into the prepared loaf pan; then, if you have time, let stand at room temperature for 10 minutes. Bake in preheated oven for 50 to 60 minutes or until a cake tester comes out clean. Let cool slightly, and drizzle with orange liqueur. Let sit at least 3 hours before serving.

Preparation time: 15 minutes. Cooking time: 50 to 60 minutes. Standing time: 3 hours. Yield: 10 servings

Nutrition analysis: 187 calories per serving; 3.5 gm. protein; 36 gm. carbohydrate; 3.5 gm. fat; 21.5 mg. cholesterol; 1 gm. fiber; 162 mg. sodium

Percent of calories from protein: 7%; from carbohydrates: 76%; from fat: 17%

Exchange values: ½ fruit; 1 bread; ½ fat

Festive Apricot Bread

Tea breads make great gifts. Adding fruit provides an exotic flavor and moistness without added fat. Apricots give this bread a lightly sweet and citrus flavor.

Vegetable oil cooking spray

2 1/2 cups unsifted, but stirred, all-purpose, unbleached, enriched flour

3 teaspoons baking powder (make sure it's fresh)

1/2 teaspoon baking soda

1/2 teaspoon salt

1/4 to 1/3 cup granulated sugar

1 whole large egg

1 cup apricot preserves (try the juice-sweetened variety)

1 cup orange juice

2 tablespoons triple sec, Cointreau, or orange liqueur

2 tablespoons canola oil

1/2 cup well-chopped dried apricots (they should be soft and pliable)

Preheat oven to 350°. Spray an 8½" x 4½" loaf pan with cooking spray. Stir the dry ingredients together, and set aside. Beat the egg, preserves, juice, 1 tablespoon liqueur, and canola oil together in a large bowl. Stir in the apricots. (If the apricots are dried out they can be rejuvenated in the microwave with a couple teaspoons of orange juice.) Stir the dry ingredients into the bowl of liquid ingredients just until everything is moistened. Spoon the batter into the loaf pan, and bake for 50 to 60 minutes or until a cake tester comes out clean. Cool for 10 minutes. Pierce the bread several times with a fork, then pour the remaining orange liqueur over the bread. Let stand for several hours before serving.

Preparation time: 10 minutes. Cooking time: 50 to 60 minutes. Yield: 1 loaf or 60 mini muffins—10 servings

Nutrition analysis: 229 calories per serving; 3 gm. protein; 45 gm. carbohydrate; 3.5 gm. fat; 21.5 mg. cholesterol; 1.5 gm. fiber; 282 mg. sodium

Percent of calories from protein: 6%; from carbohydrates: 78%; from fat: 14%

Exchange values: ½ fruit; 1½ bread; ½ fat

Creamy Corn Pudding Bread

Unlike most corn breads, the corn bread made from this recipe is very moist; in fact, it's somewhere between a corn pudding and a bread.

Vegetable oil cooking spray

1 cup cornmeal

1 cup stirred unbleached, all-purpose flour

2 teaspoons baking powder

1/2 teaspoon baking soda

1/2 teaspoon salt, or to taste

1 whole large egg

2 large egg whites

1 cup skim buttermilk

2 tablespoons canola oil or low-in-saturated-fat vegetable oil

2 tablespoons honey

1 can (14 1/2 or 14 3/4 ounces) cream-style corn

Preheat oven to 400°. Spray a 9" square baking dish with cooking spray. Stir the cornmeal, flour, baking powder, baking soda, and salt together. Set aside. In a large bowl, beat the whole egg and egg whites until frothy. Beat in the buttermilk, oil, honey, and corn. Stir in the cornmeal mixture just until everything is combined. Do not overmix. Pour the batter into the prepared dish, and let stand at room temperature for 10 minutes. Bake for 30 to 40 minutes or until a cake tester comes out clean. Serve warm or at room temperature, but refrigerate any leftovers. (The bread may fall slightly while cooling.) This corn bread goes nicely with a hearty salad or soup.

Preparation time: 10 minutes. Standing time: 10 minutes. Cooking time: 30 to 40 minutes. Yield: 12 servings

Nutrition analysis: 142 calories per serving; 4 gm. protein; 25 gm. carbohydrate; 3.5 gm. fat; 18 mg. cholesterol; 2 gm. fiber; 281 mg. sodium

Percent of calories from protein: 11%; from carbohydrates: 69%; from fat: 21%

Exchange values: 1½ bread; ½ fat

Lynsie's Bruschetta

1 loaf of Italian or French bread

1 to 1 1/2 teaspoons olive oil

1/2 to 1 teaspoon garlic salt

3 to 4 large (summer-fresh) tomatoes, thinly sliced or chopped

1/4 cup chopped fresh basil

Cut the bread on the diagonal into 1-inch slices. Lightly brush one side of each slice with a touch of olive oil. Sprinkle the same side with garlic salt. Place on the grill with the olive oil side down, and quickly brown; or broil with the olive oil side up. Top each piece with tomatoes, a sprinkle of garlic salt if you like, and chopped basil.

Preparation time: 10 minutes. Grilling or broiling time: a few minutes. Yield: about 15 slices

Nutrition analysis: 110 calories per serving; 3.5 gm. protein; 19.5 gm. carbohydrate; 2 gm. fat; 0 cholesterol; 1 gm. fiber; 333 mg. sodium

Percent of calories from protein: 13%; from carbohydrates: 71%; from fat: 16%

Exchange values: ½ vegetable; 1½ bread; ½ fat

Fear of Frying

Orange Muffins

These simple muffins are bursting with flavor and yet have very little fat and cholesterol. In addition, there are no eggs in this recipe, so these muffins can be enjoyed by people who can't eat eggs.

Vegetable oil cooking spray

2 cups unsifted, unbleached all-purpose flour

1 tablespoon baking powder

1/4 cup sugar

6-ounce can frozen orange juice concentrate, thawed

2 tablespoons canola oil or low-in-saturated-fat vegetable oil

1 tablespoon nonfat plain yogurt

1/2 cup apricot preserves (try the juice-sweetened or reduced-sugar variety)

2 tablespoons dried apricots, well chopped (optional)

Topping:

1 tablespoon sugar

1/4 teaspoon cinnamon

1/4 teaspoon nutmeg (I prefer freshly ground nutmeg)

Preheat oven to 375°. Spray 12 muffin tins with cooking spray. Mix the flour, baking powder, and ¼ cup sugar together. Set aside. In a large bowl, beat the thoroughly thawed orange juice concentrate, oil, yogurt, and apricot preserves together. Stir in the apricots. Slowly stir the flour mixture into the liquid ingredients just until everything is moistened. Do not overmix. Spoon the batter into the muffin tins. Mix the sugar, cinnamon, and nutmeg together, and sprinkle over the muffins. Bake for 20 to 25 minutes or until a cake tester comes out clean.

Preparation time: 10 minutes. Cooking time: 20 to 25 minutes. Yield: 12 muffins

Nutrition analysis: 157 calories per serving; 2 gm. protein; 33 gm. carbohydrate; 2.5 gm. fat; O cholesterol; 0.5 gm. fiber; 84 mg. sodium

Percent of calories from protein: 5%; from carbohydrates: 81%; from fat: 14%

Exchange values: ½ fruit; 1½ bread; ½ fat

Pear
Bread

This bread is not only easy to make but delicious and low in fat. The pureed pears give the bread its moisture and delicate flavor. With that winning combination, you will find yourself making it often.

Vegetable oil cooking spray

2 cups unsifted, stirred, unbleached all-purpose flour

1 teaspoon baking powder

1/2 teaspoon baking soda

1 teaspoon ground cinnamon

1/4 teaspoon salt (optional)

29-ounce can unsweetened pears, slices or halves

1 large whole egg

2 large egg whites

3/4 cup granulated sugar

1 teaspoon vanilla extract

2 tablespoons canola oil or low-in-saturated-fat oil

3 tablespoons apricot jam (try the fruit juice-sweetened variety)

Orange liqueur (optional)

Preheat oven to 350°. Spray an 8½" x 4½" loaf pan with cooking spray. Sift the dry ingredients together into a large bowl. Set aside. Drain the pears thoroughly. Purée enough pears in a food processor or blender to make 1¼ cups of puréed pears. Add the eggs, sugar, vanilla, oil, and jam to the puréed pears in the food processor and mix well. (An electric beater works, too.) Stir the pear mixture into the dry ingredients just until everything is moistened. Do not overmix. Pour into the prepared pan, and bake for 50 to 60 minutes or until a cake tester comes out clean. Let cool slightly, then drizzle with orange liqueur.

Preparation time: 10 minutes. Cooking time: 50 to 60 minutes. Yield: 10 servings

Nutrition analysis: 204 calories per serving; 3.5 gm. protein; 41 gm. carbohydrate; 3.5 gm. fat; 21.5 mg. cholesterol; 1.5 gm. fiber; 154 mg. sodium

Percent of calories from protein: 6%; from carbohydrates: 79%; from fat: 15%

Exchange values: ½ fruit; 1 bread; ½ fat

Onion-Stuffed Baguette

This is a delicious luncheon entree or appetizer.

1 fresh baguette (loaf of long, thin French bread)

2 to 3 teaspoons Dijon mustard

Vegetable oil cooking spray

1 1/2 teaspoons olive oil

3 leeks, cleaned and chopped (use mostly the white part)

1 bunch scallions, washed, trimmed, and chopped (use the white part and 2 inches of the green)

1 garlic clove, minced

1 to 3 teaspoons chicken broth or water

2 to 3 tablespoons coarsely chopped fresh dill weed

1 tablespoon finely chopped fresh basil

Salt and freshly ground pepper to taste

Cut the French bread in half lengthwise. Spread a thin layer of Dijon mustard on each half. Spray a large, heavy skillet with cooking spray. Add the oil, and heat. Sauté the leeks, scallions, and garlic over medium-low heat for 5 minutes, adding broth or water if they begin to burn. Stir in the dill, basil, and more broth or water if necessary. Cover, and simmer for 3 minutes, stirring occasionally. Add salt and pepper to taste. Spread the onion mixture on the bread. Cut each half diagonally in half or into 10 slices for appetizers.

Preparation time: 10 minutes. Cooking time: 10 minutes. Yield: 4 luncheon servings or 20 appetizers

Nutrition analysis for 4 servings: 328 calories per serving; 10.5 gm. protein; 59 gm. carbohydrate; 5.5 gm. fat; 0 cholesterol; 4 gm. fiber; 610 mg. sodium

Percent of calories from protein: 13%; from carbohydrates: 72%; from fat: 16%

Exchange values: 2½ vegetable; 3 bread; 1 fat

Pita
Pizza

There are endless varieties of pita pizzas, all of which are quick, easy, and popular with the kids. Use whatever vegetables you have in the refrigerator and you'll have a different taste each time.

1 pita, cut open to make 2 round halves. You can use pocketless pita if you prefer.

4 to 6 tablespoons pizza sauce or tomato sauce

Garlic salt (optional)

1/4 teaspoon dried oregano

2 to 3 tablespoons chopped, fresh vegetables such as onions, broccoli, spinach, peppers, and tomatoes, or shredded zucchini and carrots

2 tablespoons low-fat mozzarella cheese

Preheat oven to 400°. Spread 2 to 3 tablespoons of sauce on each half. Sprinkle some garlic salt and oregano on the sauce. Cover each half with chopped or shredded vegetables. Sprinkle with mozzarella cheese, and bake for 10 to 12 minutes or until cheese melts.

KIDS LOVE THIS

Preparation time: 10 minutes. Cooking time: 10 to 12 minutes. Yield: 2 servings

Nutrition analysis: 192 calories per serving; 10 gm. protein; 32 gm. carbohydrate; 3 gm. fat; 0 cholesterol; 2.5 gm. fiber; 794 mg. sodium

Percent of calories from protein: 21%; from carbohydrates: 66%; from fat: 13%

Exchange values: 2 vegetable; ½ bread; ½ meat

Grilled Veggie Sandwich

Whenever I make grilled or roasted vegetables, I make some extra so I can have this sandwich for lunch. This is my favorite combination of grilled vegetables for a sandwich, but you can be creative and use most any vegetable.

1 to 2 teaspoons minced or mashed sun-dried tomatoes or to taste

2 teaspoons nonfat mayonnaise

1 pita with a pocket, or 6 inches of fresh French bread cut lengthwise

1 cup grilled, sliced vegetables: onions, eggplant, zucchini, mushrooms, carrots, green and red peppers, etc.

Mix or puree the sun-dried tomatoes together with the mayonnaise. Spread this on the inside of the pita or French bread. Cover with the grilled vegetables to make a sandwich. (If you don't mind the extra fat and calories, this sandwich is delicious with a slice of fresh mozzarella cheese.)

Preparation time: 5 minutes. Yield: 1 serving

Nutrition analysis using all listed vegetables, but no cheese: 178 calories per serving; 7 gm. protein; 36.5 gm. carbohydrate; 1.5 gm. fat; 4.5 mg. cholesterol; 3.5 gm. fiber; 290 mg. sodium

Percent of calories from protein: 15%; from carbohydrates: 79%; from fat: 7%

Exchange values: 1½ vegetable; 1½ bread

Louisiana French Toast

I serve this for breakfast most Sunday mornings. It's one of the few healthier breakfast dishes that pleases everyone in my family.

1 whole large egg

2 large egg whites

1 1/2 to 2 tablespoons sugar, or to taste

2 to 3 tablespoons skim milk and 1 tablespoon orange liqueur, or 3 to 4 tablespoons skim milk if you are serving this to kids

1 tablespoon apricot preserves

2 tablespoons orange juice

1/4 teaspoon ground cinnamon

1/2 teaspoon vanilla extract

1/2 loaf French bread or 8 to 10 slices cinnamon bread

Vegetable oil cooking spray

Maple syrup and/or sliced fruit

KIDS LOVE THIS

Beat the eggs, sugar, milk, liqueur, and apricot preserves together well. Beat in the orange juice, cinnamon, and vanilla. Slice the French bread into eight to ten 1-inch diagonal slices. Generously spray a large skillet with cooking spray. Heat the skillet until moderately hot. Dip each side of each slice of bread in the egg mixture. Brown the bread in the skillet over medium heat 2 to 3 minutes on each side or until golden and hot. Serve covered with sliced fruit and/or maple syrup.

Preparation time: 10 minutes. Cooking time: 5 minutes. Yield: 10 slices

Nutrition analysis: 128 calories per serving; 5 gm. protein; 22.5 gm. carbohydrate; 2 gm. fat; 21.5 mg. cholesterol; 1 gm. fiber; 214 mg. sodium

Percent of calories from protein: 16%; from carbohydrates: 71%; from fat: 13%

Exchange values: 1½ bread; ½ fat

Southwestern Chicken Sandwich

Here's another easy and healthy sandwich.

1 hard roll (use the whole-wheat variety for a healthier sandwich)

1 teaspoon fat-free mayonnaise

1 teaspoon mild green taco sauce

2 to 3 slices skinless, baked chicken breast

2 tomato slices (optional)

1 lettuce leaf (optional)

Salt and pepper to taste

TEENS LOVE THIS

Slice the roll. Mix the mayonnaise and green taco sauce together. Spread the sauce on the roll, and add the chicken, tomato, lettuce, and salt and pepper. (If you want more sauce, mix equal parts of mayonnaise and taco sauce together.)

Preparation time: 5 minutes. Yield: 1 sandwich

Nutrition analysis: 257 calories per serving; 19 gm. protein; 31.5 gm. carbohydrate; 6 gm. fat; 39 mg. cholesterol; 2 gm. fiber; 369 mg. sodium

Percent of calories from protein: 30%; from carbohydrates: 49%; from fat: 20%

Exchange values: 2 bread; 1½ meat; ½ fat

Pita Melt

Vegetables are a nice alternative to cold cuts in sandwiches. This vegetarian pita is easy to make, low in fat and calories, and delicious.

1 pita, cut in half so you have 2 pockets

1 to 2 teaspoons Dijon mustard or your favorite gourmet mustard

1 small carrot, peeled and shredded

1 small tomato, seeded and chopped

1 scallion, chopped

1/4 cup chopped red or green pepper

1 cup alfalfa sprouts

1 to 2 tablespoons chopped Havarti cheese (plain, with dill, or with jalapeño peppers). Other cheeses that can be used are Swiss, provolone, cheddar, feta, mozzarella, or your favorite low-fat cheese.

Salt and pepper to taste

Spread some mustard inside each pita half. Mix the rest of the ingredients together. Stuff both halves with the mixture. Eat the pita cold or heat it in the microwave on high for 1 to 2 minutes or until the cheese is soft.

Preparation time: 10 minutes. Yield: 2 servings

Nutrition analysis: 118 calories per serving; 6.5 gm. protein; 19.5 gm. carbohydrate; 2.5 gm. fat; 3.5 mg. cholesterol; 3 gm. fiber; 270 mg. sodium

Percent of calories from protein: 20%; from carbohydrates: 63%; from fat: 17%

Exchange values: 1½ vegetable; ½ bread; ½ meat

Pizza Bagels

1/2 plain bagel

1 tablespoon low-fat or nonfat ricotta cheese

1 tablespoon pizza sauce

Grated Parmesan or Romano cheese

Place the bagel on a piece of aluminum foil (used for easy cleanup). Spread the ricotta cheese over the bagel. Spoon the pizza sauce over the ricotta cheese, and sprinkle with grated cheese. Toast in a toaster oven or broil until hot.

Preparation time: 5 minutes. Yield: 1 serving

Nutrition analysis: 109 calories per serving; 5 gm. protein; 18 gm. carbohydrate; 2 gm. fat; 5 mg. cholesterol; 1 gm. fiber; 203 mg. sodium

Percent of calories from protein: 18%; from carbohydrates: 65%; from fat: 16%

Exchange values: ½ vegetable; 1 bread; ½ meat; ½ fat

KIDS LOVE THIS

White Pizza Bagel

1/2 plain bagel

2 tablespoons low-fat or nonfat ricotta cheese

2 basil leaves, chopped

1/2 scallion, chopped (optional)

3 to 4 slices tomato, chopped

1/2 teaspoon Butter Buds, natural dehydrated butter (optional)

1 teaspoon grated Parmesan or Romano cheese (optional)

Salt and freshly ground pepper to taste

KIDS
LOVE
THIS

Place the bagel on a piece of aluminum foil (used for easy cleanup). Mix the rest of the ingredients together. Spread the mixture on the bagel. Toast in a toaster oven or broil until hot.

Preparation time: 10 minutes. Yield: 1 serving

Nutrition analysis: 149 calories per serving; 8 gm. protein; 20 gm. carbohydrate; 4 gm. fat; 11 mg. cholesterol; 1.5 gm. fiber; 182 mg. sodium

Percent of calories from protein: 21%; from carbohydrates: 55%; from fat: 24%

Exchange values: ½ vegetable; 1 bread; ½ meat; ½ fat

Holiday Turkey Sandwich

Fresh 6-inch French baguette (use the whole-wheat variety for a healthier sandwich)

2 slices skinless, baked turkey breast

1 to 2 tablespoons fresh cranberry relish or cranberry sauce

Slice the baguette lengthwise. Spread the cranberry relish on one side of the baguette, add the sliced turkey, and top with the other side of the baguette.

Preparation time: 5 minutes. Yield: 1 sandwich

Nutrition analysis: 325 calories per serving; 24 gm. protein; 49 gm. carbohydrate; 3 gm. fat; 47 mg. cholesterol; 2 gm. fiber; 425 mg. sodium

KIDS LOVE THIS

Percent of calories from protein: 30%; from carbohydrates: 61%; from fat: 9%

Exchange values: 1 fruit; 2½ bread; 2½ meat; ½ fat

Vegetable Pocket

Vegetable pockets are fun to make because you can use many different combinations of vegetables to give you a variety of tastes. This is a basic recipe to which fresh, chopped broccoli, cauliflower, peas, and green beans can be added.

1 flour tortilla or 1/2 pita pocket

1 to 2 tablespoons low-fat or nonfat ricotta cheese

1/2 teaspoon fresh dill weed, chopped
   or 1/4 teaspoon dried dill weed

1 tablespoon low-fat Italian salad dressing,
   or 1/2 teaspoon sweet and hot mustard

1 teaspoon Parmesan cheese (optional)

Salt and freshly ground pepper to taste

3/4 to 1 cup alfalfa sprouts

3 slices fresh summer tomatoes, chopped

1 scallion, chopped (optional)

1/4 cup red or green pepper, chopped

1 small carrot, peeled and shredded

1 roasted red pepper, sliced (optional)

Heat the tortilla in the oven or microwave for a minute or two until it's warm but not crisp. Mix the ricotta cheese, dill weed, salad dressing, Parmesan cheese, and salt and pepper together to make a dressing. Set aside. Mix the other ingredients together. Spread the vegetable mixture out on the tortilla. Cover with the dressing. Fold up the bottom of the tortilla, then fold in the sides, or roll the tortilla up, and serve.

Preparation time: 10 minutes. Yield: 1 serving

Nutrition analysis: 249 calories per serving; 10.5 gm. protein; 38.5 gm. carbohydrate; 7 gm. fat; 12 mg. cholesterol; 6 gm. fiber; 231 mg. sodium

Percent of calories from protein: 16%; from carbohydrates: 59%; from fat: 25%

Exchange values: 3½ vegetable; 1 bread; ½ meat; 1 fat

SOUPS, SALADS,
AND
DRESSINGS

Broccoli Plus Soup

Broccoli is one of those miracle vegetables that is full of vitamins and minerals. Unfortunately, though, not everybody loves its strong taste. This soup combines broccoli with other vegetables to make a rich-tasting puree that has a mild and appealing flavor.

1 1/2 teaspoons olive oil, or vegetable oil cooking spray

1 large, sweet onion, chopped

2 large garlic cloves, minced

5 cups homemade chicken broth or 3 cans (13 3/4 ounces each) low-sodium chicken broth. Skim off all visible fat.

1 1/2 pounds fresh broccoli crowns, cut-up

1 large red apple, peeled, cored, and sliced

1 medium parsnip, peeled and sliced

1 medium-large potato, peeled and sliced

1 tablespoon fresh lemon juice (optional)

Salt and freshly ground pepper to taste (optional)

Heat the oil in a large, heavy pot or spray the bottom of the pot with cooking spray. Sauté the onions and garlic over medium-low heat for 3 to 5 minutes, stirring often. (If you use cooking spray, you may need to add a teaspoon or two of water.) Stir in the chicken broth, broccoli, apple, parsnip, and potato. Bring to a boil, cover, and reduce heat. Simmer for 30 minutes or until the vegetables are very tender. Purée in small batches in a food processor or blender. Return to the pot, and reheat to boiling. Stir in the lemon juice, and taste to check seasoning. Serve immediately with crusty bread or corn bread. Freezes well.

Preparation time: 15 minutes. Cooking time: 35 minutes (mostly unattended). Yield: about 9 cups

Nutrition analysis: 93 calories per serving; 3 gm. protein; 17.5 gm. carbohydrate; 2 gm. fat; 0 cholesterol; 3.5 gm. fiber; 293 mg. sodium

Percent of calories from protein: 12%; from carbohydrates: 70%; from fat: 18%

Exchange values: 1½ vegetable; ½ bread; ½ fat

Chunky Corn Chowder

I'm sure this soup will become a family favorite in your house. Not only is it a snap to make and delicious to eat, but the colorful vegetables make it very attractive.

1 1/2 teaspoons olive oil

Vegetable oil cooking spray

1 whole bunch of scallions, washed and chopped

1 red pepper, seeded and diced

2 medium potatoes, peeled and diced

12-ounce can low-fat or skimmed evaporated milk, undiluted

1 cup skim milk, divided

1/2 to 1 teaspoon dried thyme

1 tablespoon minced fresh parsley

16-ounce can creamed corn

10-ounce box frozen corn, partially thawed, or 2 cups fresh corn

Salt and freshly ground pepper to taste

Mild green taco sauce to taste (optional)

Heat the oil and a generous spray of cooking spray for 45 seconds in a large, heavy pot. Sauté the scallions over medium-low heat for 2 minutes, stirring frequently. Add red pepper, and stir for 2 more minutes. Add the potatoes; stir for 1 minute. Stir in the evaporated milk and ½ cup of skim milk. Bring to a boil, reduce heat, stir, cover, and simmer for 15 minutes. Add thyme and parsley, cover, continue simmering for 10 minutes or until the potatoes are tender. Stir in the creamed corn and corn kernels. Add remaining skim milk until the soup reaches desired consistency. Bring to a boil and continue simmering 3 to 5 minutes or until the corn is tender. Salt and pepper to taste. Pour into soup dishes and drop 1 to 2 teaspoons of taco sauce into each bowl, if you want to add a little Southwestern flavor.

Preparation time: 10 minutes. Cooking time: 35 minutes. Yield: 6 servings

Nutrition analysis: 205 calories per serving; 9.5 gm. protein; 42 gm. carbohydrate; 2 gm. fat; 3 mg. cholesterol; 2.5 gm. fiber; 307 mg. sodium

Percent of calories from protein: 17%; from carbohydrates: 76%; from fat: 7%

Exchange values: ½ milk; 2 bread; ½ fat

Meatball Soup

1/2 pound very lean ground turkey, chicken, or beef

2 to 4 tablespoons Italian seasoned bread crumbs (beef usually needs the lower amount and chicken close to the higher amount)

Vegetable oil cooking spray

2 carrots, peeled or scrubbed and chopped

2 celery stalks, chopped

1 small onion, chopped

1 garlic clove, minced

2 cups Hunts® tomato sauce or your favorite marinara sauce

3 1/2 cups low-salt chicken broth, with fat skimmed off

1 cup water

1 tablespoon parsley

1 bay leaf

1/4 teaspoon crushed thyme

1/4 teaspoon dried basil or 1/2 teaspoon chopped fresh basil

1/2 teaspoon saffron (optional)

1/2 cup uncooked Acini Pepe pasta or Orzo (rice-shaped) pasta

Salt and freshly ground pepper to taste

Mix the ground meat and bread crumbs together until the mixture reaches a sticky consistency. Make 25 small meatballs. Generously spray a large, heavy pot with cooking spray. Cook the meatballs over medium-low heat for 5 to 7 minutes, gently turning them frequently. Remove the meatballs from the pot, and drain off any excess fat from the pot.

Generously respray the bottom of the pot, if necessary, and sauté the chopped carrots, celery, onion, and garlic for 3 minutes over medium-low heat, stirring frequently (you may have to add 1 to 2 teaspoons of water to prevent the mixture from burning). Stir in the tomato sauce, chicken broth, water, and seasonings. Bring to a boil, stir in the meatballs, cover, and simmer for 25 minutes.

Stir in the pasta, bring to a boil, and cook over medium-low heat for 15 to 20 minutes, or until the pasta is tender, stirring occasionally. Add salt and pepper to taste, and serve immediately. This soup tastes best when freshly made and is better if not frozen.

Preparation time: 15 minutes. Cooking time: 50 minutes (mostly unattended). Yield: 7½ cups or 5 to 6 servings

Nutrition analysis: 195 calories per serving; 10 gm. protein; 28 gm. carbohydrate; 5 gm. fat; 17 mg. cholesterol; 3 gm. fiber; 1,020 mg. sodium

Percent of calories from protein: 20%; from carbohydrates: 57%; from fat: 23%

Exchange values: 2½ vegetable; 1 bread; 1 meat; ½ fat

Fabulous Chick-Pea Soup

Chick-peas, also known as garbanzo beans, contain cholesterol-lowering nutrients and are an important legume to add to our diet. The chick-peas provide a surprisingly tasty, creamy base and delicious flavor to this easy-to-prepare, healthy, and delicious soup.

1 1/2 teaspoons olive oil

Vegetable oil cooking spray

1 medium onion, chopped

2 garlic cloves, minced

3 large carrots, scrubbed and sliced

1 small sweet potato, peeled and sliced

16-ounce can chick-peas, drained and rinsed or 1 3/4 cups cooked chick-peas

3 1/2 to 4 cups low-salt chicken broth with the fat skimmed off the top

1 to 2 tablespoons lemon juice

Salt and freshly ground pepper to taste

Heat the olive oil and a generous spray of the cooking spray in a large pot for 45 seconds. Stir in the onions and garlic, and sauté for 3 minutes over medium-low heat, stirring frequently. (You may have to add 1 to 2 teaspoons of water to prevent the onions from burning.) Stir in the carrots, sweet potato, chick-peas, and chicken broth. Cover and simmer for 30 to 35 minutes or until the carrots are tender.

Remove from heat and puree in small batches in a food processor or blender. Return to the pot, then stir in the lemon juice, and salt and pepper to taste. Reheat just to the boiling point, and serve immediately. Serve with a green salad and some crusty breads for a wonderful tasting and healthy meal in 40 minutes. Freezes well.

Preparation time: 10 minutes. Cooking time: 40 minutes (mostly unattended). Yield: 6 cups

Nutrition analysis: 148 calories per serving; 5 gm. protein; 24 gm. carbohydrate; 3.5 gm. fat; 2 mg. cholesterol; 6 gm. fiber; 743 mg. sodium

Percent of calories from protein: 14%; from carbohydrates: 64%; from fat: 22%

Exchange values: 1 vegetable; 1½ bread; ½ fat

Zesty Carrot Ginger Soup

This delicious, yet healthy soup has a sophisticated, clean, fresh taste. The amount of ginger you use will determine how zesty the soup will be. I prefer a lot of ginger, but my family likes the milder version.

1 1/2 teaspoons olive oil, or a generous
   spray of vegetable oil cooking spray plus
   1 to 2 teaspoons of water

1 1/2 cups well-cleaned chopped leeks, white part only

2 to 3 garlic cloves, minced

1 to 3 tablespoons fresh gingerroot, peeled and minced

6 cups low-salt chicken broth with the fat skimmed off

1 1/4 pounds fresh or frozen young carrots, peeled and sliced. (If you use frozen
   carrots, make sure they are mostly thawed.)

1/2 to 3/4 pound parsnip, peeled and sliced

1/2 to 1 cup low-fat or skim milk

Salt and freshly ground pepper to taste

Heat the oil in a large pot. Sauté the leeks and garlic over medium-low heat for 2 minutes, stirring frequently. Stir in the ginger and continue to sauté and stir for 2 more minutes, adding a drop or two of water if the onions begin to burn. Pour in the chicken broth, and quickly bring to a boil. Stir in the carrots and parsnips, and quickly bring to a boil again. Lower heat, cover, and simmer for 30 minutes or until carrots are tender.

Puree in small batches in a food processor or blender, making sure the ginger is completely pureed. Return to pot, then stir in milk, salt, and pepper. Reheat just to the boiling point and serve. Freezes well.

Preparation time: 10 minutes. Cooking time: 40 minutes. Yield: about 7 cups or 6 servings

Nutrition analysis: 178 calories per serving; 4 gm. protein; 35 gm. carbohydrate; 3 gm. fat; 0.5 mg. cholesterol; 3.5 gm. fiber; 583 mg. sodium

Percent of calories from protein: 8%; from carbohydrates: 76%; from fat: 16%

Exchange values: 5 vegetable; ½ bread; ½ fat

Butternut Squash & Apple Soup

This soup is full of healthy ingredients such as complex carbohydrates, dietary fiber, vitamin C, and the antioxidant, beta-carotene. It's easy to make, elegant to serve, and delicious to eat.

Vegetable oil spray or 1 1/2 teaspoons olive oil

1 medium yellow onion, chopped

1 garlic clove, minced

1/4 cup all-purpose flour

5 cups homemade chicken stock or 3 (13 3/4-ounce) cans low-salt chicken broth (skim off all fat)

1 butternut squash (about 3 pounds), peeled, cored, and cubed

3 large red apples, peeled, cored, and coarsely chopped

1 cup low-fat or skim milk, divided

2 tablespoons nonfat dry milk

2 tablespoons caraway seeds (optional)

Dash of nutmeg

Salt and freshly ground black pepper to taste

Heat the cooking spray or olive oil in a large, heavy pot. Stir in the onions and garlic, and sauté over medium-low heat for 3 to 5 minutes, stirring often. (If using cooking spray, add a teaspoon or two of water to the onions and garlic.) Stir in the flour, and continue stirring for 30 to 45 seconds or until the onions absorb most of the flour. Stir in the chicken stock, squash, and apples. Bring to boil, and simmer for 30 to 40 minutes.

As soon as the soup starts simmering, combine ½ cup of the milk, the dry milk, and the caraway seeds in a small microwave-proof bowl. Microwave on high for 1 to 2 minutes or until the milk starts bubbling. Stir, and let stand. (If you don't have a microwave, this may be done on the stove.)

When the squash is very tender, puree the soup in small batches in a food processor or blender. Return to the pot. Rub the caraway seed milk through a small, fine mesh sieve into the soup. (The more you rub the caraway seeds, the more caraway flavor you get in the soup, but you don't want the seeds themselves in the soup. Discard the seeds when finished.) Stir the soup and add the remaining milk until the desired consistency is reached. Reheat just to boiling. Stir in the nutmeg, salt, and pepper to taste. Serve immediately with a crusty bread. Freezes well.

Note: For a different flavor, omit the caraway seeds and mix 1 to 2 teaspoons curry powder into the pureed soup. Mix the milk and dry milk together, and stir into the pureed soup. Reheat just to boiling, and stir in remaining seasonings to taste.

Preparation time: 20 minutes. Cooking time: 35 to 45 minutes (mostly unattended). Yield: 11 to 12 cups

Nutrition analysis: 111 calories per serving; 3 gm. protein; 22.5 gm. carbohydrate; 2 gm. fat; 2.5 mg. cholesterol; 1 gm. fiber; 311 mg. sodium

Percent of calories from protein: 10%; from carbohydrates: 75%; from fat: 15%

Exchange values: ½ fruit; 1 bread; ½ fat

Continental Vegetable Soup

This recipe combines pistou (a blend of basil and garlic), with a garden full of vegetables and a touch of pasta to make a delicious and hearty soup.

2 (13 3/4-ounce) cans of low-salt chicken or vegetable broth, with excess fat skimmed off

14 1/2-ounce can Italian stewed tomatoes, undrained

1 bunch (about 40 leaves) basil, stemmed, washed, and dried

1 to 2 large garlic cloves

1 1/2 teaspoons olive oil

15 to 16-ounce can Great Northern or white beans, rinsed and drained

2 cups cut up fresh or frozen and thawed mixed vegetables (broccoli, cauliflower, carrots, celery, etc.)

1/4 cup Orzo (rice-shaped) pasta or Acini Pepe pasta, uncooked

Salt and freshly ground pepper to taste

2 tablespoons grated Parmesan cheese

Bring the chicken broth and stewed tomatoes to a boil in a large, heavy pot. Blend the basil, garlic, and olive oil in a food processor or blender until smooth or the consistency of pesto sauce (scrape the sides of the food processor once or twice during this process). Stir the basil mixture, beans, and chopped vegetables into the soup. Bring to a full boil, then stir, lower heat, cover, and simmer for 10 minutes. Stir in the pasta, and cook, stirring occasionally, for 20 minutes or until pasta and vegetables are tender. Add salt and pepper to taste. Top with Parmesan cheese and serve immediately.

Preparation time: 10 minutes. Cooking time: 35 to 40 minutes (mostly unattended). Yield: 7 cups

Nutrition analysis: 166 calories per serving; 8.5 gm. protein; 28.5 gm. carbohydrate; 2.5 gm. fat; 3 mg. cholesterol; 2.5 gm. fiber; 506 mg. sodium

Percent of calories from protein: 20%; from carbohydrates: 66%; from fat: 14%

Exchange values: 2 vegetable; 1½ bread; ½ meat; ½ fat

Cream of Zucchini Soup

This hearty soup is easy to make and delicious either hot or cold.

Vegetable oil cooking spray

1 1/2 teaspoons olive oil

1 1/2 cups chopped leeks (use the white part only)

1 large garlic clove, minced

1 2/3 cups low-salt chicken broth, with the fat skimmed off

2 pounds zucchini, cleaned, and sliced or chopped

1 tablespoon chopped fresh dill

1/4 cup nonfat plain yogurt

Salt and freshly ground pepper to taste

Spray a large, heavy pot with cooking spray. Add the olive oil, and heat for 45 seconds. Stir in the leeks and garlic. Sauté over medium-low heat for 3 minutes, stirring frequently. Add the chicken broth and zucchini (chopped zucchini cooks faster than sliced). Bring to a boil, reduce heat, cover, and simmer for 20 to 25 minutes or until the zucchini is mushy. Stir in the dill and yogurt. Puree in small batches in a food processor or blender. Return to the pot, and bring just to the boiling point. Remove from heat, and add salt and pepper to taste. Serve hot or cold.

Preparation time: 10 minutes. Cooking time: 30 minutes. Yield: 5 servings or 5 1/2 cups

Nutrition analysis: 81 calories per serving; 2.5 gm. protein; 14 gm. carbohydrate; 2 gm. fat; 1 mg. cholesterol; 1 gm. fiber; 236 mg. sodium

Percent of calories from protein: 13%; from carbohydrates: 65%; from fat: 22%

Exchange values: 1 vegetable; ½ bread; ½ fat

Idette's Hearty Lentil Soup

This hearty soup was originally made with chopped turkey kielbasa or turkey sausage. I substituted ground turkey because it has less fat. Depending upon your dietary needs, you can use any of these three meats or omit all meat.

1 1/2 teaspoons olive oil

Vegetable oil cooking spray

1 large garlic clove, minced

2 large onions, chopped (about 2 cups)

1/2 pound ground white meat turkey or chicken

2 carrots, scrubbed or peeled, and sliced

2 celery stalks, chopped

5 cans or 8 1/2 cups low-salt chicken broth (skim off all fat)

14 1/2- to 16-ounce can diced tomatoes, undrained

1 ham bone (optional)

1 bay leaf

1/2 teaspoon of each of the following: thyme leaves, cumin, marjoram, and salt (or salt to taste)

1 1/2 cups uncooked lentils, rinsed

10-ounce box chopped frozen spinach, thawed

Grated Parmesan cheese

In a large, heavy pot, heat the oil and a generous spray of cooking spray for 45 seconds. Sauté the garlic and onions, stirring often, over medium-low heat for 3 minutes or until golden. Stir in the ground turkey, and continue cooking and stirring for another few minutes until the meat is thoroughly cooked. Drain off all fat. Stir in the carrots, celery, broth, tomatoes, ham bone, bay leaf, seasonings, and lentils. Bring to a boil, lower heat, cover, and simmer for an hour, stirring occasionally. Stir in the spinach, and continue cooking for 10 minutes. Spoon into bowls, sprinkle with grated Parmesan cheese, and serve hot with a hearty bread. This soup makes a delicious, satisfying meal.

Preparation time: 15 minutes. Cooking time: 1 hour and 20 minutes (mostly unattended). Yield: 10 servings

Nutrition analysis: 105 calories per serving; 7 gm. protein; 11.5 gm. carbohydrate; 4 gm. fat; 11 mg. cholesterol; 3 gm. fiber; 773 mg. sodium

Percent of calories from protein: 25% from carbohydrates: 42%; from fat: 33%

Exchange values: 2 vegetable; ½ bread; ½ meat; ½ fat

Cream of Carrot & Potato Soup

Richard and Joyce love to spend cold Sunday afternoons in the kitchen. The result is usually a warm pot of some wonderful creation that lasts them through the week. From their many recipes, I chose one that doesn't take all day to make, but makes a large quantity that freezes well.

1 1/2 teaspoons olive oil

Vegetable oil cooking spray

2 large garlic cloves, minced

2 leeks, washed and chopped (use the white part only)

4 to 5 all-purpose potatoes (about 2 1/2 pounds total), peeled and coarsely chopped

10 fresh or frozen carrots (1 1/2 to 2 pounds), peeled and sliced

7 cups low-salt and defatted chicken broth (low-salt vegetable broth can be used if you prefer a vegetarian dish)

1 tablespoon Butter Buds, natural dehydrated butter

1 cup low-fat or skim milk or low-fat or skim evaporated milk, undiluted

Salt and freshly ground pepper to taste

2 to 4 tablespoons chopped fresh chives (optional)

Heat the olive oil and a generous spray of cooking spray in a large, heavy pot for 45 seconds. Stir in the garlic and leeks, and sauté over medium-low heat for 3 to 5 minutes, stirring frequently. If the mixture begins to brown too quickly, add 1 to 2 teaspoons of water. Stir in the potatoes, carrots, broth, and Butter Buds. Quickly bring to a boil. Reduce heat, cover, and simmer for 30 minutes or until the vegetables are tender.

Remove from heat, and purée in small batches in a large food processor or blender. Return to the pot, and stir in the milk. Bring just to the boiling point, then remove from heat. Add salt and pepper. Serve hot or cold topped with chives.

Preparation time: 15 minutes. Cooking time: 35 to 40 minutes. Yield: 15 cups

Nutrition analysis: 133 calories per serving; 3.5 gm. protein; 27 gm. carbohydrate; 1.5 gm. fat; 1 mg. cholesterol; 2 gm. fiber; 271 mg. sodium

Percent of calories from protein: 10%; from carbohydrates: 80%; from fat: 10%

Exchange values: 1½ vegetable; 1 bread; ½ fat

Ruth's Cauliflower Curry Soup

Ruth gave me this recipe one summer evening in Southampton. She loves to make soup and often uses a potato to give the soup a thicker, creamier texture.

1 1/2 teaspoons olive oil

Vegetable oil cooking spray

1 medium-sized yellow onion, peeled and chopped

3 scallions, chopped (use mostly the white part)

1 large garlic clove, minced

5 cups low-salt chicken broth, defatted

1 head cauliflower, remove the stem and chop the florets

2 medium-sized all-purpose potatoes, peeled and chopped

1 teaspoon curry powder, or to taste

1 cup 1% milk or 1 cup low-salt defatted chicken broth

Salt and freshly ground pepper to taste

1/4 cup chopped fresh chives (optional)

Heat the olive oil and a generous spray of cooking spray in a large, heavy pot for 45 seconds. Sauté the onion, scallions, and garlic over medium-low heat for 3 minutes, stirring frequently. Add 1 or 2 teaspoons of water if the mixture begins to burn. Add the chicken broth, and bring to a boil. Stir in the cauliflower and potatoes, and bring to a boil again. Lower heat, cover, and simmer for 30 minutes or until the vegetables are tender. Puree in small batches in a large food processor or blender. Return to the pot, and stir in the curry. Stir in the milk until the desired consistency is reached. Reheat to just under the boiling point. Add salt and pepper to taste. Serve hot or cold garnished with chives. This soup tastes even better the next day.

Preparation time: 10 minutes. Cooking time: 35 minutes. Yield: 10 cups

Nutrition analysis using milk (numbers in parentheses indicate nutrition analysis using chicken broth): 80 (72) calories per serving; 3 (2.5) gm. protein; 13 (12) gm. carbohydrate; 1 (1) gm. fat; 1 mg. (0) cholesterol; 1.5 (1.5) gm. fiber; 341 (393) mg. sodium

Percent of calories from protein: 16 (14)%; from carbohydrates: 70 (74)%; from fat: 13 (12)%

Exchange values: ½ vegetable; ½ bread; ½ fat

Potato & Spinach Soup

This delicious soup is particularly satisfying to eat on a cold winter night.

1 1/2 teaspoons olive oil, or vegetable oil cooking spray plus 1 to 2 teaspoons water

3 large garlic cloves, minced

1 bunch scallions, chopped

3 medium all-purpose potatoes (about 1 3/4 pounds total), peeled and sliced

5 3/4 cups or 46 ounces low-salt chicken broth with the fat skimmed off

10-ounce box frozen spinach, partially thawed

Salt and freshly ground pepper to taste

1/4 to 1/2 cup nonfat plain yogurt (optional)

3 tablespoons chopped chives

Heat the oil or cooking spray in a large, heavy pot. Sauté the garlic and scallions over medium-low heat for 3 minutes, stirring frequently. Make sure the garlic and scallions don't burn. Stir in the potatoes, chicken broth, and spinach. Bring to a boil, cover, and simmer for 35 minutes. When the potatoes are soft, remove from heat. Puree in small batches in a food processor or blender. Return to the pot and reheat. Check the seasonings. Serve in soup bowls, and garnish with yogurt and chives.

Preparation time: 10 minutes. Cooking time: 35 to 45 minutes (mostly unattended). Yield: 8 servings or about 9 cups

Nutrition analysis: 142 calories per serving; 4 gm. protein; 27.5 gm. carbohydrate; 2 gm. fat; 0.5 mg. cholesterol; 2 gm. fiber; 399 mg. sodium

Percent of calories from protein: 10%; from carbohydrates: 76%; from fat: 13%

Exchange values: ½ vegetable; 1½ bread; ½ fat

Cream of Pumpkin Soup

This soup is amazingly easy to make, yet it tastes as if you spent hours cooking it. It's also full of heart-healthy beta-carotene and other wonderful nutrients. This recipe can easily be doubled, and it freezes well.

Vegetable oil cooking spray

1 1/2 teaspoons olive oil

1 medium onion, chopped

1 garlic clove, minced

1 tablespoon flour

2 cups low-salt chicken broth, skim off the fat

16-ounce can pumpkin (not pumpkin pie filling)

1/2 cup 1% milk

Salt and freshly ground pepper to taste

Generously spray a medium pot with cooking spray. Add the olive oil, and heat for 45 seconds. Stir in the onions and garlic. Sauté over medium-low heat for 3 minutes or until translucent, stirring frequently. Add 1 to 2 teaspoons of water if the mixture starts to burn. Sprinkle the flour over the onion mixture, and stir for 10 seconds. Add the chicken broth and pumpkin, and mix thoroughly. Bring to a boil, lower heat, cover, and simmer for 20 minutes, stirring frequently. Purée the mixture in a food processor or blender. Return the mixture to the pot. Stir in the milk, and salt and pepper to taste. Reheat just to the boiling point. Serve hot with raisin walnut bread or your favorite low-fat muffins to make a delicious meal for a cold day.

Preparation time: 10 minutes. Cooking time: 25 minutes. Yield: 3 servings

Nutrition analysis: 135 calories per serving; 3.5 gm. protein; 22.5 gm. carbohydrate; 4 gm. fat; 1.5 mg. cholesterol; 3.5 gm. fiber; 356 mg. sodium

Percent of calories from protein: 10%; from carbohydrates: 64%; from fat: 26%

Exchange values: ½ vegetable; 1 bread; ½ fat

Note: If you double the recipe, keep the amount of olive oil the same at 1½ teaspoons, and increase the flour by ½ tablespoon to equal 1½ tablespoons flour.

Leek & Two Potato Soup

Since sweet potatoes are full of vitamins, beta-carotene, minerals, and fiber, I decided to use one in this traditional soup. It adds a delicate taste and color.

1 1/2 teaspoons olive oil

1 garlic clove, minced

1 medium yellow onion, chopped

3 leeks (use the white part plus 3 inches of green), washed and chopped

5 cups chicken stock, homemade or reduced-salt canned, or a combination of chicken stock and water (skim off all fat)

3 medium to large all-purpose potatoes, peeled and sliced

1 large sweet potato, peeled and sliced

1 cup low-fat or skim milk

Salt and freshly ground pepper to taste

3 tablespoons finely chopped fresh chives or fresh parsley

Heat the olive oil in a large, heavy pot. Stir in the garlic, onion, and leeks, and sauté over medium-low heat for 5 minutes, stirring often. You may have to add a few drops of water to prevent the onions from burning. Stir in the stock, and bring to a boil. Stir in the potatoes. Reduce the heat, stir, cover, and simmer for 50 to 60 minutes or until the vegetables are tender. Let cool slightly, then puree in small batches in a food processor or blender. Return the soup to the pot. Stir in the milk and check the seasonings, and stir in the milk. Reheat just to the simmering point. Serve immediately, garnished with fresh chives or parsley. This soup can be served hot or as a cold vichyssoise. It's wonderful as a main course when served with a green salad and a crusty bread or corn bread.

Preparation time: 15 minutes. Cooking time: 50 to 60 minutes (mostly unattended). Yield: 8 servings

Nutrition analysis: 141 calories per serving; 3 gm. protein; 27.5 gm. carbohydrate; 2.5 gm. fat; 1.5 mg. cholesterol; 2.5 gm. fiber; 335 mg. sodium

Percent of calories from protein: 9%; from carbohydrates: 76%; from fat: 15%

Exchange values: 1½ vegetable; 1 bread; ½ fat

Mrs. Bowers' Cold Peach Soup

This delightfully delicious and refreshing soup is wonderful to serve on a summer day. It requires almost no time to make, is elegant to serve, and is popular with just about everyone.

3 cups canned, naturally sweetened peaches, drained (keep the syrup)

1 cup nonfat plain or peach yogurt, drained

1/2 teaspoon almond extract

1 to 2 teaspoons powdered sugar or to taste (optional)

Mint leaves for garnish (optional)

Blend the first four ingredients in a large food processor or blender until foamy. Add 1 to 2 tablespoons of the peach juice if you want a thinner consistency. Cover, and chill until cold. Serve cold garnished with mint leaves.

Preparation time: 5 minutes. Chilling time: 1 to 2 hours. Yield: 4 servings

Nutrition analysis: 118 calories per serving; 4.5 gm. protein; 27 gm. carbohydrate; 0 fat; 1 mg. cholesterol; 0 fiber; 52 mg. sodium

Percent of calories from protein: 14%; from carbohydrates: 85%; from fat: 1%

Exchange values: ½ milk; 1½ fruit

Sweet Garden Green Pea Soup

This soup doesn't taste like pea soup made from dried split peas. The taste is much fresher, and the color is brighter green. I serve this soup to my family as a main course and to company as a first course.

1 1/2 teaspoons olive oil or a generous amount of vegetable oil cooking spray

1 large onion, chopped

2 garlic cloves, chopped

1 large all-purpose potato, peeled and sliced

2 stalks celery, chopped

2 (13 3/4-ounce) cans low-salt chicken broth or homemade chicken broth, skim off all fat

1 cup water

1/4 teaspoon dried basil

1/4 teaspoon dried thyme leaves

1/4 teaspoon dried rosemary leaves, crushed

1/4 teaspoon dried oregano

1/4 teaspoon celery salt

1/4 teaspoon ground marjoram

1/2 teaspoon ground nutmeg

1 bay leaf

2 (10-ounce) packages frozen peas

1/2 to 3/4 cup nonfat plain yogurt

1/2 cup skim milk

Salt and freshly ground pepper to taste

Heat the olive oil or cooking spray in a large, heavy pot. Sauté the onion and garlic over low heat for 3 minutes, stirring often. (You may have to add 1 to 2 teaspoons of water to prevent the onions from burning.) Stir in the potato, celery, chicken broth, water, seasonings, and peas. Bring to a boil. Stir, cover, and simmer for an hour.

Remove from heat and let cool slightly. Remove the bay leaf, then stir in the yogurt and milk, and purée in small batches in a food processor or blender. Return to the pot. Add salt and pepper to taste. Reheat just to the boiling point. Serve immediately with a crusty bread, garlic bread, or buttermilk biscuits, and you have a delicious meal.

Preparation time: 20 minutes. Cooking time: 1 hour (mostly unattended). Yield: 8 servings

Nutrition analysis: 123 calories per serving; 6 gm. protein; 21 gm. carbohydrate; 2 gm. fat; 0.5 mg. cholesterol; 3.5 gm. fiber; 366 mg. sodium

Percent of calories from protein: 19%; from carbohydrates: 67%; from fat: 13%

Exchange values: ½ vegetable; 1 bread; ½ fat

Sweet Potato Soup

Vegetable oil spray or 1 1/2 teaspoons olive oil

1 garlic clove, minced

1 large, sweet yellow onion, chopped

5 1/2 cups homemade chicken stock or 3 (13 3/4-ounce) cans low-salt chicken broth (skim off all fat)

1 cup water

3 1/2 pounds sweet potatoes, peeled and sliced

1 tablespoon Butter Buds, natural dehydrated butter

1 cup nonfat plain yogurt

1/4 teaspoon nutmeg

1/4 teaspoon pumpkin pie spice

Salt and freshly ground pepper to taste

KIDS LOVE THIS

Heat the cooking spray or olive oil in a large, heavy pot. Stir in the garlic and onion, and sauté over medium-low heat for 3 to 5 minutes, stirring often. If using cooking spray, you may need to add a few drops of water to prevent the onions from burning. Stir in the stock and water, and bring to a boil. Stir in the sweet potatoes and Butter Buds. Bring to a boil, then cover, and simmer for 50 to 60 minutes. Remove from heat, and let cool slightly. Stir in the yogurt, then puree the soup in small batches in a food processor or blender. Return the soup to the pot. Stir in the spices, and salt and pepper to taste. Reheat the soup just to the boiling point before serving. Sweet potato soup tastes great with corn bread and a salad.

Preparation time: 10 minutes. Cooking time: 1 hour. Yield: 10 to 12 servings

Nutrition analysis for 10 servings: 176 calories per serving; 3.5 gm. protein; 36.5 gm. carbohydrate; 1.5 gm. fat; 0.5 mg. cholesterol; 0.5 gm. fiber; 301 mg. sodium

Percent of calories from protein: 8%; from carbohydrates: 83%; from fat: 9%

Exchange values: 2 bread; ½ fat

Vegetable Bean Soup

I love homemade soups, especially ones that don't take all day to make. There's something comforting about a bowl of hearty soup on a cold day. This recipe combines the goodness of beans and other vegetables to make a thick, hearty puree that is quick, easy, and delicious.

5 1/2 cups low-salt chicken or vegetable broth, skim off all the fat

1 medium onion, chopped

3 carrots, peeled and sliced

3 celery stalks, sliced

19-ounce can black beans, undrained (Progresso® makes a 19-ounce can)

2 potatoes, peeled and chopped

10 basil leaves, chopped

1 teaspoon mild chili powder

1 teaspoon dried, crushed thyme leaves

Salt and freshly ground pepper to taste

Combine all the ingredients in a large, heavy pot. Bring to a boil, then lower heat to medium-low. Stir, cover, and simmer for 30 minutes or until the vegetables are tender. Puree the soup in small batches in a food processor or large blender. Return the puree to the pot. Add salt and freshly ground pepper to taste, and reheat just to the boiling point. Serve hot with crusty bread or homemade muffins for a great meal.

Preparation time: 10 minutes. Cooking time: 30 minutes. Yield: 9 to 10 cups

Nutrition analysis for 9 servings: 105 calories per serving; 4.5 gm. protein; 19.5 gm. carbohydrate; 1 gm. fat; 2 mg. cholesterol; 1.5 gm. fiber; 665 mg. sodium

Percent of calories from protein: 16%; from carbohydrates: 73%; from fat: 11%

Exchange values: ½ vegetable; 1 bread

Zucchini Soup

I fell in love with this soup when I had it at my brother's house. Unfortunately, a major ingredient was bacon, and that didn't fit into my low-fat diet. I started experimenting and eventually created this version, which kept the light, fresh taste that I enjoyed without the fat and preservatives.

1 1/2 teaspoons olive oil and a generous spray of vegetable oil cooking spray

1 garlic clove, minced

2 medium onions, chopped

3 pounds (6 medium) zucchini, unpeeled

2 (13 3/4-ounce) cans low-salt beef broth or homemade broth (skim off all the fat)

1 cup water

2 tablespoons all-natural bacon bits (optional)

2 tablespoons Butter Buds, natural dehydrated butter

Salt and freshly ground pepper to taste

Heat the oil and cooking spray in a large, heavy pot. Add the garlic and onions, and sauté, stirring frequently, over medium-low heat for about 3 minutes. You may need to add a few drops of water to prevent the mixture from burning. Wash and dry the zucchini, cut off both ends, and cut it into half-inch round slices. Add the broth and water to the cooked onions and garlic. Stir in the sliced zucchini and bacon bits, and bring to a boil. Lower the heat, cover, and simmer for 30 minutes or until the zucchini is tender and thoroughly cooked.

Purée small batches of the soup in a food processor or blender. Return the soup to the pot. Stir in the Butter Buds. Add salt and freshly ground pepper to taste. Reheat just to the boiling point, then serve. This soup freezes well.

Preparation time: 10 minutes. Cooking time: 40 minutes (mostly unattended). Yield: 6 to 8 servings

Nutrition analysis for 6 servings: 80 calories per serving; 4 gm. protein; 13 gm. carbohydrate; 2 gm. fat; 0 cholesterol; 1 gm. fiber; 333 mg. sodium

Percent of calories from protein: 18%; from carbohydrates: 59%; from fat: 22%

Exchange values: ½ vegetable; ½ bread; ½ meat; ½ fat

Black Bean & Corn Salad

I love salad, but when I eat it as a main course, I am often hungry soon after. This recipe solves this problem by combining a group of hearty vegetables that are not only filling, but are also attractive when mixed together.

16- to 19-ounce can black beans, rinsed and drained

1 1/2 cups fresh or frozen corn, cooked al dente (tender but not mushy), at room temperature

2 carrots, peeled and shredded

1 celery stalk, chopped

1/2 red pepper, seeded and chopped

2 to 3 scallions, chopped, use mostly the white part (optional)

2 tablespoons fresh parsley, chopped

1 tablespoon cilantro, chopped (optional)

1/2 to 1 cup cooked brown or white rice, at room temperature (optional)

Salad dressing:

1/4 cup low-fat Italian salad dressing

Dash of hot sauce

1 tablespoon sherry wine vinegar or red wine vinegar

1 teaspoon brown sugar

Salt and freshly ground pepper

8 lettuce leaves, washed and dried

Mix the salad ingredients together in a large bowl, and set aside. Mix the salad dressing ingredients together thoroughly. Pour the salad dressing over the vegetables, and toss well. Add salt and pepper to taste. Serve on a bed of lettuce.

Preparation time: 15 minutes. Yield: 4 servings

Nutrition analysis: 251 calories per serving; 10 gm. protein; 51 gm. carbohydrate; 2.5 gm. fat; 1 mg. cholesterol; 3 gm. fiber; 705 mg. sodium

Percent of calories from protein: 15%; from carbohydrates: 77%; from fat: 8%

Exchange values: 1 vegetable; 3½ bread; ½ meat; ½ fat

Soups, Salads, and Dressings   75

Cancun Rice Salad

2 cups low-salt chicken stock, with the fat skimmed off the top

3/4 cup, or 5 1/2 ounces, Spicy Hot V8® juice or tomato juice

1/4 cup water

1 1/2 cups raw white rice

1/4 cup low-fat Italian salad dressing

1 extra-full tablespoon nonfat mayonnaise

1 teaspoon Dijon mustard

1 large tomato, seeded and chopped

1 tablespoon chopped fresh basil (optional)

1 tablespoon chopped fresh parsley (optional)

1/2 large green pepper, chopped

1 to 2 scallions, chopped, with some of the green

6 1/2-ounce can water-packed tuna, well drained

Salt and freshly ground pepper to taste

Lettuce leaves

Bring the chicken stock, V8 juice, and water to a boil. Stir in the rice, cover, and simmer for 20 to 25 minutes. Remove from heat, keep covered, and let stand for 5 minutes. Mix the salad dressing, mayonnaise, and mustard together well. Stir into the hot rice. Transfer to a bowl, cover and refrigerate until cold, about 4 hours. Stir in the chopped tomato, basil, parsley, green pepper, scallions, tuna, salt, and pepper. Serve cold on a bed of lettuce.

Preparation time: 10 minutes. Cooking time: 20 to 25 minutes. Refrigeration time: 4 hours. Yield: 4 to 6 servings

Nutrition analysis: 389 calories per serving; 18.5 gm. protein; 67 gm. carbohydrate; 4.5 gm. fat; 22 mg. cholesterol; 1.5 gm. fiber; 827 mg. sodium

Percent of calories from protein: 19%; from carbohydrates: 70%; from fat: 10%

Exchange values: 1 vegetable; 4½ bread; 1½ meat; ½ fat

Broccoli and Pea Salad

I thank my friend Linda for reminding me of this well-known vegetable salad. I stopped making it years ago because it had too many calories and fat, but with a few adjustments, it is now back on my table.

2 to 3 cups raw broccoli crowns, cut into bite-size pieces

10-ounce package frozen petits peas, at room temperature

1 red apple, cored and cut into bite-size pieces

1/2 cup raisins (optional)

2 tablespoons sunflower seeds or sliced almonds (optional)

1 to 2 tablespoons real bacon bits (optional)

Sweet Creamy Dressing:

1/4 cup nonfat mayonnaise (I prefer Kraft®)

1/4 cup plain nonfat yogurt

1 to 2 tablespoons sugar

2 teaspoons red wine vinegar

Mix the first 6 ingredients together in a large salad bowl. Stir the dressing ingredients together thoroughly, and pour over the salad. Toss well, and serve.

Preparation time: 15 minutes. Yield: 4 servings

Nutrition analysis: 233 calories per serving; 9.5 gm. protein; 44 gm. carbohydrate; 4.5 gm. fat; 6.5 mg. cholesterol; 6.5 gm. fiber; 251 mg. sodium

Percent of calories from protein: 15%; from carbohydrates: 69%; from fat: 16%

Exchange values: ½ vegetable; 1½ fruit; ½ bread; ½ fat

Grilled Chicken Salad

It's amazing how quickly you can make this delicious and healthy meal. You'll have a great California-style meal in about 20 minutes.

4 single skinless, boneless chicken breasts (1 to 1 1/4 pounds total)

Maple syrup, Dijon mustard, or olive oil

1 small head romaine lettuce

Small head endive lettuce (optional)

1 large tomato, chopped

1 small cucumber, chopped

2 scallions, chopped (optional)

Vicki and Bob's Salad Dressing, Balsamic Maple Salad Dressing, or your favorite low-fat Italian salad dressing

1 to 2 large roasted red peppers, thinly sliced

Salt and freshly ground pepper to taste

Heat the grill or broiler. Lightly brush a small amount of maple syrup, Dijon mustard or olive oil on each side of the chicken breasts. Grill the chicken about 4 minutes on each side or until done. While the chicken is cooking, wash and dry the lettuce. Put the lettuce on 4 plates. Arrange the chopped tomato, cucumber, and scallions on the lettuce. Place a cooked chicken breast on top of the chopped vegetables on each plate. Place a couple slices of roasted red peppers on each chicken breast. Drizzle 1 to 2 teaspoons of salad dressing over the vegetables and chicken on each plate. Salt and pepper to taste. Serve with biscuits or a hearty, crusty bread.

Preparation time: 10 minutes. Cooking time: 8 to 10 minutes. Yield: 4 servings

Nutrition analysis: 206 calories per serving; 25.5 gm. protein; 9 gm. carbohydrate; 7.5 gm. fat; 65.5 mg. cholesterol; 2.5 gm. fiber; 255 mg. sodium

Percent of calories from protein: 49%; from carbohydrates: 18%; from fat: 33%

Exchange values: 1½ vegetable; 3 meat

Oriental Vegetable Salad

This delightfully fresh-tasting salad can be made using a variety of vegetables. I've included what I like best, but you can also use asparagus and carrots or your favorite combination. The dressing is fat-free but can be made with 1½ teaspoons olive oil if you don't mind the added calories and fat.

Creamy Chive Dressing:

2 teaspoons red wine vinegar

1 teaspoon Dijon mustard

1/4 cup nonfat plain yogurt

1/4 cup fat-free mayonnaise

1 tablespoon chopped fresh chives

1 teaspoon chopped fresh dill or to taste

1/4 teaspoon low-sodium soy sauce or to taste

Salad ingredients (at room temperature):

1/2 pound small, fresh snow peas, washed with ends snapped off

1/2 pound broccoli florets

10 cherry tomatoes, halved

1 to 2 chopped scallions (optional)

10 whole baby corn (optional), jarred or canned

8-ounce can sliced water chestnuts, drained well

4 to 6 leaves romaine lettuce, washed, dried, and cut into small pieces

1 tablespoon real bacon bits (optional)

Salt and freshly ground pepper to taste

Combine the dressing ingredients in a blender or small food processor. Puree until thoroughly blended. Taste, and add more soy sauce or dill if necessary. Combine the salad ingredients in a large salad bowl. Pour the dressing over the salad. Add salt and freshly ground pepper to taste. Let stand for 15 minutes or serve immediately. Serve with a crusty bread or rolls for an almost fat-free lunch or dinner.

Preparation time: 20 minutes. Yield: 4 servings

Nutrition analysis: 116 calories per serving; 6.5 gm. protein; 21 gm. carbohydrate; 2 gm. fat; 6.5 mg. cholesterol; 3 gm. fiber; 200 mg. sodium

Percent of calories from protein: 21%; from carbohydrates: 66%; from fat: 13%

Exchange values: 3½ vegetable

Fiesta Bean Salad

Here's a wonderfully delicious and healthy salad recipe to enjoy. The beans make the salad more filling, so you can eat it as a main course without feeling hungry right away.

2 cups canned black beans, rinsed and drained

1 green or red pepper, seeded and chopped

1 celery stalk, chopped

1 shredded carrot

1 medium-size tomato, seeded and chopped

2 tablespoons chopped scallions (optional)

1 tablespoon sherry or red wine vinegar

1 tablespoon olive oil

1 teaspoon brown sugar (optional)

1/4 teaspoon ground cumin

Salt and freshly ground pepper to taste

8 to 10 lettuce leaves, washed and dried

Mix the beans, green pepper, celery, carrot, tomato, and scallions together in a large bowl. Set aside. Stir the vinegar, olive oil, brown sugar, and ground cumin together. Pour the dressing over the salad, and toss well. (If you want to add a little more dressing, add 1 to 2 teaspoons more oil and vinegar.) Add salt and pepper to taste. Serve on a bed of lettuce.

Preparation time: 15 minutes. Yield: 4 servings

Nutrition analysis: 149 calories per serving; 6 gm. protein; 23.5 gm. carbohydrate; 4 gm. fat; 0 cholesterol; 1.5 gm. fiber; 518 mg. sodium

Percent of calories from protein: 16%; from carbohydrates: 61%; from fat: 23%

Exchange values: 1 vegetable; 1 bread; ½ meat; ½ fat

Fruit Salad

8 leaves Boston lettuce, washed and dried

1 brimming cup whole fresh cranberries, washed and dried

2 tablespoons sugar, or to taste

8 ounces low-fat (1%) cottage cheese

1 large banana, sliced

1 large red apple, cored and sliced

1 small bunch of grapes, removed from stem

1 pear, cored and sliced

TEENS
LOVE
THIS

Place the lettuce leaves on four salad plates. Chop the cranberries in a food processor or blender, then add the sugar and cottage cheese, and chop briefly. Place the fruit on the lettuce leaves, cover with the cranberry/cottage cheese mixture, and serve immediately.

Preparation time: 15 minutes. Yield: 4 side salads or 2 entree salads

Nutrition analysis for 2 servings: 336 calories per serving; 16.5 gm. protein; 68 gm. carbohydrate; 2.5 gm. fat; 5 mg. cholesterol; 6 gm. fiber; 470 mg. sodium

Percent of calories from protein: 18%; from carbohydrates: 76%; from fat: 6%

Exchange values: ½ vegetable; 3½ fruit; 2 meat

Mandarin, Spinach & Romaine Salad

If you have trouble getting your kids to eat salad, try this one. I like the combination of spinach and romaine but the salad is equally good if only spinach or only romaine is used.

Poppy Seed Dressing:

1/4 teaspoon Dijon mustard

1/4 cup nonfat, plain yogurt

1/4 cup nonfat mayonnaise

1 to 1 1/4 tablespoons sugar, or to taste

2 teaspoons white wine vinegar

Dash of lemon juice

1 to 1 1/2 teaspoons poppy seeds

1/8 to 1/4 teaspoon onion salt

Salad:

3 cups packed spinach, washed, dried, and torn into bite-size pieces

2 to 3 cups romaine lettuce, washed, dried, and torn into bite-size pieces

11-ounce can mandarin oranges, drained, or 2 cups sliced, fresh strawberries, or a combination of both

2 tablespoons sliced almonds (optional)

Mix the dressing ingredients together in a small bowl, and whisk thoroughly. Taste, and add more sugar, onion salt, or lemon juice if desired. Set aside. Place the spinach and romaine in a medium to large salad bowl, and toss well. Toss in the mandarin oranges. Toast the almonds in a toaster oven set at 350° for about 5 minutes or until golden. Let cool slightly, then toss into the salad. Pour the dressing over the salad, toss well, and serve immediately. This salad is best when eaten right after the dressing has been put on the greens.

Preparation time: 15 minutes. Yield: 4 to 6 servings

Nutrition analysis for 4 servings: 102 calories per serving; 4.5 gm. protein; 15.5 gm. carbohydrate; 3.5 gm. fat; 6.5 mg. cholesterol; 4 gm. fiber; 266 mg. sodium

Percent of calories from protein: 16%; from carbohydrates: 55%; from fat: 30%

Exchange values: ½ vegetable; ½ fruit; ½ fat

Surprise Salad

My godmother, a very good cook and salad lover, introduced me to this salad. I love the combination of crisp lettuce greens, Italian salad dressing, and steak. Through the years I've served this salad using whatever leftover meat I have in the house. Just a little meat gives a great taste, and it's a wonderful way to use leftovers.

1/2 to 1 head romaine lettuce, washed, dried, and cut into bite-size pieces

1 carrot, peeled and shredded

1 to 2 tomatoes

1/2 cucumber, sliced or chopped

1 to 2 scallions, chopped

1/2 red pepper, chopped

1/2 cup canned corn or cooked fresh corn at room temperature

1/2 to 1 cup cooked, cubed, and cooled lean steak, chicken, or pork (1/4 pound well-drained lean ground beef, chicken, or turkey can also be used)

Vicki and Bob's Salad Dressing, Maple Balsamic Vinaigrette Dressing, or low-fat Italian salad dressing

Salt and freshly ground pepper to taste

1/2 cup low-fat croutons

Toss the first 8 ingredients together in a large salad bowl. Pour 2 to 4 tablespoons of salad dressing over the salad. Toss again, check seasoning, and add a little more dressing if necessary. Toss in the croutons. Serve with a good crusty bread or corn bread for a great meal.

Preparation time: 15 minutes. Yield: 4 servings

Nutrition analysis: 168 calories per serving; 14.5 gm. protein; 15.5 gm. carbohydrate; 6 gm. fat; 32.5 mg. cholesterol; 3.5 gm. fiber; 389 mg. sodium

Percent of calories from protein: 33%; from carbohydrates: 36%; from fat: 31%

Exchange values: 1½ vegetable; ½ bread; 1½ meat; ½ fat

Taco Salad

1 cup nonfat plain yogurt

1 1/4-ounce packet low-sodium taco seasoning mix

1 head romaine lettuce

16-ounce can red kidney beans, rinsed and drained

1 small green pepper, chopped

1/4 pound cooked ground white meat turkey or chicken, well drained (omit the meat if you're on a very low-fat diet)

Sliced Bermuda onion (optional)

2 tablespoons grated low-fat cheddar cheese (optional)

1/2 cup skim buttermilk

1/4 to 1/2 cup low-fat croutons (optional)

Drain the yogurt of any excess liquid. Mix the yogurt and taco seasoning mix together to make the dressing. Cover, put the mixture in the refrigerator, and let stand for at least 2 to 4 hours. Wash and dry the lettuce, break the leaves into bite-size pieces, and place in a large salad bowl. Toss in the kidney beans, green pepper, cooked ground turkey, onion, and cheddar cheese. Thin the taco-yogurt dressing with a few tablespoons of buttermilk until it reaches the consistency you like. Pour the dressing over the salad, toss in the croutons, and serve immediately. Taco salad goes very well with a crusty whole wheat bread, corn bread, garlic bread, or biscuits.

Preparation time: 15 minutes. Refrigeration time: 2 to 4 hours. Yield: 6 servings

Nutrition analysis: 172 calories per serving; 13.5 gm. protein; 23.5 gm. carbohydrate; 3 gm. fat; 11 mg. cholesterol; 6 gm. fiber; 696 mg. sodium

Percent of calories from protein: 31%; from carbohydrates: 53%; from fat: 16%

Exchange values: ½ milk; 1 vegetable; 1 bread; ½ meat

Tomato & Mozzarella Salad

I first had this salad on the island of Capri. Since then, I make it whenever I can get deliciously ripe summer tomatoes. The secret to making this easy and delicious salad is to use only the freshest ingredients.

3 to 4 large, ripe summer tomatoes at room temperature

24 fresh basil leaves

2 to 4 tablespoons shredded low-fat mozzarella cheese, depending on dietary needs

1 to 2 teaspoons olive oil

Salt and freshly ground pepper to taste

Remove the stem, and slice each tomato into about 8 slices no wider than ¼-inch thick. Arrange the slices on a platter with a basil leaf between each pair. Sprinkle with mozzarella cheese, drizzle with olive oil, and season with salt and pepper to taste. Serve immediately, or let stand 5 minutes before serving.

Preparation time: 10 minutes. Yield: 4 servings

Nutrition analysis using 4 tablespoons mozzarella cheese : 88 calories per serving; 6 gm. protein; 6 gm. carbohydrate; 5 gm. fat; 0 cholesterol; 1.5 gm. fiber; 85 mg. sodium

Percent of calories from protein: 25%; from carbohydrates: 27%; from fat: 47%

Exchange values: 1 vegetable; ½ meat; ½ fat

Winter Fruit Salad

8 Boston lettuce leaves, washed and dried

14-ounce jar spiced apple rings

4 poached or canned pear halves

2 navel oranges, peeled and separated into sections

4 tablespoons crumbled blue cheese, or to taste

Nonfat plain yogurt (optional)

Place the lettuce on 4 salad plates. Put 2 spiced apple rings, 1 pear half, and several orange sections on the lettuce on each plate. Sprinkle about 1 tablespoon of crumbled blue cheese over the fruit salad on each plate. You can serve the salad at this point, or pour some of the pear juice on the salad, or mix some pear juice and yogurt together to make a dressing. If you want to make this salad into an entrée, add a scoop of low-fat cottage cheese to each plate.

KIDS LOVE THIS

Preparation time: 10 minutes. Yield: 4 servings

Nutrition analysis: 167 calories per serving; 3 gm. protein; 34.5 gm. carbohydrate; 3 gm. fat; 6.5 mg. cholesterol; 3.5 gm. fiber; 128 mg. sodium

Percent of calories from protein: 7%; from carbohydrates: 77%; from fat: 16%

Exchange values: 2 fruit; ½ meat; ½ fat

Creamy Chive
Salad Dressing

This fat-free dressing has a slightly oriental taste that is great on vegetable salads.

2 teaspoons red wine vinegar

1 teaspoon Dijon mustard

1/4 cup nonfat plain yogurt

1/4 cup nonfat mayonnaise

1 tablespoon chopped fresh chives

1 tablespoon chopped fresh dill

1/4 teaspoon low-sodium soy sauce

Place all the ingredients in a food processor or blender, and purée until thoroughly blended. Add more soy sauce, dill, or chives if desired.

Preparation time: 5 minutes. Yield: ½ cup or 4 servings

Nutrition analysis: 25.5 calories per serving; 1.3 gm. protein; 3 gm. carbohydrate; 1 gm. fat; 6.5 mg. cholesterol; 0 fiber; 130 mg. sodium

Percent of calories from protein: 20%; from carbohydrates: 48%; from fat: 32%

Exchange values: less than ½ milk

Poppy Seed Dressing

The slightly sweet, rich flavor of this dressing goes well with fruit salads.

1/4 teaspoon Dijon mustard

1/4 cup nonfat, plain yogurt

1/4 cup nonfat mayonnaise

1 to 1 1/4 tablespoons sugar

2 teaspoons white wine vinegar

Dash of lemon juice

1 to 1 1/2 teaspoons poppy seeds

1/8 to 1/4 teaspoon onion salt

Mix the ingredients together in a small bowl, and whisk well. Taste, and add more sugar, lemon juice, or onion salt, if desired. Serve over salad.

Preparation time: 5 minutes. Yield: about ½ cup or 4 servings

Nutrition analysis: 43 calories per serving; 1.5 gm. protein; 7 gm. carbohydrate; 1.5 gm. fat; 6.5 mg. cholesterol; 0 fiber; 228 mg. sodium

Percent of calories from protein: 12%; from carbohydrates: 62%; from fat: 26%

Exchange values: less than ½ milk

Sweet Creamy Salad Dressing

This delicious dressing is great on fruit salads and vegetable salads.

1/4 cup nonfat mayonnaise

1/4 cup plain nonfat yogurt

1 to 2 tablespoons sugar

2 teaspoons red wine vinegar

Mix everything together in a small bowl, and spoon over salad.

Yield: ½ cup or 4 servings

Nutrition analysis: 45 calories per serving; 1 gm. protein; 9 gm. carbohydrate; 1 gm. fat; 6.5 mg. cholesterol; 0 fiber; 86.5 mg. sodium

Percent of calories from protein: 9%; from carbohydrates: 75%; from fat: 16%

Exchange values: less than ½ milk

Maple Balsamic Salad Dressing

This is a great tasting salad dressing that doesn't have a heavy, oily taste. Be sure to use balsamic vinegar because its naturally sweet taste, richness, and exquisite aroma are essential to this recipe.

1/2 cup balsamic vinegar

2 tablespoons pure maple syrup

1/4 teaspoon minced garlic

1 tablespoon minced shallots

2 to 4 tablespoons olive oil

1/4 teaspoon salt

1/4 teaspoon freshly ground black pepper

Whisk all the ingredients together in a small bowl, or shake together in a small salad dressing carafe. Let stand at room temperature for 30 minutes. Stir well or shake again before serving over salad. Refrigerate any leftovers, but bring to room temperature before serving again.

Preparation time: 5 minutes. Standing time: 30 minutes. Yield: 6 servings

Nutrition analysis using 2 tablespoons olive oil (numbers in parentheses indicate nutrition analysis using 4 tablespoons olive oil): 80 (120) calories per serving; 0 (0) protein; 10 (10) gm. carbohydrate; 4.5 (9) gm. fat; 0 (0) cholesterol; 0 (0) fiber; 99.5 (99.5) mg. sodium

Percent of calories from protein: 0 (0)%; from carbohydrates: 50 (33)%; from fat: 50 (67)%

Exchange values: 1 (2) fat

Vicki and Bob's Salad Dressing

I'm always searching for salad dressings that are low in fat but high in taste, so I was thrilled when my friend served this dressing to me and was willing to share her secret. This vinaigrette doesn't use a lot of oil, but the combination of ingredients gives it a great taste.

1/2 cup balsamic vinegar

1 tablespoon Dijon mustard

2 tablespoons olive oil

1 teaspoon sugar

Dash of each of the following: salt, freshly ground pepper,
   curry powder, dried basil, dried oregano, and dried, crushed rosemary

Stir all the ingredients together, let stand a few minutes, and serve over a green salad. This dressing keeps in the refrigerator for several days but needs to be brought to room temperature before using again.

Preparation time: 5 minutes. Yield: 4 to 6 servings

Nutrition analysis for 4 servings: 85.5 calories per serving; 0 protein; 10 gm. carbohydrate; 4.5 gm. fat; 0 cholesterol; 0 fiber; 69.5 mg. sodium

Percent of calories from protein: 1%; from carbohydrates: 49%; from fat: 50%

Exchange values: 1 fat

BEANS
AND
LEGUMES

Black Beans & Rice

1 1/2 teaspoons olive oil

Vegetable oil cooking spray

1 small onion, chopped

1 garlic clove, minced

1 small green pepper, seeded and chopped

2 (16-ounce) cans black beans, undrained

1 to 2 teaspoons curry powder

1/4 teaspoon or more cumin

1/4 teaspoon dried oregano

Salt to taste

4 cups cooked white or brown rice

Heat the oil and a generous spray of cooking spray in a large, heavy skillet. Sauté and stir the onion and garlic over medium-low heat for 3 minutes, being careful not to burn the onions. Stir in the green pepper, and sauté and stir for 2 additional minutes. Stir in the black beans and seasonings, cover, and simmer for 20 minutes. Serve over rice.

Preparation time: 10 minutes. Cooking time: 25 to 30 minutes. Yield: 4 servings

Nutrition analysis: 468 calories per serving; 16.5 gm. protein; 93 gm. carbohydrate; 3 gm. fat; 0 cholesterol; 3 gm. fiber; 949 mg. sodium

Percent of calories from protein: 14%; from carbohydrates: 80%; from fat: 6%

Exchange values: ½ vegetable; 6 bread; ½ meat; ½ fat

Beans
Olé

This versatile dish is delicious eaten hot or cold, with or without rice, and as a salad, dip, or sandwich filling. Since it is such a healthy dish, you can try it many different ways.

1 1/2 teaspoons olive oil

Vegetable oil cooking spray

1 onion, chopped well

1 large garlic clove, minced

1 red pepper, chopped well

1 teaspoon minced jalapeño pepper (Note: always wear rubber gloves when working with hot peppers)

2 (16- to 19-ounce) cans black beans, rinsed and drained (red kidney beans can be used if you prefer)

1/2 cup fresh or frozen corn, thawed

1/4 cup red wine vinegar

1/4 cup brown sugar

1 teaspoon chili powder, or to taste

1 teaspoon ground cumin, or to taste

Salt and freshly ground pepper to taste

6 cups cooked white or brown rice (optional)

Heat the olive oil and a generous spray of cooking spray in a large, heavy skillet for 45 seconds. Stir in the onion and garlic, and sauté over medium-low heat for 3 minutes, stirring frequently. Add 1 to 2 teaspoons of water if the mixture starts to burn. Stir in the red pepper and jalapeño pepper. Sauté for 5 minutes, stirring frequently. Stir in the beans and corn. Mix the vinegar, brown sugar, chili powder, and ground cumin together in a small bowl. Stir this mixture into the bean mixture, bring to a boil, and simmer uncovered for 10 minutes. Add salt and pepper to taste.

Serve hot with rice; cold as a salad; at room temperature or cold as a dip with low-fat tortilla chips; or on your favorite hearty bread or tortilla as a sandwich.

Beans Olé (continued)

Preparation time: 10 minutes. Cooking time: 20 minutes. Yield: about 3½ cups. 6 to 8 main course servings

Nutrition analysis for 6 servings: 448 calories per serving; 16 gm. protein; 90 gm. carbohydrate; 3.5 gm. fat; 0 cholesterol; 9.5 gm. fiber; 605 mg. sodium

Percent of calories from protein: 14%; from carbohydrates: 79%; from fat: 7%

Exchange values: ½ vegetable; 5½ bread

Fear of Frying

Chick-Pea Casserole

I serve this dish with rice as a main course, but it makes a delicious and healthy side-dish as well.

1 1/2 teaspoons olive oil

Vegetable oil cooking spray

1 yellow onion, chopped

1 garlic clove, minced

1 green pepper, seeded and chopped

14 1/2-ounce can chopped tomatoes, undrained

1 tablespoon chopped fresh basil

16-ounce can or 2 cups cooked chick-peas, rinsed and well drained

Salt and freshly ground pepper to taste

Preheat the oven to 350°. Heat the olive oil and a generous spray of cooking spray in a large, heavy skillet for 45 seconds. Stir in the onion and garlic, and sauté over medium-low heat for 3 minutes, stirring frequently. If the mixture begins to burn, add 1 to 2 teaspoons water. Stir in the green pepper, and continue to sauté and stir for another 3 minutes. Stir in the tomatoes, basil, and chick-peas, and bring to a boil. Spoon the chick-pea mixture into the prepared casserole, cover, and bake for 35 minutes. Add salt and freshly ground pepper to taste, and serve immediately.

Preparation time: 5 minutes. Cooking time: 45 minutes (mostly unattended). Yield: 4 servings

Nutrition analysis: 163 calories per serving; 7 gm. protein; 27 gm. carbohydrate; 4 gm. fat; 0 cholesterol; 7 gm. fiber; 620 mg. sodium

Percent of calories from protein: 16%; from carbohydrates: 63%; from fat: 22%

Exchange values: 1½ vegetable; 1½ bread; ½ fat

Delhi Curried Beans

This vegetarian dish is filled with flavor, nutrition, and a hint of exotic India.

Vegetable oil cooking spray

1 1/2 teaspoons olive oil

1 cup chopped onion

1 large garlic clove, minced

1 small green pepper, seeded and chopped

1 teaspoon chopped jalapeño pepper (optional) (Note: always wear rubber gloves when working with hot peppers

1 tablespoon flour

1 teaspoon curry powder

1/4 teaspoon ground cumin

1 1/2 cups seeded and chopped tomatoes

1 tablespoon sun-dried or regular tomato paste

1 2/3 cups low-salt chicken broth with fat skimmed off the top

1 1/2 cups potatoes, peeled and diced

1 3/4 cups cooked or canned chick-peas (garbanzo beans), rinsed and drained

1/2 cup raisins

Salt and freshly ground pepper

4 cups cooked brown or white rice (optional)

2 to 3 tablespoons nonfat plain yogurt (optional)

Spray a large, heavy pot with cooking spray. Pour in the olive oil and heat for 45 seconds. Stir in the onions and garlic, and sauté over medium-low heat for 3 minutes, stirring frequently. Do not let the onions and garlic burn. Add the green pepper and jalapeño pepper. Sauté and stir for 2 more minutes. Mix in the flour, curry powder, and cumin, and stir for 30 seconds. Stir in the tomatoes, tomato paste, and chicken broth. Bring to a boil, then stir in the potatoes and chick-peas. Bring to a boil again, then reduce heat, cover, and simmer, stirring occasionally, for 30 minutes or until potatoes are very tender. Stir in the raisins, salt, and pepper. Serve in bowls as a stew or over cooked rice. Top with a dollop of yogurt, if you like.

Preparation time: 15 minutes. Cooking time: 35 minutes. Yield: 4 servings without rice; 4 to 6 servings with rice

Nutrition analysis without rice (numbers in parentheses indicate nutrition analysis with one cup of rice per serving): 294 (558) calories per serving; 8 (13.5) gm. protein; 59 (116) gm. carbohydrate; 4.5 (5) gm. fat; 0 (0) cholesterol; 8 (10) gm. fiber; 586 (590) mg. sodium

Percent of calories from protein: 11 (10)%; from carbohydrates: 76 (82)%; from fat: 13 (8)%

Exchange values: 2 (2) vegetable; 1 (1) fruit; 2½ (6) bread; ½ (½) fat

Mexican Marinated Beans

I like to serve this dish on a bed of lettuce for a delicious salad. The marinade gives these vegetables a mildly spicy taste and a lot of character.

1 3/4 to 2 cups cooked or canned white beans, rinsed and drained

3/4 to 1 cup corn, cooked al dente, tender but not mushy

3/4 cup cooked or canned chick-peas, rinsed and drained

1/4 cup chopped red pepper

1/4 cup chopped green bell pepper

1 tomato, seeded and chopped

1 chopped scallion

Marinade:

1/4 cup low-fat Italian salad dressing

1 teaspoon balsamic vinegar

1/2 teaspoon minced jalapeño pepper (Note: always wear rubber gloves when working with hot peppers)

1 teaspoon chopped scallion (use the white part only)

1/4 teaspoon minced garlic

Salt and freshly ground pepper to taste

Mix the vegetables together in a large bowl. Purée the marinade ingredients together in a food processor or blender. Pour the dressing over the vegetables, and stir well. Add salt and pepper to taste. Cover, and refrigerate for at least 4 hours.

Preparation time: 10 minutes. Marinating time: 4 hours. Yield: 6 servings

Nutrition analysis: 158 calories per serving; 8.5 gm. protein; 29 gm. carbohydrate; 1.5 gm. fat; 1 mg. cholesterol; 2 gm. fiber; 154 mg. sodium

Percent of calories from protein: 20%; from carbohydrates: 70%; from fat: 9%

Exchange values: ½ vegetable; 2 bread; ½ meat

Spanish Chick-Peas & Rice

My friend who grew up in Panama introduced me to this family recipe years ago. It makes a great tasting vegetarian dish that is brimming with healthy nutrients, fiber, and flavor.

1 1/2 teaspoons olive oil and a generous spray of vegetable oil cooking spray

1 small onion, chopped

1 large garlic clove, minced

1/2 large green pepper, chopped

2 tablespoons chopped parsley

2 tablespoons chopped cilantro

Dash or two of dried oregano

1/4 teaspoon cumin

1 tablespoon tomato paste

16-ounce can chick-peas (also known as garbanzo beans), undrained (canned kidney beans or black beans may be used)

4 cups cooked white or brown rice

Heat the oil and cooking spray in a large, heavy skillet. Sauté the onion, garlic, and green pepper over medium-low heat for 5 minutes, stirring frequently. Stir in the parsley, cilantro, oregano, cumin, tomato paste, and undrained chick-peas. Bring to a boil. Cover the skillet but leave the cover slightly ajar to allow some steam to escape. Cook over low heat for 20 minutes. If necessary, rapidly boil down the sauce a little to reach desired consistency. Serve with rice.

Preparation time: 10 minutes. Cooking time: 25 minutes. Yield: 4 servings

Nutrition analysis: 406 calories per serving; 11.5 gm. protein; 79.5 gm. carbohydrate; 4.5 gm. fat; 0 cholesterol; 8.5 gm. fiber; 490 mg. sodium

Percent of calories from protein: 11%; from carbohydrates: 79%; from fat: 10%

Exchange values: ½ vegetable; 5½ bread; ½ fat

Southwestern Beans

Here is a recipe that gives pinto beans a southwestern flavor without being too spicy. It's a good way to start incorporating beans into your diet.

1 1/2 teaspoons olive oil and a generous spray of vegetable oil cooking spray

1 medium onion, chopped

2 garlic cloves, minced

1/2 large green pepper, chopped

1/2 pound ground white meat turkey or chicken (if you're on a very low-fat diet, this can be omitted)

14 1/2-ounce can diced or stewed tomatoes, undrained

2 medium potatoes, peeled and diced

2 tablespoons minced fresh cilantro or parsley

1 to 1 1/2 teaspoons chili powder

15-ounce can partially drained pinto beans

Salt and freshly ground pepper to taste

6 cups cooked white or brown rice

Heat the oil and cooking spray in a large, heavy skillet. Sauté the onion and garlic over medium-low heat for 3 minutes or until tender, stirring frequently. You may need to add 1 to 2 teaspoons of water to prevent the mixture from burning. Stir in the green pepper and ground turkey. Continue cooking and stirring a few more minutes until the turkey is thoroughly cooked. Drain well. Stir in the tomatoes, potatoes, cilantro, chili powder, and pinto beans. Cover, and simmer for 25 to 30 minutes or until the potatoes are tender. Add salt and pepper to taste. Serve with rice.

Preparation time: 10 minutes. Cooking time: 35 to 40 minutes. Yield: 6 servings

Nutrition analysis with white rice: 443 calories per serving; 15.5 gm. protein; 83.5 gm. carbohydrate; 5 gm. fat; 14 mg. cholesterol; 4 gm. fiber; 500 mg. sodium

Percent of calories from protein: 14%; from carbohydrates: 76%; from fat: 10%

Exchange values: 1 vegetable; 5 bread; 1 meat; ½ fat

VEGETABLES

Broccoli Custard

This recipe makes eating broccoli fun.

Vegetable oil cooking spray

1 whole large egg

1 large egg white

1/4 cup skim milk

1/2 cup low-fat (1%) cottage cheese

1 tablespoon Butter Buds, natural dehydrated butter

1 teaspoon sharp prepared mustard

2 teaspoons cornstarch

1/2 teaspoon salt

1/8 teaspoon ground nutmeg

Freshly ground pepper, one or two turns on the pepper mill

1 pound of broccoli tops, cut up, and steamed for 8 to 10 minutes

Preheat oven to 350°. Spray a flat 2-quart glass baking dish with cooking spray. Put all the ingredients, except the broccoli, in a food processor. Puree on high for 15 seconds. Add the slightly cooled, steamed broccoli, and using the on/off button, process until the broccoli is well chopped but not pureed. Pour into the prepared baking dish, and bake for 35 to 45 minutes or until the custard is set. Serve immediately with chicken or fish.

Preparation time: 10 minutes. Cooking time: 45 to 55 minutes. Yield: 6 servings

Nutrition analysis: 59 calories per serving; 6.5 gm. protein; 6 gm. carbohydrate; 1.5 gm. fat; 36.5 mg. cholesterol; 0 fiber; 310 mg. sodium

Percent of calories from protein: 42%; from carbohydrates: 38%; from fat: 19%

Exchange values: 1 vegetable; ½ meat

Basic Asparagus and Zippy Dip

Choose asparagus spears that are about the same thickness, round and firm, with tightly closed, pointed tips that haven't started to flower. The thickness of the asparagus spear is not as important as the condition of the tip. Cook them the same day or the day after you buy them because they don't store very well.

Basic Asparagus:

2 pounds asparagus

2 tablespoons fresh dill (optional)

1/2 tsp. salt

1/2 tsp. sugar

Zippy Asparagus Dip:

2 tablespoons nonfat mayonnaise

2 teaspoons Dijon mustard

2 teaspoons prepared horseradish

Snap off the bottom of each spear by bending it with your fingers. It will snap at the point where the tough end of the stalk ends. Discard the bottoms, and rinse the asparagus tips. Add the dill, salt, and sugar to an inch of water in a pan. Bring the water to a boil, then add the asparagus, and cook for 4 to 7 minutes or until just tender and bright green. (Or you can steam for 4 to 7 minutes, or bundle and cook upright in an inch of boiling water in a tall asparagus pot.) Be careful not to overcook the asparagus. Remove from heat, drain well, and drop the asparagus into cold water. Now they are ready to eat plain, with a sauce, or in a salad.

For Zippy Asparagus Dip: Mix all ingredients. Serve dip with the asparagus at room temperature on a vegetable platter or as the vegetable course with dinner.

Preparation time: 5 minutes. Cooking time: 4 to 7 minutes. Yield: 4 dinner servings

Nutrition analysis with dip: 70 calories per serving; 6.5 gm. protein; 11.5 gm. carbohydrate; 1.5 gm. fat; 3 mg. cholesterol; 2.5 gm. fiber; 138 mg. sodium

Percent of calories from protein: 30%; from carbohydrates: 56%; from fat: 14%

Exchange values: 2½ vegetable

Double Baked Potatoes

These potatoes can be served as a side dish or as a main course. Their velvety smooth texture and zesty taste make them a popular choice. I love how they puff up while baking and look very elegant when served.

4 evenly-sized, large Idaho baking potatoes

Olive oil

3 tablespoons minced scallions (use mostly the white part)

1/2 small garlic clove, minced

3 tablespoons skim milk at room temperature

2 tablespoons nonfat plain yogurt at room temperature

1 teaspoon horseradish

1/2 teaspoon Worcestershire sauce

1 tablespoon Butter Buds, natural dehydrated butter

Salt and freshly ground pepper to taste

2 egg whites

1 tablespoon grated Parmesan cheese

Preheat oven to 425°. Scrub the potatoes. Dry them, and coat them lightly with a small amount of olive oil. Pierce them with a fork a few times. Bake for an hour to an hour and a quarter or until completely tender but not dried out. Remove them from the oven and cut them in half lengthwise. Scoop out the pulp without breaking the skin. Broil the potato shells for 3 to 5 minutes until golden.

Combine the potato pulp, scallions, garlic, milk, yogurt, horseradish, Worcestershire sauce, and Butter Buds in a medium bowl, and beat with an electric beater until smooth. Salt and pepper to taste. In another bowl, beat the egg whites until stiff but not dry. Fold the egg whites into the potato mixture. Fill each potato shell with the pulp mixture, then sprinkle the filled potatoes with Parmesan cheese. Bake at 425° for 15 to 20 minutes or until puffy and golden.

Preparation time: 15 minutes. Cooking time: 1½ hours. Yield: 4 to 8 servings, depending on whether they are served as a side dish or main course.

Nutrition analysis for 4 servings: 173 calories per serving; 6.5 gm. protein; 35.5 gm. carbohydrate; 0.5 gm. fat; 1.5 mg. cholesterol; 4 gm. fiber; 96 mg. sodium

Percent of calories from protein: 15%; from carbohydrates: 82%; from fat: 3%

Exchange values: 2 bread; ½ meat

Basic Baked Acorn Squash

Vegetable oil cooking spray

2 medium acorn, or similar winter squash

1 teaspoon brown sugar

1 tablespoon melted light butter (optional)

2 tablespoons Butter Buds, natural dehydrated butter

2 tablespoons light brown sugar

2 to 3 tablespoons pure maple syrup (depending on the size of the squash)

1/2 teaspoon ground cinnamon

Dash of ground nutmeg (freshly ground nutmeg is best)

1/4 teaspoon rum flavoring (optional)

Preheat oven to 400°. Spray a large baking dish with cooking spray. Cut the squash in half horizontally. Do not remove seeds. (If necessary, even off the top and bottom of each squash so it will sit flat in the baking dish when it needs to be turned over.) Place the cut squash in the baking dish, seed side down, and add about one-half inch of water mixed with a teaspoon of brown sugar. Bake uncovered for 30 minutes.

Meanwhile, combine the rest of the ingredients and stir well. Remove the baking dish from the oven, turn the squash over, and remove the seeds and any stringy matter. Brush the flesh of the squash with the sugar mixture, and pour the remaining mixture in the inside of the squash. Add some water to the bottom of the baking dish if necessary. Return the squash to the oven, and bake for 25 to 40 more minutes or until tender (cooking time depends on the type and size of the squash). Serve immediately.

Preparation time: 10 minutes. Cooking time: 60 to 70 minutes (mostly unattended). Yield: 4 servings

Nutrition analysis: 177 calories per serving; 2 gm. protein; 41.5 gm. carbohydrate; 2 gm. fat; 5 mg. cholesterol; 3 gm. fiber; 42.5 mg. sodium

Percent of calories from protein: 4%; from carbohydrates: 87%; from fat: 10%

Exchange values: 1½ bread; ½ fat

Asparagus in Orange Dijon Sauce

This delicate and slightly sweet sauce is wonderful with asparagus.

2 pounds fresh asparagus, washed, with the lower part of the stalks snapped off

Orange Dijon Sauce:

1/3 cup orange juice

1 teaspoon grated orange zest (peel), optional

1 teaspoon honey

2 teaspoons Dijon mustard

1 teaspoon cornstarch

Salt and freshly ground pepper to taste

Cook the asparagus tips in a covered pot with 1 inch of lightly salted and sweetened boiling water for 4 to 7 minutes. (See Basic Asparagus, page 107.) Stir the orange juice, orange zest, honey, mustard, and cornstarch together in a small saucepan. Slowly bring to a boil, and continue cooking for 1 to 2 minutes. Salt and pepper to taste. Serve the asparagus covered with Orange Dijon Sauce.

Preparation time: 5 minutes. Cooking time: 4 to 7 minutes. Yield: 4 servings

Nutrition analysis: 76 calories per serving; 6 gm. protein; 14.5 gm. carbohydrate; 1 gm. fat; 0 cholesterol; 3 gm. fiber; 73 mg. sodium

Percent of calories from protein: 27%; from carbohydrates: 64%; from fat: 9%

Exchange values: 2½ vegetable

Dijon Glazed Carrots

1 to 1 1/2 pounds carrots, peeled and sliced into 1/4-inch rounds

Salt to taste

1 tablespoon Dijon mustard

1 tablespoon Butter Buds, natural dehydrated butter

2 tablespoons lightly packed brown sugar

1 tablespoon honey

2 tablespoons chopped fresh parsley (optional)

KIDS LOVE THIS

Place carrots in a medium saucepan, and add enough cold water just to cover the carrots. Lightly salt the carrots, stir, cover, and bring to a boil. Reduce heat, and simmer just until carrots are tender, about 15 to 20 minutes. Drain well, remove from saucepan, and set aside. In the same saucepan, combine the rest of the ingredients. Bring the sauce just to the boiling point, stirring over medium heat. Stir in the carrots, and serve.

Preparation time: 10 minutes. Cooking time: 20 to 25 minutes. Yield: 4 servings

Nutrition analysis: 118 calories per serving; 2 gm. protein; 28 gm. carbohydrate; 0.5 gm. fat; 0 cholesterol; 0 fiber; 157 mg. sodium

Percent of calories from protein: 6%; from carbohydrates: 90%; from fat: 4%

Exchange values: 3½ vegetable

Snappy Green Beans & Onions

Were you afraid that cooking without butter would lead to boring, tasteless dishes? This recipe proves that great taste can be achieved easily and quickly by using the right combination of ingredients.

Vegetable oil cooking spray

1/3 cup lightly salted water

1/2 pound fresh green beans, washed, with the ends snapped off

1 cup frozen small whole onions

Sauce:

1 tablespoon balsamic vinegar

1 teaspoon olive oil

1 teaspoon Dijon mustard

Spray a cookie sheet with cooking spray. Bring the water to a boil in a medium saucepan. Add the green beans, then reheat the water to boiling, cover, and cook 2 minutes. Stir in the onions. Bring to boiling point again, cover, and cook 3 additional minutes. Drain well. Combine the sauce ingredients in a medium bowl, and mix thoroughly. Stir in the vegetables, and let sit for 5 minutes. Spread the vegetables in a single layer on the cookie sheet. Cover with any remaining sauce. Broil for 3 minutes. Serve hot or at room temperature.

Preparation time: 10 minutes. Cooking time: 15 minutes. Yield: 4 servings

Nutrition analysis: 58 calories per serving; 9 gm. protein; 11 gm. carbohydrate; 1.5 gm. fat; 0 cholesterol; 1.5 gm. fiber; 35.5 mg. sodium

Percent of calories from protein: 12%; from carbohydrates: 68%; from fat: 21%

Exchange values: 2 vegetable

Candied
Carrots

—————————————

6 to 8 carrots, peeled and cut into 1/4-inch rounds

1/2 tablespoon light butter or margarine, melted

1 tablespoon brown sugar

1 to 2 tablespoons Middlesex Farm's Ginger Jazz, orange marmalade, or honey

Place the sliced carrots in a saucepan, add an inch or less of lightly salted water, and bring to a boil. Cover, lower heat, and simmer for 10 to 20 minutes or just until tender. Don't overcook the carrots. Drain well. Mix the rest of the ingredients together. Stir the mixture into the carrots, and simmer until the carrots are completely glazed, about 2 to 3 minutes. Serve immediately.

KIDS LOVE THIS

Preparation time: 5 minutes. Cooking time: 15 to 20 minutes.
Yield: 6 servings

Nutrition analysis: 77 calories per serving; 1 gm. protein; 17.5 gm. carbohydrate; 1 gm. fat; 1.5 mg. cholesterol; 3 gm. fiber; 41 mg. sodium

Percent of calories from protein: 5%; from carbohydrates: 86%; from fat: 9%

Exchange values: 2 vegetable

Carrots & Parsnips

This recipe combines the complementary flavors of carrots and parsnips to create a delicious, healthy, attractive vegetable dish.

5 medium-sized carrots, peeled

1 medium-sized parsnip, peeled

2 tablespoons freshly chopped parsley

1 1/2 teaspoons olive oil

Butter Buds, natural dehydrated butter, to taste

Salt and freshly ground pepper to taste

Julienne the carrots and parsnip, or cut them into very thin sticks about 2 inches long. The thickness of the carrot sticks will determine how long you cook the vegetables. Make sure the parsnip sticks are not thinner than the carrot sticks. Place the carrots in a large skillet, and fill the skillet with just enough lightly salted water to cover the bottom. Bring to a boil, lower heat, cover, and simmer for 3 to 5 minutes.

Stir in the parsnip sticks. Add water to the skillet when necessary, being careful not to let it boil away. Bring to a boil, lower heat, cover, and simmer for 5 to 10 minutes more or until the vegetables are tender but not soft. Drain well. Stir in the rest of the ingredients, and check the seasonings for taste.

Preparation time: 10 minutes . Cooking time: 10 to 15 minutes. Yield: 4 servings

Nutrition analysis: 69 calories per serving; 1 gm. protein; 13 gm. carbohydrate; 2 gm. fat; 0 cholesterol; 4 gm. fiber; 34 mg. sodium

Percent of calories from protein: 7%; from carbohydrates: 70%; from fat: 24%

Exchange values: 2½ vegetable; ½ fat

Sweet Potato Chips

Vegetable oil cooking spray

4 long sweet potatoes

Kosher salt to taste (table salt may be used, but
   I prefer the coarser Kosher salt)

Preheat oven to 350°. Spray two cookie sheets with cooking spray. Peel or scrub and dry the potatoes. Slice each potato into ¼-inch rounds. Place potato rounds in a single layer on cookie sheets. Lightly spray the potato rounds with cooking spray. Sprinkle with salt to taste. Bake in preheated oven for 35 to 45 minutes, depending on desired crispness. (You may want to flip the potatoes after 18 minutes if you want them evenly browned, but it is not a necessary step.) You can make these chips as crispy as you want, but check them after 35 minutes because they get hard when left in the oven too long.

KIDS LOVE THIS

Preparation time: 5 minutes. Cooking time: 35 to 45 minutes. Yield: 4 servings

Nutrition analysis: 117 calories per serving; 2 gm. protein; 27 gm. carbohydrate; 0 fat; 0 cholesterol; 3.5 gm. fiber; 44.5 mg. sodium

Percent of calories from protein: 7%; from carbohydrates: 93%; from fat: 1%

Exchange values: 2 bread

Note: All-purpose potatoes, especially the Yukon Gold® variety, can be used in place of the sweet potatoes with equal success.

Easy Mashed Sweet Potatoes

Sweet potatoes are filled with healthy nutrients and are popular with kids. This dish takes little time to prepare and will disappear quickly when served to your family or friends.

4 medium sweet potatoes or yams

2 tablespoons Butter Buds, natural dehydrated butter

1/4 cup (or slightly more) skimmed evaporated milk, low-fat milk, or skim milk

2 to 6 teaspoons packed brown sugar, depending on desired sweetness

Salt to taste

Peel the sweet potatoes, then slice them into 1-inch slices, and put them in a large pot. Fill the pot with about an inch of lightly salted water. Cover, bring to a boil, reduce heat, and simmer for 20 to 25 minutes or until the potatoes are just tender enough to be mashed. Drain well. Put the potatoes in a medium bowl. Add the remaining ingredients, and beat with an electric mixer until smooth. If necessary, add more milk while beating. Serve immediately.

Preparation time: 10 minutes. Cooking time: 20 to 25 minutes. Yield: 4 to 5 servings

Nutrition analysis: 126 calories per serving; 2.5 gm. protein; 29 gm. carbohydrate; 0 fat; 0.5 mg. cholesterol; 2.5 gm. fiber; 25.5 mg. sodium

Percent of calories from protein: 8%; from carbohydrates: 91%; from fat: 1%

Exchange values: 1½ bread

KIDS LOVE THIS

Grilled Vegetables

————————————

When it's too hot to cook and I want a quick meal, I grill some chicken breasts or fish and whatever vegetables are in the house. This is always a popular meal with the family, and it takes very little effort to make. This is a basic recipe, but an endless variety of vegetables can be used.

Vegetable oil cooking spray

1 vidalia or sweet onion, cut into eighths

1/2 pound fresh small or button mushrooms, washed and dried

8 cherry tomatoes

1 small green pepper, seeded and sliced

1 small red pepper, seeded and sliced

1 tablespoon low-fat Italian dressing (don't use a fat-free dressing for this recipe)

Kosher or coarse salt

Preheat the grill. Spray a vegetable griller with cooking spray. (Vegetable grillers are metal, mesh trays or baskets. They can be bought where grills are sold.) Place the vegetables in a bowl, and cover with the Italian dressing. Toss until everything is coated. Place the vegetables on the vegetable griller, spray them with vegetable cooking spray,* and lightly sprinkle with salt. Place the vegetable griller on a medium to medium-hot grill, cover, and cook for 5 to 7 minutes on each side or until desired tenderness is reached.

Preparation time: 10 minutes. Cooking time: 10 to 15 minutes. Yield: 4 servings

Nutrition analysis: 56 calories per serving; 2.5 gm. protein; 11.5 gm. carbohydrate; 1 gm. fat; 0.5 mg. cholesterol; 3 gm. fiber; 39.5 mg. sodium

Percent of calories from protein: 16%; from carbohydrates: 71%; from fat: 13%

Exchange values: 2 vegetable

*Do not use the cooking spray near the grill.

Purée de Broccoli

The idea for this recipe started in the gourmet club I joined years ago. I have made various versions and have been most happy with this one. Remember, broccoli is one of those "super foods" filled with cancer-fighting antioxidants.

1 1/2 pounds fresh broccoli florets
1 tablespoon Butter Buds, natural dehydrated butter
1/4 to 1/2 teaspoon salt
Freshly ground pepper to taste
Pinch of freshly ground nutmeg
1/4 cup nonfat plain yogurt
1 tablespoon nonfat dried milk
1/4 to 1/2 cup skim milk

Wash and dry the broccoli. Divide into small florets. Bring an inch of salted water to boil in a large, heavy pot. Add the broccoli. Bring back to a boil, then cover and simmer for 5 to 7 minutes. While the broccoli simmers, mix the Butter Buds, salt, pepper, nutmeg, yogurt, and dry milk together in a small bowl. Drain the broccoli and put a quarter of the broccoli in a food processor. Chop the broccoli (be careful not to liquefy it). Add the rest of the broccoli in small batches. Add the yogurt mixture and some milk. Purée until smooth, adding more milk to reach desired consistency. Add salt if desired, and serve immediately.

Preparation time: 10 minutes. Cooking time: 10 minutes. Yield: 7 to 8 servings

Nutrition analysis: 34.5 calories per serving; 3.5 gm. protein; 6 gm. carbohydrate; 0.5 gm. fat; 0.5 mg. cholesterol; 2.5 gm. fiber; 171 mg. sodium

Percent of calories from protein: 35%; from carbohydrates: 58%; from fat: 8%

Exchange values: 1 vegetable

Sweet Peas in
Orange Sauce

It can be hard to get our families to eat vegetables that aren't cooked with a lot of butter or margarine. The delicious orange sauce in this recipe solves this problem quickly and easily. Best of all, this tasty sauce can be used on a variety of vegetables, such as carrots, green beans, and broccoli

2 cups or 10 ounces sweet, young
   or petite peas, fresh or frozen

Orange Sauce:

1/3 cup orange juice

1 tablespoon honey

1 teaspoon cornstarch

1/4 teaspoon Butter Buds, natural dehydrated butter (optional)

Salt to taste

Cook the peas in a little water just until they're tender but not mushy. Drain the peas, and keep them hot. Mix the orange juice, honey, and cornstarch together in a medium saucepan. Cook over medium heat, stirring frequently, until the mixture starts to boil. Stir in the cooked peas, and salt to taste. Serve immediately.

Preparation time: 5 minutes. Cooking time: 10 minutes. Yield: 4 servings

Nutrition analysis: 94.5 calories per serving; 4.5 gm. protein; 19.5 gm. carbohydrate; 0 fat; 0 cholesterol; 0 fiber; 2.5 mg. sodium

Percent of calories from protein: 18%; from carbohydrates: 80%; from fat: 2%

Exchange values: 1 bread; ½ meat

Baked Vidalia Onions

Vidalia onions are a sweet onion from the South named after the city of Vidalia, Georgia. Vidalia onions become available in the Northeast for a short time each spring. I use them often when I can buy them, and my favorite way is to bake them. Other sweet onions can also be baked. Baked onions are a wonderful addition to a barbecue.

Vegetable oil cooking spray

4 whole Vidalia onions, peeled with the ends cut off

Olive oil

Salt to taste

1/4 cup raisins

Preheat oven to 350° Spray a small baking dish with cooking spray. Brush the onions with a small amount of olive oil. Place the onions in the dish, sprinkle them with salt, and pour in the raisins. Cover with foil, and bake for 1½ hours, basting occasionally. Serve covered with the raisins and juice from the bottom of the baking dish.

Preparation time: 5 minutes. Cooking time: 1½ hours (mostly unattended). Yield: 4 servings

Nutrition analysis: 88 calories per serving; 2 gm. protein; 21 gm. carbohydrate; 0.5 gm. fat; 0 cholesterol; 3 gm. fiber; 6 mg. sodium

Percent of calories from protein: 9%; from carbohydrates: 88%; from fat: 3%

Exchange values: 2 vegetable; ½ fruit

Baked
Sweet Potatoes

Many of us know sweet potatoes are nutritious, but we often have a hard time convincing our children to eat them without slabs of butter or margarine. This recipe solves that problem without adding a lot of unnecessary fat. Kids love the taste of apricot yogurt on top of sweet potatoes.

4 medium sweet potatoes

Olive oil

3 to 6 tablespoons nonfat plain yogurt

1 to 2 tablespoons apricot jam or preserves, or to taste
  (try the fruit juice-sweetened variety)

Preheat oven to 350°. Scrub the potatoes, dry them, cut off the stems, and pierce the skin with a sharp knife. Rub each potato with a little olive oil. Place a sheet of aluminum foil on the middle rack in your oven and place the potatoes on the foil. (This will keep your oven clean since sweet potatoes can drip while cooking.) Bake for 40 to 60 minutes or until the potatoes are soft. While the potatoes are cooking, mix the yogurt and apricot jam together to desired sweetness. When the potatoes are done, slice each one open, and generously spoon some of the apricot yogurt on top of each potato. Serve immediately.

KIDS LOVE THIS

Preparation time: 5 minutes. Cooking time: 40 to 60 minutes. Yield: 4 servings

Nutrition analysis: 161 calories per serving; 3 gm. protein; 36.5 gm. carbohydrate; 0.5 gm. fat; 0.5 mg. cholesterol; 3.5 gm. fiber; 28.5 mg. sodium

Percent of calories from protein: 8%; from carbohydrates: 88%; from fat: 4%

Exchange values: 2 bread

Easy Mashed Potatoes

6 medium potatoes, peeled and quartered (or cut into eighths for quicker cooking)

2 garlic cloves, sliced

1/2 medium-size onion, sliced

1/2 teaspoon salt

1/3 to 1/2 cup hot skim milk

1 tablespoon or more Butter Buds, natural dehydrated butter

Salt and pepper to taste

KIDS LOVE THIS

Place the potatoes, garlic, and onions in a large, heavy saucepan. Add about an inch of water. Stir in the salt, and bring to a boil. Cover, lower heat, and simmer 20 to 40 minutes or until the potatoes are tender but not mushy. Drain well. Pour ⅓ cup hot milk and the Butter Buds into the potatoes, onions, and garlic. Beat with an electric beater until fluffy, adding more hot milk if necessary. Taste and adjust seasonings, and serve immediately.

Preparation time: 10 minutes. Cooking time: 20 to 40 minutes. Yield: 4 servings

Nutrition analysis: 158 calories per serving; 3 gm. protein; 36.5 gm. carbohydrate; 0 fat; 0.5 mg. cholesterol; 3.5 gm. fiber; 32 mg. sodium

Percent of calories from protein: 8%; from carbohydrates: 91%; from fat: 1%

Exchange values: 2 bread

Harvest Squash

Vegetable oil cooking spray

4 medium acorn squash

4 medium red apples, peeled and cored

1/2 cup fresh whole cranberries

1/4 cup whole walnuts (optional)

1/4 cup packed brown sugar

1 1/2 tablespoons honey

1/4 to 1/2 teaspoon cinnamon

1/8 teaspoon freshly ground nutmeg

1 tablespoon light butter or margarine, melted

1 teaspoon brown sugar

Salt to taste

Preheat oven to 375°. Spray a large baking pan with cooking spray. Split the squash in half, and do not remove the seeds. Place the squash seed side down in the baking dish. Add enough water to cover the dish with about a quarter inch of water. Bake uncovered for 30 minutes. (Microwaving saves half the time: Place the split squash upside down on a microwaveable plate, and cook on high for 10 to 15 minutes, turning once.) Meanwhile, chop the apples, cranberries, and walnuts. Combine the apples, cranberries, walnuts, brown sugar, honey, cinnamon, and nutmeg in a large bowl. Stir well. Remove the squash from the oven, and scoop out the seeds. Mix the melted butter and 1 teaspoon brown sugar together, then brush the inside of each squash with this mixture. Lightly salt the squash. Fill the squash with the apple mixture, and bake for 25 more minutes or until the inside of the squash is soft. Serve immediately.

Preparation time: 15 minutes. Cooking time: 1 hour. Yield: 8 servings

Nutrition analysis: 222 calories per serving; 3.5 gm. protein; 51 gm. carbohydrate; 3 gm. fat; 0 cholesterol; 6 gm. fiber; 24.5 mg. sodium

Percent of calories from protein: 5%; from carbohydrates: 83%; from fat: 11%

Exchange values: ½ fruit; 2 bread; ½ fat

Italian Green Beans

Don't worry if you're not fond of anchovies; most people have trouble figuring out what gives these green beans their deliciously zesty taste.

2 (9-ounce) packages frozen French-style green beans

1 1/2 to 2 teaspoons olive oil

2 to 3 teaspoons freshly squeezed lemon juice

1/4 to 1/2 teaspoon garlic powder

1 tablespoon anchovy paste, or to taste

Salt and freshly ground pepper to taste

Cook the green beans with ½ cup lightly salted boiling water in a large covered pot over medium heat until almost tender and still very green, about 8 to 10 minutes. Break up the frozen beans while they are cooking, and be sure not to overcook them. Remove from heat, drain well, and let cool slightly. Meanwhile, whisk the olive oil and lemon juice together. Whisk in the rest of the ingredients very well. Pour the sauce over the green beans, and toss thoroughly. Taste to check seasonings, and serve either hot or at room temperature. These green beans go well with a mild-tasting fish, chicken, or pasta.

Preparation time: 5 minutes. Cooking time: 8 to 10 minutes. Yield: 6 servings

Nutrition analysis: 37.5 calories per serving; 2 gm. protein; 5.5 gm. carbohydrate; 1.5 gm. fat; 1.5 mg. cholesterol; 1.5 gm. fiber; 84.5 mg. sodium

Percent of calories from protein: 17%; from carbohydrates: 52%; from fat: 31%

Exchange values: 1 vegetable

Karen's Sesame Green Beans

When I asked Karen for her family's favorite quick and easy vegetable recipe, she immediately came up with this one. I think you will find that the touch of sesame oil gives the green beans a great taste.

1 pound whole green beans, trimmed and cleaned

1 1/2 teaspoons sesame oil

1/3 to 1/2 teaspoon minced garlic

1 teaspoon sesame seeds (optional)

Salt and freshly ground pepper to taste

Bring 1 inch of lightly salted water to a boil in a large pot. Add the green beans, and stir. Cover, lower heat, and cook until tender, about 5 minutes. (Stir the beans once or twice while they cook.) Drain the beans thoroughly, cover, and set aside. Heat the oil in a large skillet. Add the garlic, and stir-fry over medium heat for 1 minute. Remove as much of the garlic as you can. Stir in the green beans until they are coated with oil. Remove from heat. Sprinkle with sesame seeds, salt, and pepper to taste.

Preparation time: 5 minutes. Cooking time: 6 minutes. Yield: 4 servings

Nutrition analysis: 60 calories per serving; 2 gm. protein; 9 gm. carbohydrate; 2 gm. fat; 0 cholesterol; 2 gm. fiber; 3.5 mg. sodium

Percent of calories from protein: 14%; from carbohydrates: 55%; from fat: 32%

Exchange values: 2 vegetable; ½ fat

Mixed
Vegetables

You'll be amazed how this simple, pure method of cooking can make such delicious vegetables. This recipe allows the natural flavors of the fresh vegetables to come out and blend together without adding any butter or sauce.

Vegetable oil cooking spray

4 carrots, peeled and cut into 1/8-inch rounds

3 stalks celery, sliced

1 small onion, cut into eighths

1 small zucchini, cut into 1/8-inch rounds

2 medium plum tomatoes, cut into quarters

1 tablespoon chopped fresh parsley

Kosher salt

Freshly ground pepper

Generously spray a large, heavy pot with cooking spray. Place all the vegetables in the pot. Sprinkle with parsley, and salt and pepper to taste. Stir well, cover the pot tightly, and cook over low heat for 10 minutes. Stir, and cook a few more minutes, if necessary. The vegetables should be tender, but not mushy. Adjust the seasonings, and serve immediately.

Preparation time: 10 minutes. Cooking time: 10 to 15 minutes. Yield 4 servings

Nutrition analysis: 61 calories per serving; 2 gm. protein; 14 gm. carbohydrate; 0.5 gm. fat; 0 cholesterol; 4.5 gm. fiber; 192 mg. sodium

Percent of calories from protein: 12%; from carbohydrates: 82%; from fat: 6%

Exchange values: 2½ vegetable

Oven-Roasted Vegetables

This recipe calls for only a few of the vegetables that can be roasted with great success. Be creative, and try new combinations, such as eggplant and carrots. All you need to remember is that some vegetables cook faster than others.

2 tablespoons low-fat Italian salad dressing (don't use nonfat dressing for this recipe)

1 brimming tablespoon Dijon mustard

6 small red new potatoes, scrubbed, dried, and cut into eighths

1 pound green beans, washed, dried, and trimmed

2 large red or green peppers, washed, dried, and quartered

1 large sweet onion, peeled and cut into eighths

1 zucchini, washed, dried, and cut into 1/2-inch rounds

Vegetable oil cooking spray

Coarse or Kosher salt to taste

KIDS LOVE THIS

Preheat oven to 375°. Mix the Italian dressing and mustard together in a very large bowl. Add the cut vegetables, and toss to coat them thoroughly with the dressing. Spray one or two large cookie sheets with cooking spray. Place the vegetables in a single layer on the cookie sheet, and sprinkle with salt to taste. Bake uncovered for 35 minutes, then check the vegetables. Remove those that are tender and cooked to desired consistency. Return the other vegetables, and continue cooking until done, anywhere from 10 to 25 more minutes. Check frequently, removing the vegetables that are tender. Serve hot or at room temperature.

Preparation time: 15 minutes. Cooking time: 35 to 60 minutes. Yield: 6 servings

Nutrition analysis: 118 calories per serving; 4 gm. protein; 25.5 gm. carbohydrate; 1 gm. fat; 0.5 mg. cholesterol; 4 gm. fiber; 131 mg. sodium

Percent of calories from protein: 12%; from carbohydrates: 80%; from fat: 8%

Exchange values: 2 vegetable; 1 bread

Parsnip & Carrot Purée

The combination of these two vegetables is only natural, because their tastes complement each other perfectly. When they are pureed with orange juice or milk, the result is not only delicious and attractive, but also very healthy.

1/2 pound parsnips, peeled and sliced

1/2 pound young carrots, peeled and sliced

1 tablespoon light butter (optional)

1/4 to 1/3 cup orange juice, skimmed evaporated milk, skim milk, or low-fat milk

1 tablespoon Butter Buds, natural dehydrated butter

Salt to taste

Place the sliced parsnips and carrots in a large pot, then add 1 inch of lightly salted boiling water. Cover, and simmer until the carrots are tender, about 20 minutes. Drain thoroughly. Stir in the butter, orange juice or milk, and Butter Buds. Purée in several batches in a food processor or blender. Add salt to taste, and serve immediately.

Preparation time: 10 minutes. Cooking time: 20 minutes. Yield: 4 servings

Nutrition analysis with orange juice: 98 calories per serving; 1.5 gm. protein; 19 gm. carbohydrate; 2 gm. fat; 5 mg. cholesterol; 5 gm. fiber; 62 mg. sodium

Percent of calories from protein: 6%; from carbohydrates: 75%; from fat: 19%

Exchange values: 3 vegetable; ½ fat

Peas & Artichokes

9-ounce box frozen artichoke hearts, slightly thawed

10-ounce box frozen petit peas, slightly thawed

1 teaspoon olive oil

1 tablespoon Butter Buds, natural dehydrated butter

2 tablespoons crumbled blue cheese

Salt and freshly ground pepper to taste

Bring ¼ to ½ cup of lightly salted water to a boil in a medium saucepan. Stir in the artichokes, and separate them with a fork or knife. Bring to a boil, cover, and simmer 2 minutes. Add the peas, and separate them with a fork or knife. Bring to a boil again, cover, and simmer 5 to 6 minutes or until the vegetables are tender. Drain well. Stir in the olive oil, Butter Buds, blue cheese, salt, and pepper. Serve immediately.

Preparation time: 5 minutes. Cooking time: 10 minutes. Yield: 4 servings

Nutrition analysis: 114 calories per serving; 7 gm. protein; 17.5 gm. carbohydrate; 2.5 gm. fat; 3 mg. cholesterol; 2.5 gm. fiber; 181 mg. sodium

Percent of calories from protein: 22%; from carbohydrates: 57%; from fat: 20%

Exchange values: 1½ vegetable; ½ bread; ½ fat

Roasted Potatoes

Vegetable oil cooking spray

4 small baking potatoes

2 tablespoons low-fat Italian salad dressing
(Do not use nonfat dressing)

1 teaspoon dried rosemary

Kosher salt or table salt

Preheat oven to 450°. Spray a cookie sheet with cooking spray. Scrub or peel the potatoes. Cut each potato lengthwise into 8 wedges, then cut those wedges in half so they are no more than 2 inches long. Mix the salad dressing and rosemary together in a large bowl. Toss the potato wedges in the salad dressing mixture until thoroughly coated. Place the potato wedges in a single layer on the cookie sheet. Sprinkle with salt to taste. Bake for 15 to 25 minutes, turning the potatoes over with a spatula every 5 minutes, or until each wedge is golden brown and tender.

KIDS LOVE THIS

Preparation time: 5 minutes. Cooking time: 15 to 25 minutes. Yield: 4 servings

Nutrition analysis: 154 calories per serving; 3 gm. protein; 3.5 gm. carbohydrate; 1 gm. fat; 0.5 mg. cholesterol; 4 gm. fiber; 67 mg. sodium

Percent of calories from protein: 8%; from carbohydrates: 87%; from fat: 5%

Exchange values: 2 bread

Roasted Spicy Eggplant

The beauty of this recipe is that it is so simple to prepare and yet still delicious. The combination of the garlic and spices complement the normally bland-tasting eggplant without adding any fat or cholesterol.

1 tablespoon chopped fresh parsley

1 tablespoon chopped fresh basil

1 medium to large garlic clove

1 scallion (use some of the green)

1 medium-size eggplant (about 1 to 1 1/2 pounds)

Olive oil (optional)

Salt and pepper to taste

2 to 3 teaspoons Dijon mustard

2 teaspoons grated Parmesan cheese

Preheat oven to 350°. Place the parsley, basil, garlic, and scallion in a food processor (the small size works well), and process on high until well minced. If you don't have a food processor, mince these ingredients together by hand. Scrub the eggplant thoroughly under hot water to remove most of the wax coating. Cut off the stem. Cut the eggplant lengthwise into halves. Cut six to eight deep slits into the white flesh of each half of the eggplant without puncturing the skin. Push the minced seasonings and garlic into the slits. Lightly brush the white part of the eggplant with olive oil. Sprinkle with salt and pepper. Spread the mustard over the white part of the eggplant, then sprinkle with grated cheese. Place skin side down on a cookie sheet, and bake for 30 to 40 minutes or until the eggplant is soft and tender at its thickest point. Cut lengthwise, and serve hot or at room temperature. This eggplant goes well with a mild tasting chicken, fish, or beef dish.

Preparation time: 10 minutes. Cooking time: 30 to 40 minutes. Yield: 4 servings

Nutrition analysis: 51 calories per serving; 2 gm. protein; 10 gm. carbohydrate; 1 gm. fat; 1 mg. cholesterol; 0 fiber; 119 mg. sodium

Percent of calories from protein: 14%; from carbohydrates: 72%; from fat: 14%

Exchange values: ½ bread

Sweet Potatoes in Orange Cups

My neighbor Adelaide served this to us one wintry evening. I was immediately intrigued by the delicious, pure taste of the pureed sweet potatoes, while being impressed at the creative, elegant manner in which they were served.

2 1/2 pounds sweet potatoes

3 juice oranges and fresh orange juice
  (for a total of 1 cup of orange juice)

Salt to taste

Peel the potatoes, and slice them into 1-inch rounds. Boil 1 inch of lightly salted water in a large pot. Stir in the potatoes, bring to a boil again, then cover, and simmer for about 30 minutes or until the potatoes are very tender but not mushy. Drain well. (A healthier way to cook sweet potatoes is to scrub them, bake them in a moderately hot oven for 45 to 60 minutes or until soft, then to scoop out all the soft flesh.)

KIDS LOVE THIS

Meanwhile, cut the oranges in half, and squeeze out and save all the orange juice, being careful to remove the seeds. Clean out the inside of each orange half so the oranges can be used as cups. Purée the cooked sweet potatoes with about 1 cup of orange juice in a food processor or blender. Taste, and add salt if necessary. Fill each orange half with the puréed sweet potato mixture, and serve immediately.

Preparation time: 10 minutes. Cooking time: 30 to 40 minutes. Yield: 6 servings

Nutrition analysis: 217 calories per serving; 3.5 gm. protein; 50 gm. carbohydrate; 0.5 gm. fat; 0 cholesterol; 6 gm. fiber; 25 mg. sodium

Percent of calories from protein: 6%; from carbohydrates: 91%; from fat: 3%

Exchange values: ½ fruit; 3 bread

Two-Potato Purée

2 medium-sized all-purpose potatoes, peeled and quartered

2 small sweet potatoes, peeled and quartered

1 small yellow onion, chopped

1 clove garlic, chopped

1 1/2 cups boiling water

1 teaspoon salt

2 to 4 tablespoons hot skim milk

1 tablespoon nonfat plain yogurt at room temperature

1 tablespoon Butter Buds, natural dehydrated butter

Salt and pepper to taste

KIDS LOVE THIS

Place the potatoes, sweet potatoes, onions, and garlic in a medium pot. Pour the boiling water and salt over the vegetables, and bring to a boil. Reduce the heat, cover, and simmer over medium-low heat for 20 to 30 minutes or until the potatoes are tender (check the potatoes while they're cooking to make sure the water hasn't boiled away). Drain the vegetables thoroughly, and place them in a large food processor. Add the milk, yogurt, and Butter Buds. Process on high until the mixture is completely puréed. Add salt and pepper, check the seasonings, and serve. This dish goes well with chicken, fish, or beef. Add some broccoli or peas, and you'll have a dinner that will please your eyes as well as your palate.

Preparation time: 10 minutes. Cooking time: 20 to 30 minutes. Yield: 6 servings

Nutrition analysis: 91 calories per serving; 2 gm. protein; 20.5 gm. carbohydrate; 0 gm. fat; 0 cholesterol; 2 gm. fiber; 369 mg. sodium

Percent of calories from protein: 9%; from carbohydrates: 89%; from fat: 2%

Exchange values: ½ vegetable; 1 bread

Quick Red Potatoes

Boiling new red or white potatoes with a little garlic and salt gives them a great flavor that is enhanced by adding a drop of olive oil and Butter Buds. What could be easier?

Lightly salted water

1 pound small, new red or white potatoes, very well scrubbed and cut in half

1 large garlic clove, peeled and cut in half

1 teaspoon olive oil

Butter Buds, natural dehydrated butter

Salt and freshly ground pepper to taste

KIDS
LOVE
THIS

Bring one inch of lightly salted water to a boil in a large pot. Stir in the potatoes and garlic. Return to boiling point, cover, and simmer for about 30 minutes or until the potatoes are tender when pierced with a fork. Drain well, remove garlic halves, and return potatoes to pot. Stir in the olive oil, and season to taste with Butter Buds, salt, and freshly ground pepper.

Preparation time: 10 minutes. Cooking time: 30 minutes. Yield: 4 servings

Nutrition analysis: 123 calories per serving; 2.5 gm. protein; 26.5 gm. carbohydrate; 1 gm. fat; 0 cholesterol; 0 fiber; 8 mg. sodium

Percent of calories from protein: 8%; from carbohydrate 84%; from fat 9%

Exchange values: 2 bread

Dilled Butternut Squash

_____

When we were served this dish at my brother's house, I was immediately attracted to it because I love butternut squash and the heart-healthy beta carotene it contains. Not only is this delicious recipe healthy, it takes little time to make.

1 butternut squash (about 3 pounds), peeled, seeded, and cut into 1 1/2-inch cubes

1 tablespoon Butter Buds, natural dehydrated butter

1 tablespoon butter or margarine

1 tablespoon dried dill weed

Salt and freshly ground pepper to taste

Bring a large pot filled with about 2 inches of lightly salted water to a boil. Stir in the squash. Return to boiling point, cover, reduce heat, and simmer for 20 to 25 minutes or until the squash is tender (not mushy) when pierced with a fork. Drain very well. Using an electric blender, beat in Butter Buds, butter, and dill. Season to taste and serve immediately. The dish freezes well, so it can be served even when butternut squash is not readily available.

Preparation time: 10 minutes. Cooking time: 20 to 25 minutes. Yield: 6 to 8 servings

Nutrition analysis for 6 servings: 95 calories per serving; 2 gm. protein; 20.5 gm. carbohydrate; 2 gm. fat; 5 mg. cholesterol; 0 fiber; 50 mg. sodium

Percent of calories from protein: 7%; from carbohydrate: 76%; from fat 18%

Exchange values: 1 1/2 bread; 1/2 fat

Dutch Baked Corn Pudding

Corn is always a popular vegetable with the younger set. This recipes features a way of preparing corn that is popular with everyone and can be served at any occasion.

Vegetable oil cooking spray

1 large egg yolk

1/2 cup skim milk

2 tablespoons nonfat powdered milk

1 teaspoon cornstarch

1/2 tablespoon Butter Buds, natural dehydrated butter

1/4 to 1/2 teaspoon salt

Freshly ground pepper, one turn of pepper mill

1 tablespoon sugar

2 cups corn (fresh, or frozen that has been thawed)

2 large egg whites that have been stiffly beaten

Preheat oven to 350°. Spray a 1 1/2-quart flat baking dish with cooking spray. Beat the egg yolk, milk, powdered milk, cornstarch, Butter Buds, salt, pepper, and sugar together. Stir in the corn. Fold in the egg whites well. Bake uncovered for 30 to 40 minutes or until a knife inserted in the center comes out clean. Serve immediately.

Preparation time: 10 minutes. Cooking time: 30 to 40 minutes. Yield: 4 servings

Nutrition analysis: 123 calories per serving; 6.5 gm. protein; 23.5 gm. carbohydrate; 1.5 gm. fat; 327 mg. sodium

Percent of calories from protein: 20%; from carbohydrate: 70%; from fat: 9%

Exchange values: 1 bread; 1/2 meat

Fear of Frying

PASTA

 **AND**

RICE

Dijon
Rice

The Dijon mustard gives this rice its great flavor.

2 cups water

1/4 teaspoon salt (optional)

1 tablespoon Dijon mustard

1 tablespoon Butter Buds, natural dehydrated butter

1 teaspoon olive oil

1/4 teaspoon lemon juice

1 cup raw white rice (I prefer Uncle Ben's® original)

Place the first 6 ingredients in a medium saucepan. Stir thoroughly, then bring to a boil. Stir in the rice, lower heat, cover, and simmer for 20 minutes. Remove from heat, keep covered, and let stand for 5 minutes or until all liquid is absorbed. Stir and serve immediately.

Preparation time: 5 minutes. Cooking time: 20 minutes. 4 servings

Nutrition analysis: 185 calories per serving; 3.5 gm. protein; 37.5 gm. carbohydrate; 1.5 gm. fat; 0 cholesterol; 0.5 gm. fiber; 233 mg. sodium.

Percent of calories from protein: 8%; from carbohydrates: 84%; from fat: 8%

Exchange values: 2½ bread

Creamy Green Pasta Sauce

Pasta sauce doesn't have to be tomato based. Several vegetables and herbs make delicious sauces. This recipe combines the flavors of green pepper, broccoli, and cheese to make a delicious, creamy sauce.

1 1/2 teaspoons olive oil

Vegetable oil cooking spray

1 large yellow onion, chopped

2 garlic cloves, minced

1 large green pepper, seeded and chopped

2 cups chopped broccoli florets

1 cup low-fat or skimmed evaporated milk, undiluted

1 tablespoon cornstarch

1/3 cup (1 ounce) shredded low-fat, sharp cheese

Salt and freshly ground pepper to taste

1 pound dry noodles or pasta cooked al dente (tender but not mushy)

Freshly grated Parmesan or Romano cheese

Heat the olive oil and a generous spray of cooking spray in a large, heavy skillet for 45 seconds. Stir in the onion and garlic, and sauté over medium-low heat for 3 minutes, stirring frequently. If the mixture begins to burn, add 1 to 2 teaspoons of water. Stir in the green pepper and broccoli, cover, and sauté for 15 minutes, stirring frequently and adding a drop of water, if necessary. Mix the milk and cornstarch together, then add it to the vegetable mixture. Stir constantly over medium heat until the sauce thickens and begins to bubble, about 2 to 3 minutes. Remove from heat, and puree in a food processor or large blender. Return the mixture to the skillet, stir in the shredded cheese, and reheat until the cheese is melted. Add salt and freshly ground pepper to taste. Serve over cooked pasta, and top with freshly grated Parmesan cheese.

Preparation time: 10 minutes. Cooking time: 20 minutes. Yield: 2 1/2 cups sauce, 6 to 8 servings

Nutrition analysis for 6 servings: 430 calories per serving; 16.5 gm. protein; 83 gm. carbohydrate; 3 gm. fat; 5 mg. cholesterol; 1.5 gm. fiber; 492 mg. sodium

Percent of calories from protein: 15%; from carbohydrates: 78%; from fat: 7%

Exchange values: ½ milk; 1 vegetable; 5 bread; ½ fat

Fruity Rice

The juice gives the rice a delightfully fruity taste which replaces the need for butter or cheese.

1 cup light peach or pear juice*

1 cup water

2 teaspoons Butter Buds, natural dehydrated butter

1/4 teaspoon salt

1 teaspoon olive oil

1/4 teaspoon lemon juice

1 cup raw white rice (I prefer Uncle Ben's original)

1/4 cup raisins (optional)

KIDS LOVE THIS

Bring the juice, water, Butter Buds, salt, olive oil, and lemon juice to a boil in a medium saucepan. Stir in the rice and raisins. Reduce heat, cover, and simmer for 20 minutes or until all the liquid is absorbed. Remove from heat, keep covered, and let stand for 5 minutes. Serve immediately.

*Note: 2 cups of cranberry juice cocktail can be used instead of the fruit juice and water.

Preparation time: 5 minutes. Cooking time: 20 to 25 minutes. Yield: 4 servings

Nutrition analysis: 217 calories per serving; 3.5 gm. protein; 46 gm. carbohydrate; 1.5 gm. fat; 0 cholesterol; 1 gm. fiber; 139 mg. sodium

Percent of calories from protein: 7%; from carbohydrates: 87%; from fat: 6%

Exchange values: ½ fruit; 2½ bread

Fear of Frying

Pasta With Creamy Fresh Tomato Sauce

When making a tomato sauce that is not cooked for hours, the trick is to combine garden-fresh ingredients quickly. This recipe blends some of my favorite ingredients together to make a quick and deliciously fresh-tasting tomato sauce.

1 1/2 teaspoons olive oil and a generous spray of vegetable oil cooking spray

1/4 cup sweet onions, chopped well

1 bunch scallions with 2 inches of green, chopped

3 garlic cloves, minced

2 tablespoons chopped fresh basil

1/2 teaspoon dried oregano

1 teaspoon dried tarragon

1 tablespoon sun-dried tomato paste or regular tomato paste

1/4 cup dry white wine

2 to 2 1/2 pounds fresh plum tomatoes, seeded and chopped

1/2 cup skimmed evaporated milk, undiluted

Salt and freshly ground pepper to taste

3/4 pound dry small shell pasta or your favorite fresh pasta, cooked and drained

Freshly grated Parmesan or Romano cheese

Heat the oil and vegetable oil spray in a large skillet. Sauté the onions, scallions, and garlic over a medium-low heat for 5 minutes or until golden, stirring frequently. You may have to add 1 to 2 teaspoons water to prevent this mixture from burning. Stir in the herbs, sun-dried tomato paste, wine, and plum tomatoes. While stirring, bring this mixture to a boil, lower heat, cover, and simmer for 3 minutes. Stir in the evaporated milk, and cook uncovered over medium heat for 5 additional minutes. Stir occasionally. Salt and pepper to taste, and serve over hot pasta. Sprinkle grated cheese.

Pasta With Creamy Fresh Tomato Sauce (continued)

Preparation time: 10 minutes. Cooking time: 15 minutes. Yield: 4 to 5 servings

Nutrition analysis for 5 servings: 350 calories per serving; 13 gm. protein; 67 gm. carbohydrate; 3.5 gm. fat; 1 mg. cholesterol; 3 gm. fiber; 59 mg. sodium

Percent of calories from protein: 15%; from carbohydrates: 75%; from fat: 8%

Exchange values: trace milk, 2 vegetable, 3½ bread, ½ fat

Parsleyed Rice

This is my family's favorite rice dish. It's too good to be covered with a sauce, so use this recipe when you want rice as a side dish. I always use Uncle Ben's Converted Rice when I need the rice to be firm.

1 (3 3/4-ounce) can low-salt chicken broth or 1 2/3 cups homemade broth

1 1/3 cups water

1 teaspoon olive oil

1/4 teaspoon lemon juice

2 chopped scallions (use two inches of green)

1 tablespoon Butter Buds, natural dehydrated butter

1/4 teaspoon salt (optional)

1 1/2 cups raw white rice

1/2 cup chopped fresh Italian parsley

In a medium saucepan, bring the chicken broth, water, olive oil, lemon juice, and scallions to a boil. Stir in the Butter Buds, salt, and rice. Reduce heat to low, then cover, and simmer for 20 minutes. Sprinkle with chopped parsley, cover, and let stand for 5 minutes. Stir well and serve.

Preparation time: 5 minutes. Cooking time: 25 minutes. Yield: 5 to 6 servings

Nutrition analysis for 5 servings: 227 calories per serving; 5.5 gm. protein; 45.5 gm. carbohydrate; 1.5 gm. fat; 0 cholesterol; 1 gm. fiber; 361 mg. sodium

Percent of calories from protein: 10%; from carbohydrates: 82%; from fat: 7%

Exchange values: 3 bread

Pasta Primavera

In 30 minutes you can create a delicious and healthy fresh tomato sauce. The wonderful combination of ingredients adds flavor and zest to this dish.

1 1/2 teaspoons olive oil

Vegetable oil cooking spray

1 large yellow onion, chopped

1 large garlic clove, minced

1 tablespoon water

2 teaspoons anchovy paste or 2 mashed anchovies

3/4 pound broccoli florets, chopped

1 1/4 pounds fresh plum tomatoes, seeded and chopped (and peeled, if desired)

1 tablespoon capers

2 to 3 tablespoons chopped black olives

1 to 1 1/2 tablespoons chopped fresh basil

Salt and freshly ground pepper to taste

3/4 pound dry linguine cooked al dente (tender but not mushy)

Freshly grated Parmesan or Romano cheese

Heat the olive oil and a generous spray of cooking spray in a large, heavy skillet for 45 seconds. Stir in the onion and garlic, and sauté over medium-low heat for 5 minutes, stirring frequently. If the mixture begins to burn, add 1 to 2 teaspoons of water. Stir in 1 tablespoon of water and the anchovy paste. Stir in the broccoli, tomatoes, capers, olives, and basil. Bring just to the boiling point, then cover and simmer for 10 to 15 minutes. Add salt and pepper to taste. Serve over hot, cooked linguine, and top with grated cheese.

Preparation time: 10 minutes. Cooking time: 20 minutes. Yield: 4 servings

Nutrition analysis: 502 calories per serving; 17 gm. protein; 99.5 gm. carbohydrate; 4.5 gm. fat; 1.5 mg. cholesterol; 4 gm. fiber; 689 mg. sodium

Percent of calories from protein: 14%; from carbohydrates: 78%; from fat: 8%

Exchange values: 3 vegetable; 5½ bread; ½ fat

Paulette's Black Bean Pasta

My neighbor, Paulette, gave me this recipe and described it as her family's favorite quick, easy, and healthy dinner. After trying it, I agree it's a winner.

1 1/2 teaspoons olive oil

Vegetable oil cooking spray

1 small yellow onion, chopped

1 large garlic clove, minced

1/2 green pepper, seeded and chopped

1 cup chopped, ripe plum tomatoes, seeded

15-ounce can Goya black bean soup or 1 3/4 cups thick homemade black bean soup; do not use the canned condensed type

Salt and freshly ground pepper to taste

1 pound dry spinach linguine or spinach noodles, cooked al dente (tender but not mushy)

Freshly grated Parmesan or Romano cheese

Heat the olive oil and a generous spray of cooking spray in a large, heavy skillet for 45 seconds. Sauté the onion and garlic over medium-low heat for 3 minutes, stirring frequently. If the mixture begins to burn, add 1 to 2 teaspoons of water. Stir in the green pepper, cover, and continue to sauté for 5 more minutes, stirring frequently. Put the chopped tomato in a food processor or blender, and purée. Stir the puréed tomato and the black bean soup into the onion mixture. Bring just to the boiling point, then cover and simmer for 5 to 10 minutes. Add salt and freshly ground pepper to taste. Pour over the cooked linguine, top with grated cheese, and serve immediately.

Preparation time: 10 minutes. Cooking time: 20 minutes. Yield: 6 servings

Nutrition analysis: 303 calories per serving; 11.5 gm. protein; 54 gm. carbohydrate; 4.5 gm. fat; 61 mg. cholesterol; 0.5 gm. fiber; 376 mg. sodium

Percentage of calories from protein: 15%; from carbohydrates: 71%; from fat: 14%

Exchange values: 1 vegetable; 3 bread; ½ fat

Rice
Pilaf

My family loves rice, so I'm always looking for creative ways to serve it. This recipe is not only quick and easy, but delicious as well.

1 1/2 teaspoons olive oil

1/2 cup uncooked Uncle Ben's original converted rice

1/2 cup uncooked orzo (rice-shaped) pasta

13 3/4-ounce can low-salt chicken broth or homemade chicken broth

Water

1 tablespoon freshly chopped parsley

1 tablespoon Butter Buds, natural dehydrated butter

1 tablespoon lemon juice

1/4 teaspoon salt (optional)

KIDS
LOVE
THIS

Heat the oil in a large skillet. Stir in the rice and orzo. While stirring constantly, cook the rice and orzo over medium heat for a minute or two, until golden. Add enough water to the chicken broth to make just slightly less than 2 cups of liquid. Bring the liquid to a boil, then stir into the rice mixture. Stir in the remaining ingredients, then lower the heat, cover, and simmer for 25 minutes or until the rice and pasta are tender and the liquid is absorbed. Remove from heat, keep covered, and let stand for 5 minutes. Stir, and serve immediately.

Preparation time: 5 minutes. Cooking time: 25 minutes. Yield: 4 to 5 servings

Nutrition analysis for 4 servings: 161 calories per serving; 3.5 gm. protein; 29 gm. carbohydrate; 2.5 gm. fat; 1 mg. cholesterol; 0.5 gm. fiber; 400 mg. sodium

Percent of calories from protein: 10%; from carbohydrates: 75%; from fat: 15%

Exchange values: 2 bread; ½ fat

Dirty Rice

This is not the traditional dirty rice recipe that originated in New Orleans. I borrowed the name because it looks like the New Orleans version, but the taste is quite different.

2 cups low-salt and defatted chicken broth or water

1/4 teaspoon salt

1/4 teaspoon lemon juice

1 tablespoon Butter Buds, natural dehydrated butter

2 tablespoons spicy black bean dip (I use Guiltless Gourmet)

1 cup raw white rice

Bring the chicken broth, salt, lemon juice, Butter Buds, and bean dip to a boil in a medium saucepan. Stir well. Stir in the rice, lower heat, cover, and simmer for 20 minutes or until all the liquid is absorbed. Remove from heat, keep covered, and let stand for 5 minutes before serving.

Preparation time: 5 minutes. Cooking time: 25 minutes. Yield: 4 servings

Nutrition analysis: 199 calories per serving; 3.5 gm. protein; 41 gm. carbohydrate; 1.5 gm. fat; 0.5 mg. cholesterol; 0.5 gm. fiber; 424 mg. sodium

Percent of calories from protein: 8%; from carbohydrates: 86%; from fat: 6%

Exchange values: 2½ bread

Fresh Tomato & Basil Pasta

Most of us don't like to cook on hot summer days. This recipe combines the freshest ingredients to make a tomato sauce that is marinated instead of cooked.

4 cups (about 2 1/2 pounds) seeded and chopped vine-ripened tomatoes (Use the best and ripest tomatoes you can find. Winter tomatoes are usually not good enough.)

4 tablespoons minced fresh basil

1 tablespoon minced fresh parsley

1/4 teaspoon dried oregano or 1/2 teaspoon minced fresh oregano

1 tablespoon chopped scallions

1 tablespoon olive oil

1 to 2 garlic cloves, cut in half and slightly pressed with spoon

Salt and freshly ground pepper to taste

3/4 pound dry linguine or your favorite fresh pasta

Freshly grated Parmesan or Romano cheese

Combine the tomatoes, basil, parsley, oregano, scallions, olive oil, garlic, salt, and pepper in a large bowl. Toss well. Let stand at room temperature for 30 to 60 minutes, tossing occasionally. While the sauce marinates, cook the pasta al dente (tender but not mushy). Drain the pasta. Remove the garlic cloves from the tomato sauce, check seasonings, and serve the sauce over the hot pasta. Sprinkle with grated cheese.

Preparation time: 10 minutes. Standing time: 30 to 60 minutes. Yield: 4 to 5 servings

Nutrition analysis for 5 servings: 339 calories per serving; 11.5 gm. protein; 64.5 gm. carbohydrate; 4.5 gm. fat; 0 cholesterol; 1.5 gm. fiber; 28 mg. sodium

Percent of calories from protein: 13%; from carbohydrates: 75%; from fat: 12%

Exchange values: 2 vegetable; 3½ bread; ½ fat

Macaroni & Cheese

Macaroni and cheese from a box is popular because it's easy to make and children like it, but some varieties have a lot of fat. I decided to come up with a healthier version that's easy to make and popular with the kids. Even though there are a lot of ingredients, it's very quick and easy to prepare.

Vegetable oil cooking spray

2 cups uncooked elbow macaroni

2 cups low-fat (1%) cottage cheese

2 to 3 teaspoons sharp prepared mustard

3/4 cup skim milk

1 tablespoon nonfat powdered milk

1 tablespoon cornstarch

1/2 cup (2 ounces) shredded low-fat sharp cheddar cheese

1 large egg white

1/4 teaspoon salt

Freshly ground pepper (one or two turns on the pepper mill)

1/8 teaspoon paprika

1 tablespoon grated Parmesan cheese

2 tablespoons seasoned bread crumbs

KIDS
LOVE
THIS

Cook the macaroni according to directions on the package to make it al dente (not too soft). Drain, then pour the macaroni into a 2-quart baking dish sprayed with cooking spray. Set aside. Preheat the oven to 350°. Place the next 10 ingredients in a food processor or a blender. Process on high for 60 seconds. Scrape the sides of the bowl once during this process. Mix the macaroni and cheese sauce together in the baking dish. Mix the Parmesan cheese and bread crumbs together, and sprinkle over the macaroni. Bake uncovered for 30 to 40 minutes or until the top is golden and the sauce is bubbling. Serve immediately.

Preparation time: 10 minutes. Cooking time: 50 to 60 minutes. Yield: 6 servings

Nutrition analysis: 249 calories per serving; 19.5 gm. protein; 33.5 gm. carbohydrate; 3.5 gm. fat; 9.5 mg. cholesterol; 0 fiber; 516 mg. sodium

Percent of calories from protein: 32%; from carbohydrates: 55%; from fat: 13%

Exchange values: 2 bread; 2 meat

Baked Ziti

Vegetable oil cooking spray

3 to 3 1/2 cups all-natural, good-quality tomato sauce

1 to 1 1/4 cups low-fat Ricotta cheese (nonfat or a mixture of nonfat and low-fat also can be used)

1 whole large egg

1 large egg white

1 tablespoon Butter Buds, natural dehydrated butter

1/2 teaspoon dried basil or 1/2 tablespoon minced, fresh basil

1 tablespoon chopped, fresh parsley

Freshly ground pepper (a few turns of the pepper mill)

1 pound dry ziti, cooked al dente (tender but not soft) and drained

Grated Parmesan cheese

Preheat oven to 350°. Spray a 13" x 9" baking dish with cooking spray. Spread 1 cup of tomato sauce on the bottom of the pan. Mix the cheese, eggs, Butter Buds, basil, parsley, and pepper together, and mix into the well-drained ziti. Pour the ziti mixture into the pan, and spread evenly. Cover with remaining tomato sauce. Sprinkle with Parmesan cheese, and bake uncovered for 30 minutes.

Preparation time: 10 minutes. Cooking time: 40 to 45 minutes. Yield: 4 to 6 servings

Nutrition analysis for 4 servings: 356 calories per serving; 20 gm. protein; 51 gm. carbohydrate; 7.5 gm. fat; 1,100 mg. sodium

Percentage of calories from protein: 23%; from carbohydrates: 58%; from fat 20%

Exchange values: 3½ vegetable; 2 bread; 1½ meat; ½ fat

Linda's Fresh Tomato & Pepper Pasta

Linda has a busy household filled with teenagers. Since both her children are involved in team and school activities, meals must be quick. This is the dish they ask for the most.

1 tablespoon olive oil or a generous spray of vegetable oil cooking spray

1 to 2 garlic cloves, minced

1 medium large onion, peeled, quartered, and cut into thin slices

1/4 to 1/2 pound ground white-meat turkey or chicken (optional)

1 large green pepper, quartered and cut into long, thin slices

3 to 4 large plum tomatoes, seeded, quartered and cut into long, thin slices

1 tablespoon minced fresh basil or 1 teaspoon dried basil

1/4 teaspoon dried oregano

Salt and freshly ground pepper to taste

1 pound dry pasta, cooked and drained

1 to 3 tablespoons freshly grated Parmesan or Romano cheese

Heat the olive oil in a large, heavy skillet, or spray a nonstick skillet with cooking spray. Add the garlic and onion, and sauté over medium-low heat for 3 minutes, stirring often. (You may have to add 1 to 2 teaspoons of water to prevent the onions from burning.) Stir in the ground turkey and sliced peppers. Break up the ground meat, cover, and cook 5 more minutes or until the meat is thoroughly cooked, stirring often. Drain well. Stir in the tomatoes, basil, and oregano. Cover, and continue cooking 3 to 5 more minutes, stirring occasionally. Stir in the salt and pepper, and check for taste. Serve over your favorite cooked pasta, and top with a little grated cheese.

Linda's Fresh Tomato & Pepper Pasta (continued)

Preparation time: 10 minutes. Cooking time: 20 minutes. Yield: 4 to 6 servings

Nutrition analysis for 4 servings: 561 calories per serving; 26.5 gm. protein; 85.5 gm. carbohydrate; 12.5 gm. fat; 123 mg. cholesterol; 3 gm. fiber; 144 mg. sodium

Percent of calories from protein: 19%; from carbohydrates: 61%; from fat: 20%

Exchange values: 2 vegetable; 5 bread; 1½ meat; 1½ fat

Pasta à la Wendy

1 1/2 teaspoons olive oil

Vegetable oil cooking spray

1 medium yellow onion, chopped

1 large garlic clove, minced

1 small green pepper, seeded and chopped (optional)

1 teaspoon chopped jalapeño pepper
   (Note: always wear rubber gloves
   when working with hot peppers)

1/2 pound lean ground turkey, chicken, or beef (optional)

8 ounces fresh mushrooms, sliced

10 3/4-ounce can Campbell's Healthy Request® cream of mushroom or cream of
   broccoli soup, undiluted

1 teaspoon anchovy paste or 1 mashed anchovy (optional)

1 tablespoon sun-dried tomato paste or 1 tablespoon mashed sun-dried tomatoes

1 cup top-quality tomato or marinara sauce

1/2 cup low-fat evaporated milk, undiluted, or 1/4 cup low-fat evaporated milk and
   1/4 cup vodka

1 pound dry fusilli pasta or your favorite pasta, cooked al dente
   (tender but not mushy)

Salt and freshly ground pepper to taste

Freshly grated Parmesan or Romano cheese

Heat the olive oil and a generous spray of cooking spray in a large, heavy pot for 45 seconds. Stir in the onion and garlic, and sauté over medium-low heat for 3 minutes, stirring frequently. Add 1 to 2 teaspoons of water if the mixture begins to burn. Stir in the bell pepper, jalapeño pepper, and ground meat. Sauté for an additional 5 minutes or until the meat is thoroughly cooked, stirring frequently. Drain very well.

Pasta à la Wendy (continued)

Stir in the mushrooms, and cook and stir for 3 more minutes. Stir in the cream of mushroom soup, anchovy paste, tomato paste, tomato sauce, and evaporated milk. Bring to a boil, and simmer for 5 minutes, stirring frequently. Stir in the cooked pasta, and add salt and pepper to taste. Serve hot sprinkled with grated cheese.

Preparation time: 15 minutes. Cooking time: 20 minutes. Yield: 6 to 8 servings

Nutrition analysis for 8 servings (using milk): 374 calories per serving; 16 gm. protein; 65 gm. carbohydrate; 5 gm. fat; 22 mg. cholesterol; 1 gm. fiber; 592 mg. sodium

Percent of calories from protein: 17%; from carbohydrates: 71%; from fat: 12%

Exchange values: 1 vegetable; 4 bread; ½ meat; ½ fat

Pasta Rustica

This pasta dish combines the wonderful tastes of tomatoes and spinach to create a quick, easy, and tasty sauce.

10-ounce package frozen, chopped spinach or about
   1 pound washed, fresh spinach cooked in a little
   water just until tender, yielding 1 cup of cooked
   spinach with the excess liquid squeezed out

1 1/2 teaspoons olive oil and a generous spray
   of vegetable oil cooking spray

1 large onion, chopped

1 to 2 large garlic cloves, minced

2 pounds plum tomatoes, seeded and chopped
   (cut the tomatoes in half and squeeze out the seeds)

1 to 1 1/2 tablespoons sun-dried or regular tomato paste

2 tablespoons chopped fresh basil

2 tablespoons capers

3 tablespoons chopped black olives

2 to 3 tablespoons chopped roasted red peppers (optional)

Salt and freshly ground pepper to taste

1 pound dry linguine, cooked al dente and drained

Grated Parmesan or Romano cheese

Cook the frozen spinach in a little water according to directions on the package just until defrosted and hot, then drain, and squeeze out excess liquid. Set aside. If you're using dried pasta, start heating the water now. Heat the oil and cooking spray in a large, heavy skillet. Stir in the onions and garlic. Sauté over medium-low heat for 3 minutes, stirring frequently. Add 1 or 2 teaspoons of water if the mixture begins to burn. Stir in the tomatoes and tomato paste. Cover, and cook for 5 minutes, stirring occasionally. Stir in the basil, capers, olives, roasted peppers, and spinach. Cover, and cook for 5 additional minutes. Season with salt and freshly ground pepper to taste. Serve over linguine, and sprinkle with grated cheese.

Pasta Rustica (continued)

Preparation time: 15 minutes. Cooking time: 15 minutes. Yield: 5 to 6 servings

Nutrition analysis for 5 servings: 448 calories per serving; 16.5 gm. protein; 87 gm. carbohydrate; 5.5 gm. fat; 0 cholesterol; 4.5 gm. fiber; 188 mg. sodium

Percent of calories from protein: 14%; from carbohydrates: 75%; from fat: 11%

Exchange values: 3 vegetable; 4½ bread; 1 fat

Fear of Frying

Pasta With Spinach Pesto

We all know spinach is a healthy food packed with nutrients, and we probably should eat more of it. This recipe provides a creative new way to eat spinach. Spinach is used along with fresh basil and parsley to create a pesto-type sauce that is both delicious and good for you.

2 tablespoons extra-virgin olive oil

2 tablespoons low-fat Italian dressing

2 to 2 1/2 tablespoons fresh lemon juice

1 large garlic clove, chopped

2 cups packed fresh spinach, washed, dried, stemmed, and chopped

1/2 cup lightly-packed chopped fresh parsley

1/4 cup lightly-packed chopped fresh basil

2 tablespoons freshly grated Romano or Parmesan cheese

2 tablespoons pine nuts (also called pignoli nuts) (optional)

Salt and freshly ground pepper to taste

1 pound dry thick eggless noodles cooked al dente (soft but not mushy) and drained

Freshly grated Romano or Parmesan cheese

Place the olive oil, Italian dressing, lemon juice, and garlic in a large food processor. Process on high for 10 seconds. Add the spinach, parsley, basil, 2 tablespoons grated cheese, and pine nuts. Process for 30 to 45 seconds more until smooth and sauce-like. Add salt and freshly ground pepper to taste, then stir, and pour over cooked noodles. Sprinkle with grated cheese, and serve immediately.

Preparation time: 15 minutes. Cooking time for the pasta: 8 to 12 minutes. Yield: 8 servings

Nutrition analysis: 271 calories per serving; 9 gm. protein; 45 gm. carbohydrate; 6 gm. fat; 1.5 mg. cholesterol; 0.5 gm. fiber; 76 mg. sodium

Percent of calories from protein: 13%; from carbohydrates: 66%; from fat: 21%

Exchange values: 3 bread; 1 fat

Specialty Rice

My children love rice, but plain rice can get boring. This recipe adds a slight taste of seafood and almost no extra fat and goes well with fish.

1 cup clam juice

1 cup low-salt chicken broth,
 skim off all excess fat

1 teaspoon olive oil

1/4 teaspoon lemon juice

1 tablespoon Butter Buds, natural dehydrated butter

1 cup raw long-grain white rice

Stir the clam juice, chicken broth, olive oil, lemon juice, and Butter Buds together in a small saucepan. Bring to a boil. Stir in rice, reduce heat, cover, and simmer for 20 minutes. Remove from heat, keep covered, and let stand for 5 minutes or until all the liquid is absorbed. Serve immediately.

Preparation time: 5 minutes. Cooking time: 25 minutes. Yield: 4 servings

Nutrition analysis: 220 calories per serving; 4 gm. protein; 44 gm. carbohydrate; 2 gm. fat; 0.5 mg. cholesterol; 0.5 gm. fiber; 564 mg. sodium

Percent of calories from protein: 8%; from carbohydrates: 84%; from fat: 8%

Exchange values: 1½ vegetable; 2½ bread; ½ fat

Creamy, Spicy Tomato Sauce on Pasta

This tomato sauce is quick and easy to make. The delightful pink color makes it a treat for the eyes, and the slightly spicy taste makes it a treat for the taste buds.

1/2 cup low-fat (1%) cottage cheese

1 teaspoon balsamic vinegar

1 tablespoon olive oil

1 teaspoon chopped jalapeño pepper, or to taste
(note: always wear rubber gloves when working with hot peppers)

1 to 2 large garlic cloves, chopped

10 fresh basil leaves, washed, stemmed, and chopped

2 pounds vine-ripened tomatoes, quartered and seeded

1 teaspoon dried oregano

Salt and freshly ground pepper to taste

1 pound dry angel hair pasta, cooked and drained

3 to 4 teaspoons grated Romano cheese or grated cheese]

Place the cottage cheese, vinegar, oil, jalapeño pepper, garlic, and basil in a large food processor. Process on high for 2 to 3 minutes, stopping to scrape the sides once or twice. The resulting mixture should be very creamy. Add the tomatoes and oregano. Process briefly until the tomatoes are well chopped but not puréed. Add salt and pepper to taste. Pour the sauce over the hot angel hair pasta, and top with freshly grated cheese. Serve immediately.

Preparation time: 10 minutes. Cooking time: a few minutes for angel hair pasta. Yield: 3 cups sauce or 6 servings

Nutrition analysis: 355 calories per serving; 14 gm. protein; 65 gm. carbohydrate; 5 gm. fat; 2 mg. cholesterol; 2 gm. fiber; 129 mg. sodium

Percent of calories from protein: 16%; from carbohydrates: 73%; from fat: 12%

Exchange values: 1½ vegetable; 3½ bread; ½ meat; ½ fat

Pasta and Rice

Lemon Pesto
Pasta

This pesto sauce takes the fresh taste of basil and combines it with lemon juice and other ingredients to create a lighter-tasting pesto sauce.

3 garlic cloves

1/4 teaspoon salt

1/4 cup fresh lemon juice

1 tablespoon olive oil

2 tablespoons sun-dried tomatoes, chopped

1 1/2 cup packed fresh basil leaves, washed with stems removed

2 tablespoons pine nuts

2 to 4 tablespoons freshly grated Parmesan cheese

Salt and freshly ground pepper to taste

1 pound dry linguine, cooked al dente (tender but not mushy), and drained

Place the garlic, salt, lemon juice, olive oil, and sun-dried tomatoes in a food processor or blender. Process on high for 30 seconds, scrape the sides, then process for another 10 seconds. Add the basil and pine nuts, and process for another 30 to 60 seconds until everything is finely chopped. Add the grated cheese, and process for 10 additional seconds. Taste, and add salt and pepper if necessary. Pour over hot linguine, toss well, and serve immediately.

Preparation time: 15 minutes. Yield: 4 to 6 servings or ⅔ cup pesto sauce

Nutrition analysis for 4 servings: 555 calories per serving; 20 gm. protein; 98 gm. carbohydrate; 10 gm. fat; 5 mg. cholesterol; 1 gm. fiber; 270 mg. sodium

Percent of calories from protein: 14%; from carbohydrate: 70%; from fat: 16%

Exchange values: 5½ bread; ½ meat; 1½ fat

MEAT

AND

POULTRY

Beef & Broccoli Stir-Fry

Here's a quick, easy, and tasty way to get your children to eat broccoli.

Have ready:

Vegetable oil cooking spray

1/2 pound boneless top round steak
  or very lean steak, thinly sliced

1 tablespoon sesame oil or peanut oil

1 large garlic clove, minced

5 scallions with 2 inches of green, chopped into 1-inch pieces

1 teaspoon fresh ginger, peeled and finely chopped

1 pound broccoli crowns, washed and separated into small florets

15-ounce can whole baby corn, drained

Sauce:

1 tablespoon cornstarch

1 tablespoon reduced-sodium soy sauce

1 tablespoon oyster sauce

2 to 3 tablespoons water

Note: If you plan to serve rice or noodles, start cooking them before you prepare the stir-fry so everything will be ready at the same time.

Spray a large, heavy skillet with cooking spray. Heat quickly over medium heat. Add the beef, and stir-fry for 2 to 3 minutes or until beef is browned. Remove the beef, cover, and set aside. Carefully pour the oil into the same skillet, and heat over medium heat for 30 to 60 seconds. Stir in the garlic, scallions, and ginger. Stir-fry for 2 minutes. Remove as many of the scallions as you can with a slotted spoon. Add the scallions to the cooked beef, cover, and set aside. Add the broccoli and baby corn to the skillet. Cover and cook for 3 to 5 minutes, stirring frequently. Mix the sauce ingredients together. Stir the cooked beef, scallions, and sauce into the broccoli mixture. Continue stirring until sauce thickens, about 60 seconds. Serve immediately over rice or noodles.

Preparation time: 10 minutes. Cooking time: 10 minutes. Yield: 5 servings

Nutrition analysis: 243 calories per serving; 20.5 gm. protein; 29 gm. carbohydrate; 7 gm. fat; 38 mg. cholesterol; 2.5 gm. fiber; 406 mg. sodium

Percent of calories from protein: 32%; from carbohydrates: 44%; from fat: 24%

Exchange values: 1 vegetable; 1½ bread; 2 meat; ½ fat

Maria's
Shredded Beef

This recipe came from the Venezuelan family of one of my close friends. This dish takes quite a while to cook, but it is easy to prepare and requires very little attention. Furthermore, I think its great taste is worth the wait.

1 1/2 teaspoons olive oil, or a generous spray
of vegetable oil cooking spray plus
1 or 2 teaspoons of water

2 garlic cloves, minced

1 medium onion, chopped

1/2 large green pepper, seeded and chopped

14 1/2-ounce can Del Monte® pasta-style chunky tomatoes
or canned chopped tomatoes, undrained

1 1/2 tablespoons chopped fresh cilantro or parsley

1 teaspoon Worcestershire sauce

1 to 1 1/4 pounds flank steak

1/2 to 1 cup water

Salt and freshly ground pepper to taste

4 cups cooked rice, white or brown

Heat the oil in a large, heavy pot. Sauté the garlic and onions over medium-low heat for 3 minutes, stirring frequently. Stir in the chopped green pepper, and sauté for another minute, adding a drop or two of water if necessary to prevent burning. Stir in the canned tomatoes, cilantro, and Worcestershire sauce. Place the steak in the pot, and add enough water (about 1 cup) to just barely cover the steak. Bring to a boil, lower the heat, and cover, but leave the cover slightly ajar. Simmer for an hour or until steak is tender. Flip the steak once or twice while cooking.

Remove the steak from the pot, and shred the meat by pulling apart the strands. Return shredded steak to the pot, and continue to simmer for 20 to 30 minutes with or without the cover, depending on how runny the sauce is. If still too runny, reduce the sauce by boiling on high for a few minutes. Taste and correct seasoning, and serve with rice covered with the sauce. The shredded beef and sauce also make great sloppy joe-type sandwiches.

Preparation time: 10 minutes. Cooking time: 1 hour and 30 minutes (mostly unattended). Yield: 4 to 6 servings

Nutrition analysis for 4 servings: 607 calories per serving; 45.5 gm. protein; 65 gm. carbohydrate; 17 gm. fat; 95 mg. cholesterol; 3.5 gm. fiber; 302 mg. sodium

Percent of calories from protein: 31%; from carbohydrates: 44%; from fat: 26%

Exchange values: 1½ vegetable; 4 bread; 5½ meat; ½ fat

German Chops

Vegetable oil cooking spray

4 boneless pork chops (about 1 1/4 pounds total)*

1 cup drained sauerkraut

1 1/2 tablespoons brown sugar, or to taste

Preheat oven to 400°. Spray a shallow baking dish, just big enough to fit the chops, with cooking spray. Remove all visible fat from the chops. Place the trimmed chops in the prepared baking dish. Spoon the sauerkraut over the chops, and sprinkle brown sugar on the sauerkraut. Bake uncovered for 35 to 50 minutes, or until the inside meat of the thickest chop is no longer pink. Serve immediately.

TEENS
LOVE
THIS

*Note: It will take longer, but this is also a great way to cook a pork roast.

Preparation time: 5 minutes. Cooking time: 35 to 50 minutes.
Yield: 4 servings

Nutrition analysis: 228 calories per serving; 22 gm. protein; 7.5 gm. carbohydrate; 12 gm. fat; 74 mg. cholesterol; 1.5 gm. fiber; 449 mg. sodium

Percent of calories from protein: 39%; from carbohydrates: 13%; from fat: 48%

Exchange values: ½ vegetable; 3½ meat

My Mother's Roast Beef

My mother spent the first years of her marriage in Italy. It was there she learned to cook beef with garlic to give it a delicious flavor. Keep in mind that we should all be eating less red meat, so serve small portions of this meat with a healthy selection of vegetables.

Vegetable oil cooking spray

3 1/2 pounds lean beef, top round or oven roast, at room temperature

1 large garlic clove, cut into 15 to 20 long, thin slivers

Salt and freshly ground pepper

1/4 teaspoon olive oil

2 tablespoons water

Preheat oven to 500°. Spray a shallow 2-quart baking pan with cooking spray. Mix the garlic slivers, ¼ teaspoon salt, and freshly ground pepper together. Make a 1-inch-deep slit in the meat with the point of a sharp knife, and push in one seasoned garlic sliver. Repeat this process, piercing the meat and filling each slit with a garlic sliver, until you've used all the garlic. Rub ¼ teaspoon of olive oil all over the roast, then generously salt and pepper it. Set the roast upright in the pan, and add 2 tablespoons of water to the bottom of the pan. Put the roast in the oven, and immediately reduce the temperature to 350°.

If you started with the meat at room temperature, cook it about 60 to 70 minutes for rare to medium-rare meat with an internal temperature of 130° to 140°. (It's best to use a meat thermometer to check the internal temperature of the meat; 130° for rare, 160° for medium, and 180° for well done.) But if you took the meat straight from the refrigerator you will have to cook it at least 5 minutes longer per pound. When the roast is cooked the way you like it, remove it from the oven, and slice into thin slices. Serve immediately in its own juices with the fat skimmed off. This dish goes particularly well with baked, mashed, or boiled potatoes and green beans or peas.

My Mother's Roast Beef (continued)

Preparation time: 10 minutes. Cooking time: about 20 minutes a pound for rare to medium-rare meat if the uncooked meat is at room temperature; about 25 minutes a pound if it is cold, but not frozen. Yield: 10 servings

Nutrition analysis: 231 calories per serving; 38 gm. protein; 0 carbohydrate; 7.5 gm. fat; 101 mg. cholesterol; 0 fiber; 73.5 mg. sodium

Percent of calories from protein: 69%; from carbohydrates: 0%; from fat: 31%

Exchange values: 5½ meat

Note: If you use a fillet of beef, it should be removed from the refrigerator an hour before cooking, and it usually only needs 30 minutes to cook to medium-rare.

Mrs. Bowers' Quick & Easy Chili

This chili is mild, but if you want a spicier version, just add the optional ingredients. To make this a vegetarian meal, just omit the ground meat and add a half cup of corn and a shredded carrot.

1 1/2 teaspoons olive oil

Vegetable oil cooking spray

1 large onion, chopped

1 large garlic clove, minced

1 medium green pepper, chopped

1 small cubanelle (Italian frying pepper), chopped

1 teaspoon or more minced jalapeño pepper (optional for a hotter chili)
   (Note: always wear rubber gloves when working with hot peppers.)

1/2 pound very lean ground beef, chicken, or turkey

15- or 16-ounce can red kidney beans, undrained

15- or 16-ounce can Hunt's tomato sauce

1/2 teaspoon salt

1 to 1 1/2 tablespoons chili powder, or to taste

1 teaspoon or more ground cumin (optional for a hotter chili)

Heat the oil and a generous spray of cooking spray in a large, heavy pot for 30 seconds. Stir in the onion and garlic, and sauté over medium-low heat for 2 minutes, stirring frequently. Add 1 to 2 teaspoons of water if the mixture begins to burn. Stir in all the chopped peppers, and sauté for 2 additional minutes, stirring frequently. Stir in the ground meat, and break it up with a fork or spoon. Cover, and cook over medium heat for 3 more minutes or until the meat is browned. Drain thoroughly. Add the rest of the ingredients. Stir, and bring to a boil. Lower heat and simmer uncovered for 30 to 60 minutes, stirring occasionally. The longer you cook the chili, the thicker it gets and the better the flavors meld. Serve hot with rice and/or cornbread. Freezes well.

Preparation time: 10 minutes. Cooking time: 40 to 70 minutes. Yield: 4 servings

Nutrition analysis: 289 calories per serving; 20 gm. protein; 33.5 gm. carbohydrate; 10 gm. fat; 35 mg. cholesterol; 9 gm. fiber; 1,385 mg. sodium

Percent of calories from protein: 26%; from carbohydrates: 44%; from fat: 29%

Exchange values: 2½ vegetable; 1½ bread; 1½ meat; 1 fat

Ginny's Sloppy Joes

When you come home from a busy day at work and have to decide what to feed the kids (who want absolutely nothing that tastes "healthy") this is the recipe for you. In 20 minutes, you or the kids can put together this crowd-pleaser and put a smile on everyone's face.

1 1/2 teaspoons olive oil, or a generous spray of vegetable oil cooking spray

1/2 cup minced onion

1 large garlic clove, minced

1/2 pound lean ground beef, turkey, or chicken

1/2 cup chopped green pepper (optional)

14 1/2-ounce can chunky tomatoes, undrained, or Italian-style stewed tomatoes

1 to 2 tablespoons chili sauce (optional)

1 loaf fresh Italian bread or French bread, or 4 hamburger buns

Heat the olive oil or cooking spray a large, heavy skillet, and stir in the onion and garlic. Sauté over low heat for 3 minutes, stirring frequently. (You may need to add 1 to 2 teaspoons of water to prevent the mixture from burning.) Add the ground meat and green pepper, and break up the meat with a fork while it browns. When the meat is completely browned, about 5 minutes, drain it thoroughly. Stir in the tomatoes and chili sauce, and slowly bring the mixture to a boil, stirring frequently. You can boil down the mixture if you prefer a thicker sauce. Serve immediately over 4- to 6-inch Italian bread wedges or hamburger buns.

Preparation time: 10 minutes. Cooking time: 10 minutes. Yield: 4 servings

Nutrition analysis: 330 calories per serving; 15 gm. protein; 32.5 gm. carbohydrate; 15.5 gm. fat; 42 mg. cholesterol; 2.5 gm. fiber; 644 mg. sodium

Percent of calories from protein: 18%; from carbohydrates: 39%; from fat: 43%

Exchange values: 2 vegetable; 1½ bread; 1½ meat; 2 fat

Natalie & Michael's Favorite Pork Chops

My friend Idette shared a version of this recipe with me recently, and ever since we have enjoyed the delicious, zippy taste that it gives to pork chops.

Vegetable oil cooking spray

4 center cut (on the thick side), boneless pork chops, just over a pound total

1 1/2 teaspoons olive oil

1 medium onion, chopped

6 tablespoons tarragon vinegar (use cider vinegar if you don't have tarragon)

1/4 teaspoon of each of the following: dried tarragon, dried thyme leaves, and dried parsley

1 cup low-salt chicken broth, skim off all fat

1 to 2 teaspoons Dijon mustard

1 whole medium-size Kosher dill pickle, chopped, about 1/2 cup (Claussen's® are best)

Spray a large skillet with cooking spray. Remove all the visible fat from the pork chops, and brown them on both sides. Remove the pork chops, and set aside. In the same skillet, heat the olive oil over medium heat. Stir in the onions, and sauté, stirring frequently, over medium-low heat for 3 minutes. Be sure not to burn the onions. Add the vinegar and spices. Turn the heat up, and rapidly boil down most of the vinegar. Stir in the chicken broth, and return the pork chops to the skillet. Bring to a boil, reduce heat to medium-low, and simmer, uncovered, for 20 to 35 minutes or until pork chops are done. Flip the pork chops several times during this process.

Remove the chops from the pan and cover them. Stir the mustard into the sauce left in the pan, and quickly boil down the sauce for 2 to 3 minutes, or until desired consistency is reached. Stir in the chopped pickle, then return the pork chops to the pan, and cook for 1 more minute. Serve immediately. This dish goes very well with mashed potatoes.

Natalie and Michael's Favorite Pork Chops (continued)

Preparation time: 10 minutes. Cooking time: 40 to 45 minutes. Yield: 4 servings

Nutrition analysis: 207 calories per serving; 19 gm. protein; 5 gm. carbohydrate; 12.5 gm. fat; 63 mg. cholesterol; 0.5 gm. fiber; 468 mg. sodium

Percent of calories from protein: 36%; from carbohydrates: 10%; from fat: 54%

Exchange values: ½ vegetable; 2½ meat; 1 fat

Peter's Mom's Tacos

Peter's mother shared her version of this recipe with her daughter-in-law and my friend, Kathy, who told me her children liked it better than other tacos. I've adapted it to fit our needs.

Vegetable oil cooking spray

3/4 pound lean ground beef (use ground white meat turkey or chicken if you prefer)

1 1/2 teaspoons olive or canola oil

2 large garlic cloves, minced

1 medium onion, chopped

2 chopped scallions (use 2 inches of the green)

1/2 green pepper, chopped

1 medium plum tomato, seeded and chopped

3 to 4 tablespoons salsa or taco sauce, mild or hot, to taste

Louisiana Hot Sauce or Red Devil Hot Sauce (optional)

Salt to taste

Have ready:

4 flour tortillas

1 to 3 chopped scallions (use 2 inches of the green)

1 1/2 cups chopped fresh tomatoes

1 1/2 cups shredded lettuce

1/4 to 1/2 cup salsa or taco sauce

4 tablespoons low-fat shredded cheddar cheese (optional)

Spray a large, heavy skillet with cooking spray. Brown the ground meat over medium heat, breaking up and stirring the meat as it browns. Drain the meat thoroughly, then put meat on a paper towel to continue to drain. Set aside.

Pour the olive oil into the skillet, and heat for about 40 seconds over medium heat.

Lower the heat, and sauté the garlic, onion, and scallions for 3 minutes, stirring often. Stir in the green pepper and tomato. Cover, and cook for 3 additional minutes. Stir in the cooked ground meat and salsa, and cook for 2 more minutes. Stir in the hot sauce, then salt to taste. Remove from heat, and cover.

Sprinkle each tortilla with a few drops of water. Place on a microwavable plate, cover with a paper towel, and cook each one in the microwave for 10 to 15 seconds. (Or place the tortillas on a cookie sheet, sprinkle them with a few drops of water, cover with aluminum foil, and bake in a medium-hot oven for 5 minutes.) Fill the lower half of each tortilla with a quarter of the meat mixture, some scallions, chopped tomatoes, shredded lettuce, salsa, and shredded cheese. Fold up the bottom of the tortilla to cover the meat, then fold in each side. Serve immediately.

Preparation time: 15 minutes. Cooking time: 15 minutes. Yield: 4 servings

Nutrition analysis using ground beef (numbers in parentheses indicate nutrition analysis using ground turkey): 407 (315) calories per serving; 25.5 (21) gm. protein; 29.5 (29.5) gm. carbohydrate; 22 (14) gm. fat; 64.5 (39) mg. cholesterol; 2.5 (2.5) gm. fiber; 411 (393) mg. sodium

Percent of calories from protein: 24 (25)%; from carbohydrates: 28 (36)%; from fat: 47 (38)%

Exchange values: 1½ (1½) vegetable; 1 (1) bread; 3 (2½) meat; 2½ (1) fat

Marinated London Broil

1 1/2 pounds top round London broil or steak (about 1 1/2 to 2 inches thick)

1 cup dry red wine

2 garlic cloves, minced

2 scallions, chopped

1 tablespoon Worcestershire sauce

2 teaspoons dry mustard

2 teaspoons Dijon mustard or sweet and hot mustard

3 tablespoons chili sauce

1 1/2 teaspoons sun-dried tomato paste (optional)

1 teaspoon brown sugar or molasses

Dash of Tabasco or hot sauce

Freshly ground black pepper, a few turns of the pepper mill

TEENS LOVE THIS

Remove all visible fat from the steak. Mix all the other ingredients together thoroughly. Place the steak in a flat dish with sides high enough to hold the steak and the marinade. Pour the marinade over the steak. Pierce both sides of the steak with a fork several times, and flip the steak to cover all sides with the marinade. Marinate at least an hour or overnight in the refrigerator. Remove the steak from the refrigerator an hour before grilling so it can reach room temperature. Preheat the grill or broiler to hot, remove the steak from the marinade, and grill 8 minutes on each side for rare meat or longer for more cooked meat. While the meat is cooking, bring the marinade to a boil, then stir, and simmer for a few minutes. Serve the marinade over the sliced steak.

Preparation time: 10 minutes. Marinating time: at least an hour. Grilling time: 16 to 20 minutes. Yield: 6 servings

Nutrition analysis: 182 calories per serving; 28 gm. protein; 5 gm. carbohydrate; 5.5 gm. fat; 72 mg. cholesterol; 0 fiber; 192 mg. sodium

Percent of calories from protein: 62%; from carbohydrates: 11%; from fat: 27%

Exchange values: 4 meat

Patty's
Pork Chops

Vegetable cooking oil spray

4 to 6 thin boneless center-cut pork chops (about 1 1/4 pounds total)

1 small onion, chopped

2 red apples, peeled, cored, and sliced

3/4 cup apple cider or juice

1 tablespoon cornstarch

Salt to taste

KIDS LOVE THIS

Spray a large, heavy skillet with cooking spray. Heat the skillet, then brown the pork chops on both sides. Remove them from the skillet. Generously spray the skillet again, and sauté the onions for 30 seconds over medium-low heat. Stir in the apples, and continue stirring for 1 minute. Pour in ½ cup apple cider over medium-low heat, and bring to a boil. Return the chops to the skillet, cover, lower heat, and simmer for 15 to 20 minutes or until chops are done, flipping the chops a few times.

Mix the cornstarch and the rest of the apple cider together. Remove the chops and apples from the skillet using a slotted spoon. Stir the cornstarch mixture into the juice in the skillet. Bring to a boil, and continue cooking until the sauce thickens. Stir the chops and apples into the sauce, check seasoning, and serve immediately. Tastes great with raisins.

Preparation time: 5 minutes. Cooking time: 20 to 25 minutes. Yield: 4 servings

Nutrition analysis: 275 calories per serving; 22 gm. protein; 19.5 gm. carbohydrate; 12 gm. fat; 74 mg. cholesterol; 2 gm. fiber; 60 mg. sodium

Percent of calories from protein: 32%; from carbohydrates: 28%; from fat: 40%

Exchange values: ½ vegetable; 1 fruit; 3½ meat

Quicker Vegetable Beef Stew

My friend Joanne served this stew one winter evening. I've adapted it to fit our dietary needs. Chopping the meat in a food processor can cut the cooking time in half. If you prefer a chunkier, more traditional stew, cut the meat into cubes, and cook it 30 to 40 minutes longer.

1 1/2 teaspoons olive oil

Vegetable oil cooking spray

2 large garlic cloves, minced

1 large onion, chopped

1 pound boneless sirloin steak, beef loin, with all visible fat removed (lean ground chicken, turkey, or beef can also be used)

1 tablespoon flour

2 (13 3/4-ounce) cans or 3 1/3 cups low-salt beef broth, skim off the fat

1 medium sweet potato, peeled and cut into quarters

15-ounce can or 1 2/3 cups tomato sauce

5 carrots, peeled or scrubbed and chopped

4 ribs, celery, chopped

3 potatoes, diced

2 bay leaves

1/4 teaspoon crushed thyme leaves

1/4 teaspoon crushed rosemary

1/2 teaspoon dried basil

Salt and freshly ground pepper to taste

Wondra flour

Heat the olive oil and a generous spray of cooking spray in a large, heavy pot for 45 seconds. Sauté the garlic and onion over medium-low heat for 3 minutes, stirring frequently. If the mixture begins to burn, add 1 to 2 teaspoons of water. Cut the sirloin into chunks. Put the chunks of meat in a large food processor, and coarsely chop them; do not purée. Stir the chopped meat into the onion mixture, and sauté another 5 minutes. Drain the mixture thoroughly. Stir 1 tablespoon flour into the mixture.

Purée 1 cup of broth with the sweet potato in the food processor. Stir the puréed sweet potato, the rest of the broth, and the tomato sauce into the pot. Bring to a boil. Stir in the carrots, celery, potatoes, bay leaves, and herbs. (Chop the vegetables into very small pieces if you want the stew to be done quickly.) Bring the stew to a boil again, cover, and simmer for 30 to 40 minutes or until everything is tender. (If you have time, let it cook 20 or 30 minutes longer.) Add salt and pepper to taste. If you want the stew to be thicker, stir in a few shakes of Wondra flour, and bring to a boil. Remove bay leaves before serving.

Preparation time: 20 minutes. Cooking time: 40 to 50 minutes (mostly unattended). Yield: 10 (1 cup) servings

Nutrition analysis: 178 calories per serving; 13.5 gm. protein; 20 gm. carbohydrate; 5 gm. fat; 30 mg. cholesterol; 3 gm. fiber; 481 mg. sodium

Percent of calories from protein: 30%; from carbohydrates: 45%; from fat: 26%

Exchange values: 1½ vegetable; 1 bread; 1½ meat

Skillet Stroganoff

Here is a quick and easy alternative to beef stroganoff. This version cuts down the cooking time by using chopped meat and reduces the fat and cholesterol (but not the rich and creamy taste) by using non-fat yogurt.

1 1/2 teaspoons olive oil

Vegetable oil cooking spray

1 medium yellow onion, chopped

1 large garlic clove, chopped

3/4 pound very lean ground turkey, chicken, or beef

1 pound sliced mushrooms

1 teaspoon tomato paste

1 tablespoon Worcestershire sauce

1/4 cup dry white wine

1 cup low-fat or nonfat plain yogurt

1 tablespoon nonfat powdered milk

1 tablespoon cornstarch

Salt and freshly ground pepper to taste

1 pound dry eggless noodles, cooked al dente (tender but not mushy)

Heat the olive oil and a generous spray of cooking spray in a large, heavy skillet for 45 seconds. Sauté the onion and garlic over medium-low heat for 3 minutes, stirring frequently. (You may have to add 1 to 2 teaspoons of water to prevent the mixture from burning.) Stir in the ground meat, and break it up with a fork. Sauté over medium heat for 3 to 5 minutes or until thoroughly cooked. Drain thoroughly. Stir in the mushrooms, then cover and cook for 5 additional minutes over medium-low heat, stirring frequently.

Mix the tomato paste, Worcestershire sauce, white wine, yogurt, powdered milk, and cornstarch together. Add this mixture to the skillet. Stir, and continue cooking over medium heat for 3 to 5 additional minutes, or until desired consistency is reached. Add salt and pepper to taste. Serve over cooked noodles.

Skillet Stroganoff (continued)

Preparation time: 10 minutes. Cooking time: 25 minutes. Yield: 4 servings

Nutrition analysis: 654 calories per serving; 35.5 gm. protein; 99.5 gm. carbohydrate; 11 gm. fat; 66 mg. cholesterol; 2 gm. fiber; 188 mg. sodium

Percent of calories from protein: 22%; from carbohydrates: 61%; from fat: 16%

Exchange values: ½ milk; 1½ vegetable; 5½ bread; 2 meat; ½ fat

Fear of Frying

Cutlets Supremo

When Jo heard I was collecting recipes for this book, she sent some family favorites. Her daughter, a close friend of mine, raves about Jo's healthy cooking, so I immediately tried them and adapted them for the book. This recipe gives a delicious continental flavor to veal, chicken, or turkey cutlets.

Vegetable oil cooking spray

1 1/2 teaspoons olive oil and a generous spray of cooking spray

1 small yellow onion, well chopped

1 garlic clove, minced

1 (8-ounce) can Italian style stewed tomatoes (undrained)

1 (8-ounce) can tomato sauce or homemade tomato sauce

1 tablespoon Worcestershire sauce

2 to 3 tablespoons dry white wine

2 cups petite peas, fresh or partially thawed frozen peas

Freshly ground pepper to taste (I usually do not add salt, but check seasonings before serving)

1 to 1 1/4 pounds veal, chicken, or turkey cutlets

4 cups cooked white or brown rice or your favorite pasta

Preheat oven to 350°. Spray a 7 1/2" x 11" baking dish with cooking spray. Heat the olive oil and a generous amount of cooking spray in a medium-size saucepan. Sauté the onion and garlic over medium-low heat for 3 minutes, stirring frequently. Add 1 or 2 teaspoons of water if the onions brown too quickly. Stir in the stewed tomatoes, tomato sauce, Worcestershire sauce, white wine, peas, and pepper. Quickly bring to the boiling point. Pour some of the sauce in the prepared baking dish. Place the cutlets in the dish so they are not touching. Cover with the rest of the sauce. Bake the cutlets uncovered for 30 to 40 minutes or until done. Be sure to baste frequently. Taste and adjust seasonings. Serve immediately with rice or pasta.

Preparation time: 10 minutes. Cooking time: 35 to 45 minutes. Yield: 4 servings

Nutrition analysis: 496 calories per serving; 28 gm. protein; 78 gm. carbohydrate; 6.5 gm. fat; 71 mg. cholesterol; 3.5 gm. fiber; 516 mg. sodium

Percentage of calories from protein: 23%; from carbohydrates: 64%; from fat: 12%

Exchange values: 1½ vegetable; 4½ bread; 2½ meat; ½ fat

Meat and Poultry   **183**

Simply Delectable Pork Chops

This recipe is so easy and delicious, it's bound to become one of your favorites. The pork chops are very popular with my family, and I serve the dish often at dinner parties.

Vegetable oil cooking spray

4 to 5 center cut, boneless pork loin chops
   (about 1 to 1 1/4 pounds total)*

1 medium apple, peeled, cored, and chopped

10 pitted prunes, chopped

1/2 cup Madeira wine

1 teaspoon packed brown sugar

Preheat oven to 350°. Spray a medium- to small-size baking dish with cooking spray. Place the pork chops in the dish so they are not touching. Mix the apple, prunes, wine, and brown sugar together. Pour over the pork chops. Bake uncovered for 25 to 35 minutes, basting frequently. Do not over cook the pork chops. They should be done when the center of the thickest pork chop is no longer pink and has turned white. Serve immediately with rice or noodles and your favorite green vegetable.

Preparation time: 5 minutes. Cooking time: 25 to 35 minutes. Yield: 4 servings

Nutrition analysis: 245 calories per serving; 25.5 gm. protein; 19 gm. carbohydrate; 4.5 gm. fat; 80.5 mg. cholesterol; 2 gm. fiber; 61 mg. sodium

Percentage of calories from protein: 42%; from carbohydrates: 30%; from fat: 16%

Exchange values: 1 fruit; 3 meat

It takes longer, but this is a delicious way to cook pork roast.

Baked Chile Chicken

My teenagers love this dish because it has a rich taste with just enough spice to make it interesting, but not too spicy for the average palate. Those who like it spicier, though, can add more chile peppers and taco seasoning. I want to thank my friend Linda for giving me the idea for this recipe and many others.

Vegetable oil cooking spray

1 1/2 teaspoons olive oil

1 bunch of scallions (use the white part and 3 inches of the green part), trimmed and chopped

1 large garlic clove, minced

16 ounces nonfat sour cream

2 tablespoons taco seasoning mix

4 1/2-ounce can or 8 tablespoons mild green chopped chiles, undrained

1/4 cup shredded low-fat sharp cheddar cheese

Salt and freshly ground pepper to taste

4 skinless chicken breasts

Preheat oven to 350°. Spray a 7½" x 11" baking dish or a medium baking pan with cooking spray. Heat the olive oil plus a generous spray of cooking spray in a medium skillet. Sauté the scallions and garlic over medium-low heat for 3 minutes, stirring frequently. Set aside. Mix the sour cream, taco seasoning, chopped chiles, and cheddar cheese together. Mix in the sautéed scallions and garlic. Taste and check the seasonings, adding more taco seasoning, chile peppers, salt, and pepper if needed. Place the chicken breasts in the prepared baking dish. Cover the chicken on all sides with all the sauce. Bake uncovered, basting frequently, for 45 to 55 minutes or until the chicken is done. Serve with rice or pasta covered with the sour cream sauce.

Preparation time: 10 minutes. Cooking time: 50 to 60 minutes. Yield: 4 servings

Nutrition analysis: 504 calories per serving; 41 gm. protein; 53 gm. carbohydrate; 14.5 gm. fat; 109 mg. cholesterol; 0.5 gm. fiber; 4,052 mg. sodium

Percent of calories from protein: 32%; from carbohydrates: 42%; from fat: 26%

Exchange values: 5 meat; ½ fat

Curried
Chicken

My friend Sue introduced me to this recipe one afternoon in the grocery store. It's easy to understand why it's one of her favorites, since the dish has a marvelous taste and is very easy to make.

Vegetable oil cooking spray

1/4 cup mild-tasting honey

2 tablespoons Dijon mustard

1/4 teaspoon salt

1 tablespoon Butter Buds, natural dehydrated butter

1 teaspoon curry powder

1/4 teaspoon ground ginger

1 tablespoon low-sodium soy sauce

5 to 6 boneless, skinless, single chicken breasts (about 1 3/4 pounds total)

12 fresh asparagus tips (optional)

4 cups cooked rice, white or brown

Preheat oven to 350°. Spray a flat casserole dish that is not much bigger than the chicken breasts with cooking spray. Mix the next 7 ingredients together in the casserole dish to make the sauce. Place the chicken breasts in the dish, and baste well with all the sauce. Bake uncovered for 30 minutes, basting frequently. Remove the chicken breasts. Put the asparagus tips in the sauce, place the chicken breasts over them, and baste the chicken. Bake for 5 to 10 more minutes or until the chicken breasts are thoroughly cooked. Serve the sauce-covered chicken with rice and asparagus.

Preparation time: 10 minutes. Cooking time: 30 to 40 minutes. Yield: 4 servings

Nutrition analysis: 517 calories per serving; 41 gm. protein; 63.5 gm. carbohydrate; 10 gm. fat; 91 mg. cholesterol; 3.5 gm. fiber; 538 mg. sodium

Percent of calories from protein: 32%; from carbohydrates: 50%; from fat: 17%

Exchange values: 1 vegetable; 4 bread; 4 meat

Chicken Melba

The wonderful combination of ingredients gives this dish an exotic taste reminiscent of the Pacific islands.

Vegetable oil cooking spray

4 skinless chicken breasts

1/2 cup nonfat plain yogurt

2 tablespoons nonfat mayonnaise

1/2 teaspoon Dijon mustard

1 tablespoon grated Parmesan cheese

1/4 teaspoon onion salt, or to taste

1 teaspoon dried chives or 2 teaspoons chopped fresh chives

1/4 cup light peach juice

2 tablespoons sliced almonds

29-ounce can peach halves in light syrup, drain and save juice

Preheat oven to 350°. Generously spray a 9" x 13" pan with cooking spray. Place the chicken in the pan. Mix the yogurt, mayonnaise, mustard, Parmesan cheese, onion salt, and chives together in a small bowl. Spread 1 tablespoon of the yogurt mixture on each chicken breast. Set the rest of the yogurt mixture aside. Pour peach juice in the bottom of the pan but not on the chicken breasts. Bake for 35 minutes. While the chicken is baking, toast the almonds until golden brown. Let them cool, then grind them in a food processor or blender. Remove the pan from the oven.

Place the peach halves sliced side up in a single layer in the pan next to the chicken breasts. Spoon the remainder of the yogurt mixture into the peach halves. Bake for 15 to 20 additional minutes or until the chicken breasts are cooked. Sprinkle the chicken and peaches with the ground almonds, and broil for 2 minutes. Serve immediately.

Chicken Melba (continued)

Preparation time: 10 minutes. Cooking time: 50 minutes (mostly unattended). Yield: 4 servings

Nutrition analysis: 423 calories per serving; 42 gm. protein; 35.5 gm. carbohydrate; 13 gm. fat; 109 mg. cholesterol; 0.5 gm. fiber; 320 mg. sodium

Percent of calories from protein: 39%; from carbohydrates: 33%; from fat: 28%

Exchange values: 2 fruit; 5 meat; ½ fat

Chicken Stir-Fry

My college friend Donna taught me that when you're in a hurry, stir-frying is an easy and healthy way to make dinner. This is a basic stir-fry recipe that can be made with chicken, pork, beef, or no meat at all.

Have ready:

2 teaspoons sesame or peanut oil

1 to 2 garlic cloves, minced

1 small onion, quartered and thinly sliced

2 chopped scallions (use the white part with two inches of green)

2 single boneless, skinless chicken breasts (about 1/2 pound total), cut into thin strips

1 pound broccoli crowns, cut into small florets

3 carrots, peeled and sliced into thin 2-inch strips

1 green pepper, cored and thinly sliced

1 small can chopped water chestnuts, drained (optional)

If you want to serve rice or noodles, start cooking them before you prepare the stir-fry so everything will be ready at the same time.

Sauce:

2 tablespoons reduced-sodium soy sauce

1 teaspoon sugar

1/2 teaspoon dry mustard

1 tablespoon cornstarch

1/3 cup cold water

Dash of hot sauce (optional)

Heat a large skillet or wok over medium-hot heat for 1 minute. Add the oil, and heat for about 30 seconds. Stir in the garlic, onion, and scallions, and stir-fry for 2 minutes. Stir in the chicken, and stir-fry for 3 to 5 minutes or until chicken is just about cooked through. Stir in the vegetables, cover, and cook for 5 minutes, stirring often. While the vegetables are cooking, stir all the sauce ingredients together in a small

Chicken Stir-Fry (continued)

bowl. Stir the sauce into the stir-fry mixture for 1 to 2 minutes or until thickened. Serve immediately with rice or over noodles.

Preparation time: 15 minutes. Cooking time: 15 minutes. Yield: 4 servings

Nutrition analysis: 198 calories per serving; 15 gm. protein; 25.5 gm. carbohydrate; 5.5 gm. fat; 26 mg. cholesterol; 5.5 gm. fiber; 580 mg. sodium

Percent of calories from protein: 29%; from carbohydrates: 48%; from fat: 23%

Exchange values: 4½ vegetable; 1 meat; ½ fat

Grilled
Maple Chicken

My friend Diane gave me the idea of using maple syrup to enhance the taste of chicken. The syrup gives it a very appealing, slightly sweet taste. This is definitely one of my children's favorite ways to prepare chicken.

4 boneless and skinless chicken breasts, about 1/3 to 1/2 pound each

1 to 1 1/2 tablespoons pure maple syrup, or to taste

Preheat grill to 425°. Rinse and pat dry the chicken breasts. Place them in a bowl, and stir in the maple syrup until the chicken is completely covered with the syrup. Place the chicken breasts on the preheated grill. Cover and grill for 15 to 20 minutes or until done, flipping the chicken every 3 to 5 minutes and basting with maple syrup. Be sure not to overcook the chicken; it's ready to eat when the middle of the thickest part of the chicken breast is white with no pink. Serve immediately.

KIDS LOVE THIS

Preparation time: a few minutes. Grilling time: 15 to 20 minutes. Yield: 4 servings

Nutrition analysis: 274 calories per serving; 38 gm. protein; 5.5 gm. carbohydrate; 10 gm. fat; 104 mg. cholesterol; 0 fiber; 93 mg. sodium

Percent of calories from protein: 57%; from carbohydrates: 8%; from fat: 35%

Exchange values: 5 meat

Note: The chicken can be broiled instead of grilled if you prefer.

Green Taco Chicken

Vegetable oil cooking spray

1 1/2 teaspoons olive oil

1 garlic clove, minced

1/4 cup chopped yellow onion

1/4 cup chopped green pepper

4 single skinless chicken breasts (about 2 pounds total)

1/2 cup low-salt chicken broth, skim off the fat

2 tablespoons mild green taco sauce

Salt and freshly ground pepper to taste

TEENS LOVE THIS

Preheat oven to 350°. Spray a medium baking dish with cooking spray. Heat the olive oil and a generous spray of cooking spray in a medium skillet for 45 seconds. Stir in the garlic and onion, and sauté over medium-low heat for 1 minute. Add the green pepper, and sauté for 2 to 3 more minutes, stirring frequently. Place the chicken breasts in the prepared baking dish. Stir the chicken broth and taco sauce into the onion/pepper mixture. Quickly bring it to a boil. Pour the sauce over the chicken, and bake uncovered for 40 to 55 minutes, basting frequently. Make sure the chicken is thoroughly cooked (juices should run clear and the meat should not be pink), before removing it from the oven. Add salt and freshly ground pepper to taste, and serve immediately.

Preparation time: 10 minutes. Cooking time: 45 to 60 minutes. Yield: 4 servings

Nutrition analysis: 286 calories per serving; 38 gm. protein; 3.5 gm. carbohydrate; 12 gm. fat; 104 mg. cholesterol; 0.5 gm. fiber; 179 mg. sodium

Percent of calories from protein: 55%; from carbohydrates: 5%; from fat: 40%

Exchange values: ½ vegetable; 5 meat; ½ fat

All-in-One Chicken Dinner

This dinner combines chicken with a variety of vegetables that are all cooked together in a balsamic vinegar sauce. The vegetables in this recipe are only a suggestion. I make this meal with whatever vegetables I have in the refrigerator, so it rarely tastes the same.

Vegetable oil cooking spray

1/4 cup balsamic vinegar

1 teaspoon Dijon mustard

1 tablespoon olive oil

1/2 to 1 teaspoon salt

1/2 to 1 teaspoon sugar

1 teaspoon dried basil

Dash of pepper

Dash of curry powder

4 skinless chicken breasts

1 medium zucchini, washed, dried, and sliced into 1/2-inch rounds

1 very small eggplant, washed, dried, and cut into 1/2-inch rounds

1 red pepper, seeded and sliced into quarters

1 green pepper, seeded and sliced into quarters

1 large yellow onion, peeled and sliced into eighths

2 potatoes, peeled and sliced into 1/4-inch rounds

1/4 to 1/2 cup water

Preheat oven to 375°. Generously spray a large baking dish with cooking spray. Mix the vinegar, mustard, olive oil, salt, sugar, basil, pepper, and curry powder together in a small bowl. Set aside. Place the chicken in the baking dish. Arrange the vegetables around the chicken. Brush the vinegar sauce over all sides of the chicken and vegetables, using up all the sauce. Bake for 20 minutes, then baste the chicken and vegetables with the drippings, and turn the vegetables over with a spatula. If necessary, add 2 to 4 tablespoons of water to the bottom of the pan. Return to the oven, and bake for 30 to 50 minutes or until the chicken and vegetables are done, basting occasionally. Check the seasoning, and serve immediately.

All-in-One Chicken Dinner (continued)

Preparation time: 15 minutes. Cooking time: 50 to 70 minutes. Yield: 4 servings

Nutrition analysis: 267 calories per serving; 21 gm. protein; 26.5 gm. carbohydrate; 8.5 gm. fat; 52 mg. cholesterol; 3 gm. fiber; 618 mg. sodium

Percent of calories from protein: 31%; from carbohydrates: 40%; from fat: 29%

Exchange values: 1½ vegetable; 1 bread; 2½ meat; ½ fat

Chicken Stroganoff à la Vicki

I sat down one rainy afternoon with my friend Vicki and she gave me a whole list of recipes to use. This is one of my favorites because it is simple, yet absolutely delicious. Its sophisticated continental taste makes it a nice choice for dinner parties.

Vegetable oil cooking spray

4 to 6 pieces of chicken with the skin removed, about 2 pounds (white meat has less fat)

10 3/4-ounce can Campbell's Healthy Request cream of mushroom soup

1/2 cup dry white wine

1 cup nonfat plain yogurt

1 teaspoon cornstarch

1/2 cup sliced seedless grapes (optional)

4 cups cooked white or brown rice

Preheat oven to 350°. Spray a baking dish that's not much bigger than the chicken with cooking spray. Place the chicken in the dish. Stir the cream of mushroom soup and wine together, and pour over the chicken. Bake uncovered for 45 minutes. Stir the yogurt and cornstarch together. Remove the chicken from the baking dish. Stir the yogurt mixture into the sauce on the bottom of the baking dish. Return the chicken to the dish, then spoon the soup/yogurt sauce over the chicken, and continue baking for 10 to 15 minutes or until the chicken is thoroughly cooked. Remove from the oven, and stir in the grapes. Serve over hot rice.

Preparation time: 5 minutes. Cooking time: 60 minutes. Yield: 4 to 6 servings

Nutrition analysis for 4 servings with white rice: 560 calories per serving; 47 gm. protein; 67 gm. carbohydrate; 11.5 gm. fat; 107 mg. cholesterol; 2.5 gm. fiber; 284 mg. sodium

Percent of calories from protein: 34%; from carbohydrates: 48%; from fat: 18%

Exchange values: ½ milk; 4 bread; 5 meat

East Indian Chicken

The unusual combina-
tion of tomatoes and
curry gives this chicken
dish an exotic and
slightly spicy taste.

Vegetable oil cooking spray

1 1/2 teaspoons olive oil

1 large garlic clove, minced

1 1/2 cups cleaned and chopped leeks (use the white part only)

1 green pepper, seeded and chopped

1 teaspoon minced jalapeño pepper (optional) (Note: always wear rubber gloves
 when working with hot peppers)

2 1/2 cups seeded and chopped plum tomatoes

1 tablespoon regular or sun-dried tomato paste

1/2 cup chicken broth or water

2 tablespoons dry vermouth

1 1/2 teaspoons curry powder, or to taste

1/2 to 1 teaspoon salt, or to taste

Freshly ground pepper to taste

5 single chicken breasts, with the skin removed

5 cups cooked white or brown rice

5 tablespoons chutney (optional)

Heat the cooking spray and olive oil in a large, heavy pot. Stir in the garlic and leeks,
and sauté over medium-low heat for 2 minutes, stirring frequently. You may have to
add 1 to 2 teaspoons of water to prevent the mixture from burning. Stir in the green
pepper and jalapeño pepper, and sauté for 3 more minutes, stirring frequently. Stir in
the tomatoes, tomato paste, broth, vermouth, curry, salt, and pepper. Bring the mixture to a boil, then stir in the chicken. Bring the mixture to a boil again, cover, and
simmer for 45 minutes or until the chicken is done, stirring the mixture occasionally and covering the chicken with the sauce.

Remove the chicken from the pot, and boil down the sauce for a few minutes until it reaches the desired consistency. You may want to thicken it with a little flour. Serve the chicken with the rice, and cover both with the sauce. Serve with chutney if desired.

Preparation time: 10 minutes. Cooking time: 55 minutes (mostly unattended).
Yield: 5 servings

Nutrition analysis: 549 calories per serving; 31 gm. protein; 84 gm. carbohydrate; 9 gm. fat; 62.5 mg. cholesterol; 4.5 gm. fiber; 621 mg. sodium

Percent of calories from protein: 23%; from carbohydrates: 61%; from fat: 15%

Exchange values: 2½ vegetable; ½ fruit; 4 bread; 3 meat; ½ fat

Roasted Pepper Chicken

This chicken dish is a family favorite. It tastes as if I spent hours instead of a few minutes preparing it.

Vegetable oil cooking spray

4 chicken breasts, remove skin and all visible fat

12-ounce jar Italian-style roasted peppers, rinsed, drained, and chopped

1 large garlic clove, minced

1 large yellow onion, chopped

1 cup low-salt chicken broth, with fat skimmed off

Preheat oven to 350°. Spray a 9" x 13" baking dish with cooking spray. Place the chicken in a single layer in the baking dish. Mix the other ingredients together, and pour over the chicken. Bake uncovered for 60 minutes, basting the chicken frequently. If the basting juices run low while cooking, add a little water. Serve with white rice covered with the roasted peppers and baking juices.

Preparation time: 5 minutes. Cooking time: 60 minutes. Yield: 4 servings

Nutrition analysis (without rice): 213 calories per serving; 21.5 gm. protein; 19.5 gm. carbohydrate; 6 gm. fat; 52.5 mg. cholesterol; 2.5 gm. fiber; 499 mg. sodium

Percent of calories from protein: 40%; from carbohydrates: 36%; from fat: 25%

Exchange values: ½ vegetable; 1 bread; 2½ meat

California Turkey Burgers

I serve these turkey burgers on fresh whole wheat rolls or on pita bread with tomatoes, bean sprouts, and non-fat mayonnaise.

1 pound ground white meat turkey

1/4 to 1/3 cup seasoned bread crumbs

1 tablespoon fat-free, cholesterol-free mayonnaise

1 egg white

1 teaspoon lemon juice

1 teaspoon Worcestershire sauce

1/4 teaspoon salt

Freshly ground pepper

KIDS LOVE THIS

Mix all the ingredients together, and form into 4 to 6 patties. Grill, fry, or broil for 6 to 9 minutes on each side or until cooked through but not dried out. (Don't serve turkey burgers that are still pink inside; turkey must be thoroughly cooked before eating.) This dish goes well with a fruit salad or green salad.

Preparation time: 5 minutes. Cooking time: 12 to 18 minutes. Yield: 4 to 6 servings

Nutrition analysis for 4 servings: 153 calories per serving; 23.5 gm. protein; 7 gm. carbohydrate; 3 gm. fat; 51 mg. cholesterol; 0.5 gm. fiber; 285 mg. sodium

Percent of calories from protein: 64%; from carbohydrates: 19%; from fat: 18%

Exchange values: ½ bread; 2½ meat

Krispy Baked Chicken

The cereal coating gives this chicken a slightly sweet taste that kids love. When my children were very young they used to help me roll the chicken in the crushed cereal. To save time, you can buy Corn Flake crumbs in most grocery stores.

Vegetable oil cooking spray

2 cups Rice Krispies® or corn flakes

Pinch of salt and pepper

1 tablespoon plain, nonfat yogurt

1 large egg white

6 to 8 pieces skinless chicken (white meat has less fat)

Preheat oven to 350°. Spray a shallow baking pan or cookie sheet with cooking spray. Put the Rice Krispies, salt, and pepper in a food processor or blender, and process until completely crushed into crumbs. Beat the yogurt and egg white together with a fork. Roll each piece of chicken in the egg white mixture, and shake off excess liquid. Then roll each piece in the cereal crumbs. Place the chicken in the prepared pan or cookie sheet, and bake for 40 to 60 minutes, depending on the size of the pieces, or until completely cooked. Serve immediately, and watch them disappear.

KIDS LOVE THIS

Preparation time: 10 minutes. Cooking time: 40 to 60 minutes. Yield: 6 to 8 servings

Nutrition analysis for chicken breasts for 8 servings (numbers in parentheses indicate nutrition analysis for chicken legs): 195 (210) calories per serving; 26.5 (26.5) gm. protein; 5.5 (5.5) gm. carbohydrate; 6.5 (8) gm. fat; 72 (89) mg. cholesterol; 0 (0) fiber; 144 (172) mg. sodium

Percent of calories from protein: 56 (53)%; from carbohydrates: 12 (11)%; from fat: 32 (36)%

Exchange values: ½ bread; 3½ meat

Lemon Yogurt Chicken

This is my favorite "I'm in a rush and I have to feed the hungry kids quickly" recipe.

1 teaspoon olive oil

Vegetable oil cooking spray

4 single boneless, skinless chicken breasts, cut into bite-sized pieces (about 1 1/2 pounds total)

2 to 3 tablespoons low-fat lemon yogurt

1 teaspoon cornstarch

Heat the olive oil and a generous spray of cooking spray in a large, heavy skillet over medium heat for 45 seconds. Stir in the chicken pieces, then cover and sauté for 5 to 8 minutes, stirring occasionally, or until the chicken is thoroughly cooked. Mix the yogurt and cornstarch together. Stir this mixture into the chicken, and cook for another minute or two. If the yogurt sauce is too thin, remove the chicken, stir in an additional teaspoon of cornstarch and cook a minute or two more. Serve the chicken covered with the yogurt sauce. This dish goes well with rice.

KIDS LOVE THIS

Preparation time: 5 minutes. Cooking time: 8 to 10 minutes. Yield: 4 servings

Nutrition analysis: 144 calories per serving; 22 gm. protein; 3 gm. carbohydrate; 4.5 gm. fat; 59 mg. cholesterol; 0 fiber; 57.5 mg. sodium

Percent of calories from protein: 64%; from carbohydrates: 9%; from fat: 28%

Exchange values: 3 meat; ½ fat

Meat and Poultry

Marinated Curried Chicken

I like to marinate this chicken overnight, although it's delicious even if marinated just a few hours or not at all.

Marinade:

1/4 cup honey

1/4 cup cider or apple juice

2 tablespoons vermouth or dry white wine

Juice of 1/2 lemon

1 teaspoon curry powder

1 whole chicken, with skin removed and cut into serving-sized pieces

Vegetable oil cooking spray

2 Vidalia or sweet onions

1/4 cup raisins (optional)

Mix the marinade ingredients in a large bowl. Place the chicken pieces in the bowl, and stir until well coated with marinade. Cover the bowl, place in the refrigerator for an hour or more if desired, and baste several times.

Preheat the oven to 350°. Spray a large baking pan with cooking spray. Place the chicken in a single layer in the pan. Cut the onions into eighths, and place them and the raisins in the pan. Cover the contents of the pan with the marinade. Bake uncovered for 40 to 60 minutes or until the chicken is thoroughly cooked, basting the chicken several times while baking. Remove chicken from pan. Skim the fat off the pan juices. Thicken the juices to make gravy, and serve over the chicken.

Preparation time: 10 minutes. Cooking time: 40 to 60 minutes (or 25 to 35 minutes if you use boneless chicken breasts). Yield: 6 servings

Nutrition analysis: 382 calories per serving; 37.5 gm. protein; 22 gm. carbohydrate; 15 gm. fat; 109 mg. cholesterol; 1.5 gm. fiber; 66 mg. sodium

Percent of calories from protein: 40%; from carbohydrates: 24%; from fat: 35%

Exchange values: ½ vegetable; ½ fruit; 5½ meat

Pretzeled Chicken

Vegetable oil cooking spray

25 to 30 low-salt thin and light pretzels
(use unsalted pretzels for salt-restricted diets)

1 large egg white

1 tablespoon nonfat plain yogurt

4 to 6 pieces skinless chicken (white meat has less fat)

Preheat oven to 350°. Spray a cookie sheet with cooking spray. Put the pretzels in a food processor or blender, and process on high until about ¾ cup of pretzel flour is produced. Beat the egg white and yogurt together with a fork. Dip each piece of chicken in the egg white mixture, shake off the excess, then roll it in the pretzel flour. Place the chicken on the prepared cookie sheet, and bake for 40 to 60 minutes, depending on the size of the chicken pieces, or until the chicken is thoroughly cooked.

KIDS LOVE THIS

Preparation time: 10 minutes. Cooking time: 40 to 60 minutes. Yield: 4 to 6 servings

Nutrition analysis for chicken breasts (numbers in parentheses indicate nutrition analysis for chicken legs): 272 (305) calories per serving; 26 (29.5) gm. protein; 24 (24) gm. carbohydrate; 7 (9) gm. fat; 64 (89) mg. cholesterol; 0 (0) fiber; 547 (581) mg. sodium

Percent of calories from protein: 40 (40)%; from carbohydrates: 37 (33)%; from fat: 24 (28)%

Exchange values: 1½ bread; 3½ meat

Salsa Chicken

Vegetable oil cooking spray

4 to 6 pieces skinless chicken,
   about 2 pounds total (white meat has less fat)

10- to 12-ounce jar low-sodium chunky salsa
   (try Guiltless Gourmet® or Newman's Own Bandito®)

Preheat oven to 350°. Choose a baking dish that's just big enough to hold the chicken in a single layer, and spray it with cooking spray. Place the chicken pieces in the dish. Cover them with the salsa. Bake uncovered for 45 to 60 minutes or until the chicken is thoroughly cooked. Baste the chicken a couple of times while it is baking, and add a few tablespoons of water if the salsa starts to dry out. Serve the chicken with rice covered with the baked salsa, add some corn as a side dish, and you have a crowd-pleaser for the teenage set.

TEENS LOVE THIS

Note: If you are not on a very low-fat diet, this chicken is delicious sprinkled with a few tablespoons of low-fat cheddar cheese before baking.

Preparation time: 5 minutes. Cooking time: 60 minutes. Yield: 4 to 6 servings

Nutrition analysis for 6 servings using white meat: 197 calories per serving; 26 gm. protein; 7 gm. carbohydrate; 9 gm. fat; 69.5 mg. cholesterol; 0 fiber; 451 mg. sodium

Percent of calories from protein: 49%; from carbohydrates: 13%; from fat: 38%

Exchange values: 3 meat

Sea Island Chicken

The unusual combination of ingredients gives this chicken dish an exotic taste that reminds me of the Pacific Islands. It's quick and easy to make and very popular at my house.

Vegetable oil cooking spray

1 pound skinless chicken breast cutlets

2 tablespoons duck sauce

1 teaspoon low-sodium soy sauce

1 teaspoon hot and creamy mustard (not the Chinese type)

1 bunch scallions, chopped (use mostly the white part with some green)

1 teaspoon light margarine or butter, melted

1 tablespoon brown sugar

1 1/2 teaspoons low-fat milk

3 ripe pears, peeled, cored, and cut into eighths (optional)

Preheat oven to 375°. Spray a 9" x 13" baking pan with cooking spray. Cut the cutlets into long strips about 1 inch wide. Mix the duck sauce, soy sauce, and mustard together. Stir in the chicken and scallions. Set aside. Mix the melted margarine, brown sugar, and milk together in a bowl. Toss in the pears, and coat well. Spread the chicken out flat on one side of the pan. Spread the pears out on the other side, and drizzle with their marinade. Spray the pears with cooking spray. Bake 15 to 20 minutes or until the chicken is thoroughly cooked.

Preparation time: 10 minutes. Cooking time: 20 minutes. Yield: 4 servings

Nutrition analysis: 212 calories per serving; 19 gm. protein; 22 gm. carbohydrate; 5.5 gm. fat; 52 mg. cholesterol; 3 gm. fiber; 147 mg. sodium

Percent of calories from protein: 35%; from carbohydrates: 41%; from fat: 23%

Exchange values: 1 fruit; 2½ meat

Susan's Chicken Fingers

One serving of baked chicken nuggets often contains 13 to 17 grams of fat . This low-fat recipe from my neighbor makes deliciously tender chicken with a crunchy coating. If you start marinating the chicken in the morning, it will be ready to cook when you get home.

4 single skinless, boneless chicken breasts
(about 1 pound total)

1 cup nonfat plain yogurt

2 teaspoons lemon juice

1 small garlic clove, minced (optional)

1/4 teaspoon salt (optional)

Vegetable oil cooking spray

2 cups dried herb seasoned stuffing mix
(the crumbled variety, not cubed; I use Pepperidge Farm®),
or seasoned bread crumbs

Cut the chicken breasts into long, ½-inch wide fingers. Combine the yogurt, lemon juice, garlic, and salt in a large bowl. Add the chicken fingers, and stir until they're completely coated with the yogurt marinade. Cover, and refrigerate for at least 6 hours (this makes the chicken very tender).

Preheat oven to 350°. Spray a cookie sheet with cooking spray. Place the stuffing mix in a bowl. Remove the chicken from the marinade, shake off the excess marinade, and roll the chicken in the stuffing mix. Place the chicken on the prepared cookie sheet, and bake for 15 to 20 minutes or until thoroughly cooked. Serve immediately.

Preparation time: 10 minutes. Marinating time: 6 to 12 hours. Cooking time: 15 to 20 minutes. Yield: 4 to 5 servings

Nutrition analysis for 4 servings: 210 calories per serving; 23.5 gm. protein; 15.5 gm. carbohydrate; 5.5 gm. fat; 53 mg. cholesterol; 0 fiber; 420 mg. sodium

Percent of calories from protein: 46%; from carbohydrates: 30%; from fat: 24%

Exchange values: ½ milk; ½ bread; 2½ meat

Dijon Honey Chicken

Honey and Dijon make a delicious sauce for any type of chicken. If you have time, brush a skinless roasting chicken with this sauce and bake it 20 minutes a pound, basting frequently. If in a rush, use chicken cutlets and bake for 20 to 30 minutes.

Vegetable oil cooking spray

1 tablespoon Dijon mustard

1 tablespoon honey

4 boneless, skinless, single chicken breasts (1 1/4 to 1 1/2 pounds total)

1/4 to 1/2 cup water

2 to 4 tablespoons skim milk or water

1 to 2 teaspoons Wondra flour

Salt and freshly ground pepper to taste

KIDS LOVE THIS

Preheat oven to 350°. Spray a medium-size metal baking pan with cooking spray. Mix the Dijon and honey together. Brush all sides of the chicken breasts with the mixture. Place the chicken in the prepared pan. Add water to the bottom of the pan to keep the chicken from burning. Bake uncovered, basting often and adding water when needed, for 30 to 40 minutes or until the chicken breasts are thoroughly cooked but not dried out. Remove the chicken from the baking dish.

To make a delicious gravy, after skimming off the fat from the juices in the pan, stir in 2 to 4 tablespoons of skim milk or water. Put the pan on the stove, and bring to a boil, stirring frequently. Sprinkle in 1 or 2 teaspoons Wondra flour, and continue cooking until desired consistency is reached. Add more flour if necessary. Add salt and pepper to taste. Serve with noodles, rice, or mashed potatoes.

Preparation time: 10 minutes. Cooking time: 30 to 40 minutes. Yield: 4 servings

Nutrition analysis: 220 calories per serving; 29 gm. protein; 6 gm. carbohydrate; 8 gm. fat; 78 mg. cholesterol; 0 fiber; 167 mg. sodium

Percentage of calories from protein: 55%; from carbohydrates: 12%; from fat: 34%

Exchange values: 3½ meat

SEAFOOD

Basic Baked Fish

Many people don't cook fish because they don't know how. The general rule is that fish fillets cook in a hot to moderately-hot oven for 10 to 12 minutes for each inch of thickness. Some firm fish, like catfish, take longer.

Vegetable oil cooking spray

1 to 1 1/4 pounds white fish fillets
(flounder, sole, etc.), no more than 1 inch thick

Salt

1 to 2 teaspoons Dijon mustard

1 to 2 teaspoons seasoned bread crumbs

1/4 cup dry white wine or low-salt chicken, vegetable, or fish broth

Sliced lemons

Preheat oven to 375° (Make sure the oven is hot before you start to bake the fish.) Spray a shallow broiler-proof pan with cooking spray. Rinse fish and pat dry. Lightly salt both sides of the fish, and place the fillets in the pan. Mix the mustard and bread crumbs together. Spread this mixture on the fish. (An alternative is to brush the fish lightly with olive oil and not use any other topping.) Pour the wine around the fish but not on top of the bread crumb mixture. Bake the fish uncovered in a thoroughly preheated oven for 8 to 12 minutes; do not flip or turn the fish. Add more liquid to the pan if most of the liquid evaporates during the baking or broiling process.

Place the top oven rack 3 inches from the top of the oven. Place the pan with the fish on that rack, and carefully broil the fish for 2 to 3 minutes or until the fish is flaky and no longer translucent. Be careful not to overcook the fish. Serve immediately with sliced lemon.

Preparation time: 10 minutes. Cooking time: 15 minutes. Yield: 4 servings

Nutrition analysis: 191 calories per serving; 27.5 gm. protein; 1 gm. carbohydrate; 8.5 gm. fat; 85 mg. cholesterol; 0 fiber; 143 mg. sodium

Percent of calories from protein: 58%; from carbohydrates: 2%; from fat: 40%

Exchange values: 4 meat

Baked Catfish

Even though my family doesn't love fish, this is one of their favorite dishes. They like it because it doesn't have a fishy taste. I like making it because it's quick, easy, and healthy, and doesn't leave my kitchen smelling too fishy.

Vegetable oil cooking spray

1 pound fresh catfish fillets, about 1 1/2 inches thick

1 tablespoon nonfat mayonnaise

1 tablespoon Dijon mustard

2 tablespoons cornmeal

2 tablespoons dried seasoned Italian bread crumbs

Preheat oven to 350°. Spray a cookie sheet or shallow baking pan with cooking spray. Wash and dry the catfish. Mix the mayonnaise and mustard together in a small bowl. Mix the cornmeal and bread crumbs together. Spread the mayonnaise mixture all over the catfish, then roll the fillets in the cornmeal mixture. Place the fillets in a single layer on the cookie sheet, and bake for 25 to 35 minutes or until completely cooked but not dried out.

Preparation time: 10 minutes. Cooking time: 25 to 35 minutes. Yield: 4 servings

Nutrition analysis: 166 calories per serving; 21.5 gm. protein; 6 gm. carbohydrate; 5.5 gm. fat; 67 mg. cholesterol; 0.5 gm. fiber; 210 mg. sodium

Percent of calories from protein: 54%; from carbohydrates: 15%; from fat: 31%

Exchange values: ½ bread; 3 meat

California Grilled Fish

This is a delightfully refreshing and delicious way to serve salmon or swordfish. The salsa, which is very mild, complements the fish beautifully.

4 individual salmon steaks, about 1 1/2 inches thick,
   or a swordfish steak (about 1 to 1 1/2 pounds total)

1/2 large red pepper with seeds and stem removed

1/2 medium cucumber, peeled, with seeds removed

1 small garlic clove

1 teaspoon to 1/2 tablespoon olive oil (optional)

Salt and freshly ground pepper to taste

Preheat grill to medium-hot or use oven broiler. Grill the salmon steaks about 8 minutes per side or the swordfish steaks about 6 minutes a side for each inch of thickness or until done and opaque. Be careful not to overcook the fish.

While the fish is grilling, puree the rest of the ingredients in a food processor or blender. Serve the salsa with the fish.

Preparation time: 10 minutes. Cooking time: 15 to 20 minutes. Yield: 4 servings

Nutrition analysis (numbers in parentheses indicate nutrition analysis without olive oil): 230 (215) calories per serving; 34 gm. protein; 2 gm. carbohydrate; 8.5 (7) gm. fat; 67 mg. cholesterol; 0.5 gm. fiber; 154 mg. sodium

Percent of calories from protein: 62 (66)%; from carbohydrates: 4 (4)%; from fat: 35 (30)%

Exchange values: ½ vegetable; 4½ meat; ½ (0) fat

Chowdery Fish Stew

This hearty fish stew is a satisfying meal by itself. Like the French bouillabaisse, it is a fisherman's delight.

Vegetable oil cooking spray and 1 1/2 teaspoons olive oil

2 garlic cloves, minced

1 large onion, chopped

1 small (4-ounce) all-purpose potato, peeled and sliced

8 ounces clam juice or fish broth

16-ounce can stewed tomatoes, undrained

12-ounce can evaporated skimmed milk, undiluted

1/2 teaspoon dried thyme leaves

1 pound fresh or frozen mild white fish (hake, flounder, turbot, etc.)
   Only partially defrost frozen fish, so it doesn't get mushy.

1 cup of fresh, frozen, or canned corn, drained

Freshly ground pepper to taste; salt if you desire

Heat a generous amount of vegetable oil spray and the olive oil in a large, heavy pot. Stir in the garlic and onions, and sauté over medium-low heat for 3 minutes, stirring frequently (you may have to add 1 to 2 teaspoons of water to prevent the onions from burning). Puree the potato in a food processor or blender. Scrape the sides of the container, then add the clam juice, and puree for 15 seconds more. Pour the mixture into the pot. Stir in the stewed tomatoes, evaporated milk, and thyme. Bring just to a boil, then reduce heat, stir, cover, and simmer for 10 minutes. Stir occasionally. Cut the fish into 1-inch cubes, and stir into the stew. Stir in the corn, and bring to the boiling point over medium-high heat. Immediately reduce the heat, cover, and simmer for 20 to 25 minutes, stirring occasionally. Season to taste, and serve with bread and a salad.

Preparation time: 10 minutes. Cooking time: 45 minutes. Yield: 6 servings

Nutrition analysis: 248 calories per serving; 21 gm. protein; 28 gm. carbohydrate; 6.5 gm. fat; 47.5 mg. cholesterol; 2 gm. fiber; 460 mg. sodium

Percent of calories from protein: 34%; from carbohydrates: 44%; from fat: 22%

Exchange values: ½ milk; 2 vegetable; ½ bread; 2 meat; ½ fat

Fish Kebobs

My teenagers love it when I make this recipe. Somehow it makes them feel like they're not eating fish.

Marinade:

2 tablespoons honey

1 tablespoon Dijon mustard

1/4 teaspoon curry powder

1 tablespoon lemon juice

1/2 pound sea scallops or large shrimp, peeled

3/4 pound tuna, swordfish, or salmon fillets, or firm, grillable white fish

1 large red pepper, sliced into eighths and cut in half

1 yellow onion, peeled and sliced into eighths

1/2 pound mushrooms, washed, dried, and stemmed (optional)

1 small zucchini, cut into 1/2-inch rounds (optional)

8 cherry tomatoes

Vegetable oil cooking spray

4 long skewers

Mix the marinade ingredients together in a medium bowl. Cut fish into 1-inch cubes. Stir the cubed fish into the marinade, and set aside for a few minutes. Preheat the grill or broiler. If you use metal skewers, spray them with cooking spray. Assemble the kebobs, starting each skewer with a piece of fish, then alternate 2 pieces of vegetables with a piece of fish. Generously brush the vegetables and fish with marinade. Grill on a medium-hot grill for 6 to 7 minutes. Brush with marinade, then flip the skewers. Grill 5 to 6 more minutes or until the fish is cooked. Remove the fish and vegetables from the skewers, and serve with white or brown rice if desired.

Preparation time: 15 minutes. Grilling time: 15 minutes. Yield: 4 servings

Nutrition analysis: 233 calories per serving; 32.5 gm. protein; 21.5 gm. carbohydrate; 2 gm. fat; 57 mg. cholesterol; 2.5 gm. fiber; 227 mg. sodium

Percent of calories from protein: 55%; from carbohydrates: 37%; from fat: 8%

Exchange values: 2 vegetable; 4 meat

Fish With
Cucumber Salsa

I prefer to cook fresh fish in a simple manner and serve it with fresh salsa or lemon. This cucumber salsa is great on grilled swordfish or tuna, but it's also good on baked sole or most any fish.

1 1/4 pound fresh fish fillets (sole, flounder, salmon, tuna, or swordfish), about 1 inch thick

1/2 teaspoon olive oil

Vegetable oil cooking spray

Juice of 1/2 lemon

Cucumber Olive Salsa:

3/4 cup peeled, chopped, and seeded cucumber

8 to 10 medium-sized pimento-stuffed green olives, chopped

1 scallion, chopped (use the white with some green)

4 medium-sized basil leaves, chopped

1 teaspoon olive oil

2 to 4 teaspoons lime juice

1/2 teaspoon anchovy paste (optional)

Salt and freshly ground pepper to taste

To grill or broil fish: Salmon, swordfish, or tuna can be grilled over medium-hot heat or broiled for 5 to 6 minutes per side for each inch of thickness or until the fish is no longer translucent. You may want to brush the fish with a touch of olive oil first.

To bake fish fillets (sole, flounder, etc.): Preheat oven to 375°. Generously spray a broiler-proof, shallow baking pan with cooking spray. Brush both sides of the fish with a touch of olive oil, then sprinkle with some lemon juice. Bake the fish uncovered in a preheated oven for 10 to 11 minutes for each inch of thickness. Do not flip or turn the fish. (A ½-inch-thick fillet would bake for 5 to 6 minutes, and a ¾ inch fillet would bake for 7 to 8 minutes). Baste the fish with some more lemon juice, then broil one side only of the fish 3 inches from the flame for about 2 minutes or until the fish is opaque and flaky. (Firm fish like halibut or monk fish may require more baking time.)

To make the salsa: Put all the salsa ingredients in a food processor or blender. Process until everything is well chopped but not pureed. Salt and pepper to taste. Serve the fish covered with salsa.

Preparation time: 10 minutes. Cooking time: 10 to 12 minutes for each inch of thickness. Yield: 4 servings

Nutrition analysis: 147 calories per serving; 24.5 gm. protein; 2 gm. carbohydrate; 5 gm. fat; 67.5 mg. cholesterol; 0.5 gm. fiber; 343 mg. sodium

Percent of calories from protein: 67%; from carbohydrates: 5%; from fat: 28%

Exchange values: 3½ meat; ½ fat

Fish Sticks

───────────

Vegetable oil cooking spray

1 pound white fish fillet, about 1 inch thick
(sole, flounder, etc.)

Salt, pepper, paprika, and ground mace

Flour

2 large egg whites, slightly beaten

1/3 cup seasoned bread crumbs

2 tablespoons grated Parmesan or Romano cheese

2 teaspoons Butter Buds, natural dehydrated butter

Getting children to eat fish can be a challenge; that's why I invented this quick, easy, and delicious dish. These fish sticks are popular with adults as well as children, and they're much healthier and better tasting than the frozen variety.

KIDS
LOVE
THIS

Preheat the oven to 350°. Spray a cookie sheet with cooking spray. Wash and dry the fillets, then cut them into sticks about 1 inch wide and 5 to 6 inches long. Lightly season the fish with salt, pepper, paprika, and ground mace. Dust the fish with flour, then dip into the beaten egg whites. Mix the bread crumbs, grated cheese, and Butter Buds together. Roll the fish sticks into the bread crumb mixture. Place them on the prepared cookie sheet, and bake for 10 to 20 minutes or until the fish is thoroughly cooked without being dried out. (The cooking time will depend on the thickness and type of fish; you should check them after 10 minutes.)

Preparation time: 10 minutes. Cooking time: 10 to 25 minutes. Yield: 4 servings

Nutrition analysis: 180 calories per serving; 28 gm. protein; 6.5 gm. carbohydrate; 4 gm. fat; 39 mg. cholesterol; 0.5 gm. fiber; 208 mg. sodium

Percent of calories from protein: 64%; from carbohydrates: 15%; from fat: 21%

Exchange values: ½ bread; 3 meat

Grilled Swordfish

Buy swordfish steak that is translucent and shiny with red bloodlines. Gray, dull flesh with brown bloodlines is old or previously frozen and should be avoided. Grill or broil the swordfish steak 5 to 6 minutes a side for each inch of thickness. This helps to prevent over-cooking the fish, which can become dry very quickly.

Tomato tapenade for fish:

1/2 cup seeded and finely chopped ripe tomatoes

2 tablespoons finely chopped black olives

1 tablespoon capers

1 finely chopped scallion (use both the white and green parts)

1 tablespoon anchovy paste, or less to taste (usually sold in tubes next to the anchovy tins, or you can make your own by mashing anchovy fillets)

1 teaspoon olive oil (optional)

1 tablespoon lemon juice

Freshly ground pepper to taste

Juice of 1/2 lemon

1 pound swordfish or tuna steak, about 1 inch thick

Preheat grill or broiler. Combine the first 8 ingredients in a small bowl to make the tomato tapenade. Set aside, and let marinate at room temperature while you prepare the fish. Pour the lemon juice over both sides of the fish. Grill over medium-hot heat or broil the fish about 5 to 6 minutes a side for each inch of thickness or until done and the swordfish has turned opaque. Remove from heat, and cover with the tomato tapenade. Grilled swordfish is also good served with a little lemon juice, salt, and pepper.

Preparation time: 10 minutes. Cooking time: 10 minutes. Yield: 4 servings

Nutrition analysis: 179 calories per serving; 24 gm. protein; 3.5 gm. carbohydrate; 7.5 gm. fat; 47 mg. cholesterol; 0.5 gm. fiber; 282 mg. sodium

Percent of calories from protein: 54%; from carbohydrates: 7%; from fat: 38%

Exchange values: ½ vegetable; 3 meat; ½ fat

Grilled Tuna

Marinating your tuna steak will enhance its flavor and help keep it moist.

1 pound tuna steak, about 1 inch thick

Marinade:

1/4 cup dry white wine

2 teaspoons lemon juice

1 tablespoon olive oil

1/2 teaspoon Dijon mustard

1 garlic clove, crushed

10 peppercorns, crushed

1/2 tablespoon of a minced, fresh herb such as rosemary, dill, or thyme can be added for a different flavor (optional)

Wash and dry the tuna steak. Mix the marinade together in a shallow pan big enough to fit the tuna steak. Dip both sides of the tuna in the marinade. Place the tuna in the marinade, cover, and refrigerate for 2 to 6 hours. Flip the tuna once or twice while marinating. Preheat the grill or broiler to medium-hot. Remove the tuna from the marinade, and grill the tuna about 5 minutes on each side or until done and opaque.

Preparation time: 5 minutes. Marinating time: 2 to 6 hours. Cooking time: 10 minutes. Yield: 4 servings

Nutrition analysis: 151 calories per serving; 26.5 gm. protein; 1 gm. carbohydrate; 4.5 gm. fat; 51 mg. cholesterol; 0 fiber; 59 mg. sodium

Percent of calories from protein: 70%; from carbohydrates: 3%; from fat: 27%

Exchange values: 4 meat; ½ fat

Poached Fish
With Marinated
Artichokes

1 pound fresh, firm fish fillets or steak,
  such as salmon or halibut, about 1 inch thick

Water or a mixture of water, fish stock,
  and dry white wine

Juice of 1 small lemon

1/2 teaspoon salt

1 tablespoon chopped fresh parsley

6-ounce jar marinated artichoke hearts, drained and chopped

Rinse the fish and pat dry. Pour 2 to 3 inches of water or a water/fish stock/white wine combination into a wide skillet or pan. Stir in the lemon juice, salt, and parsley. Bring to a boil, then carefully place the fish in the pan. Return just to a boil, then immediately reduce heat. Cover, and simmer for 8 to 12 minutes for each inch of thickness, or until the fish is opaque. Remove the fish with a slotted spatula or spoon, drain the fillets well, and serve the fish covered with chopped marinated artichoke hearts.

Preparation time: 5 minutes. Cooking time: 8 to 12 minutes per inch. Yield: 4 servings

Nutrition analysis: 150 calories per serving; 24 gm. protein; 2.5 gm. carbohydrate; 4 gm. fat; 36.5 mg. cholesterol; 0.5 gm. fiber; 418 mg. sodium

Percent of calories from protein: 68%; from carbohydrates: 7%; from fat: 26%

Exchange values: 2½ meat; ½ fat

Fish Fry

1 pound thin white fish fillets (sole, flounder, etc.)

Paprika, salt, and pepper

2 to 3 teaspoons Dijon mustard or your
favorite gourmet mustard

1/4 to 1/3 cup cornmeal

Vegetable oil cooking spray

2 teaspoons canola oil or low-in-saturated-fat vegetable oil

Wash and dry the fillets. Lightly season them, and spread Dijon mustard on each side. Roll the fillets in the cornmeal. Spray a large skillet with cooking spray; add the oil, and heat it over medium heat until hot, but not burned. Place the fillets in the skillet so they are not on top of each other. Cook each side for 3 to 5 minutes, being careful not to burn or dry out the fish. (You may have to spray the skillet again before flipping the fish.)

KIDS
LOVE
THIS

Preparation time: 5 minutes. Cooking time: 10 minutes. Yield: 4 servings

Nutrition analysis: 153 calories per serving; 20 gm. protein; 8 gm. carbohydrate; 4 gm. fat; 53 mg. cholesterol; 1.5 gm. fiber; 180 mg. sodium

Percentage of calories from protein: 54%; from carbohydrates: 22%; from fat: 25%

Exchange values: ½ bread; 2½ meat; ½ fat

DESSERTS
AND
OTHER DELIGHTS

Strawberry Royale

1 quart cleaned and hulled strawberries

1 banana

1 to 2 tablespoons banana liqueur

Sugar to taste

Place 3 large strawberries, half of the banana, and the banana liqueur in a food processor or blender. Purée completely. Slice, then sweeten the remaining strawberries and banana. Place the fruit in individual dessert bowls, and cover with the strawberry purée.

Preparation time: 10 minutes. Yield: 4 servings

Nutrition analysis: 93 calories per serving; 1 gm. protein; 20 gm. carbohydrate; 1 gm. fat; 0 cholesterol; 4.5 gm. fiber; 2 mg. sodium

Percent of calories from protein: 4%; from carbohydrates: 86%; from fat: 10%

Exchange values: 1 fruit

Cranberry Cheese Mousse

This combination of tart cranberries with sweet, whipped cottage cheese creates a wonderful light and delicious taste. I usually serve this dish as a dessert, but it is also delicious when served with turkey.

Vegetable oil cooking spray

1/4 cup orange juice

1 envelope plus 1 1/2 teaspoons unflavored gelatin

1 cup low-fat (1%) cottage cheese

1/2 cup nonfat plain yogurt

4 tablespoons powdered sugar, or to taste

1 tablespoon honey

16-ounce can or 1 2/3 cups whole-cranberry sauce

2 tablespoons orange, peach, or raspberry liqueur (optional),
   Or 2 tablespoons orange juice plus a little more powdered sugar

KIDS LOVE THIS

Spray a 6-cup mold with cooking spray. Pour the orange juice into a small saucepan. Sprinkle gelatin over the juice. Let soften for 5 minutes. Heat the gelatin mixture over low heat until dissolved. Remove from heat, and let cool slightly. Put the cottage cheese and yogurt in a large food processor. Process on high for 3 minutes, scraping the sides often. Add the powdered sugar, honey, cranberry sauce, and liqueur, and process on high for 1 more minute. Stir in the gelatin mixture, check for sweetness, and process 10 more seconds. Pour the mixture into the mold. Refrigerate for at least 2 hours or until firm. Unmold the mousse, and serve cold.

Preparation time: 10 minutes. Refrigeration time: 2 to 4 hours. Yield: 6 servings

Nutrition analysis: 207 calories per serving; 8 gm. protein; 42.5 gm. carbohydrate; 0.5 gm. fat; 2 mg. cholesterol; 1 gm. fiber; 193 mg. sodium

Percent of calories from protein: 16%; from carbohydrates: 82%; from fat: 2%

Exchange values: 2 fruit; ½ meat

Cindy's Crumb Cake

Vegetable oil cooking spray

2 tablespoons canola oil or low-in-saturated-fat vegetable oil

2/3 to 3/4 cup sugar

1 large whole egg, slightly beaten

2 tablespoons ripe, well-mashed banana

1/2 teaspoon vanilla extract

2 cups stirred unbleached all-purpose flour

1/8 teaspoon salt

3 teaspoons baking powder (don't use old baking powder; it loses its leavening ability)

1 cup skim or 1% milk

Crumb topping:

2/3 cup unbleached all-purpose flour

1 teaspoon cinnamon

1/2 cup brown sugar

2 tablespoons honey

1 tablespoon canola oil or low-in-saturated-fat vegetable oil

Preheat oven to 350°. Spray a 9" x 9" pan with cooking spray. In a large bowl, beat the oil, sugar, egg, banana, and vanilla extract together. Set aside. Sift together the flour, salt, and baking powder. Quickly beat the dry ingredients into the banana/sugar mixture alternating with the milk until everything is mixed well. Pour into the prepared pan.

Mix the crumb topping ingredients in a small bowl until crumbly. Sprinkle the topping on the batter. Bake for 30 to 35 minutes or until a cake tester comes out clean. Let cool completely before serving.

Preparation time: 15 minutes. Cooking time: 30 to 35 minutes. Yield: 9 servings

Nutrition analysis: 303 calories per serving; 4.5 gm. protein; 59.5 gm. carbohydrate; 5.7 gm. fat; 25 mg. cholesterol; 1 gm. fiber; 165 mg. sodium

Percent of calories from protein: 6%; from carbohydrates: 78%; from fat: 17%

Exchange values: 1½ bread; 1 fat

Cranberry Crisp

Vegetable oil cooking spray

2 cups whole cranberries, washed and dried

1/4 cup sweet sherry

2/3 to 3/4 cup granulated sugar

1 tablespoon unbleached all-purpose flour

Crisp Topping:

2/3 cup unbleached all-purpose flour

1 teaspoon cinnamon

1/2 cup brown sugar

1 tablespoon honey

2 tablespoons canola oil or low-in-saturated-fat vegetable oil

Preheat oven to 325°. Spray a 9-inch glass pie plate with cooking spray. Pour in the cranberries, and stir in the sherry. In a small bowl, mix the sugar and flour together. Stir into the cranberry mixture.

Mix the topping ingredients together until crumbly. Sprinkle the topping over the cranberry mixture. Bake for 45 to 50 minutes. Let cool, then serve plain or topped with nonfat frozen vanilla yogurt.

Preparation time: 10 minutes. Cooking time: 45 to 50 minutes. Yield: 6 to 8 servings

Nutrition analysis for 6 servings: 284 calories per serving; 1 gm. protein; 60 gm. carbohydrate; 4.5 gm. fat; 0 cholesterol; 0.5 gm. fiber; 7 mg. sodium

Percent of calories from protein: 1%; from carbohydrates: 85%; from fat: 14%

Exchange values: ½ fruit; ½ bread; 1 fat

Raspberry Delight

This delightfully light dessert is easy to make and delicious to eat.

1 envelope unflavored gelatin

3 to 4 tablespoons sugar (use 4 tablespoons if you omit the liqueur)

1/2 cup orange juice

12-ounce bag frozen raspberries, thawed

2 tablespoons orange or raspberry liqueur (optional) or 2 additional teaspoons orange juice

1 cup nonfat plain yogurt

Vegetable oil cooking spray

KIDS LOVE THIS

Stir the gelatin, sugar, and orange juice together in a medium saucepan. Heat and stir over medium-low heat, just to the boiling point, until the gelatin is dissolved. Remove from heat, and stir in well the raspberries (and juice, if any), liqueur, and yogurt. Mix thoroughly. Pour into a 3-cup mold or six individual dessert bowls that have been sprayed with cooking spray. Cover, and chill until set. Serve plain or garnished with fresh raspberries.

Preparation time: 10 minutes. Chilling time: 4 hours. Yield: 6 servings

Nutrition analysis: 128 calories per serving; 4 gm. protein; 28 gm. carbohydrate; 0 fat; 1 mg. cholesterol; 2.5 gm. fiber; 31.5 mg. sodium

Percent of calories from protein: 12%; from carbohydrates: 88%; from fat: 0

Exchange values: 1 fruit

Pear Creme

This delicious, light dessert has captured my heart because its rich, creamy taste hides the fact that it has very little fat. So serve it often when pears are in season.

Vegetable oil cooking spray

1 teaspoon sugar

2 large, ripe Bartlett pears

1/2 cup low-fat evaporated milk, undiluted

1/2 cup 1% milk

2 tablespoons sugar

1 tablespoon banana liqueur or sweet creme sherry

1 teaspoon Butter Buds, natural dehydrated butter

1/2 teaspoon vanilla extract

1 1/2 tablespoons all-purpose flour

1 1/2 tablespoons cornstarch

Preheat oven to 400°. Spray a 10-inch glass pie plate with cooking spray. Sprinkle the bottom of the pie plate with 1 teaspoon sugar. Peel the pears, cut them in half from the stem down, and remove the cores. Put the pears cut side down in the pie plate. Mix all the other ingredients together well, then pour the mixture over the pears. Bake the pears for 25 to 30 minutes or until tender but not mushy, basting them often with the sauce on the bottom of the pie plate. Serve warm.

Preparation time: 10 minutes. Cooking time: 25 to 30 minutes. Yield: 4 servings

Nutrition analysis: 149 calories per serving; 4 gm. protein; 31 gm. carbohydrate; 1 gm. fat; 3 mg. cholesterol; 2 gm. fiber; 50.5 mg. sodium

Percent of calories from protein: 11%; from carbohydrates: 83%; from fat: 6%

Exchange values: ½ milk; 1 fruit; ½ bread

230   Fear of Frying

Chocolate Marshmallow Cookies

These cookies taste almost too rich to be in a low-fat and low-cholesterol cookbook. They're definitely a family favorite.

Vegetable oil cooking spray

2 cups unsifted but well-stirred unbleached, all-purpose flour

1/2 teaspoon baking soda

1/4 teaspoon salt (optional)

3/4 cup granulated sugar

1/4 cup unsweetened cocoa powder

1 ounce square unsweetened baking chocolate, melted

3 tablespoons canola oil or low-in-saturated-fat vegetable oil

1/4 cup marshmallow topping

1/2 cup nonfat plain yogurt

1 teaspoon vanilla extract

1 large egg

Preheat the oven to 350°. Spray cookie sheets with cooking spray. Mix the flour, baking soda, salt, sugar, and cocoa powder together. Set aside. Beat the rest of the ingredients together in a large bowl. Stir in the dry ingredients until a sticky but firm batter is formed. Drop teaspoonfuls of the batter about 2 inches apart on the prepared cookie sheets. Bake for 8 to 9 minutes or until the cookies start to get firm on the top. Remove cookies from the cookie sheet immediately.

Preparation time: 15 minutes. Cooking time: 8 to 9 minutes. Yield: 50 cookies

Nutrition analysis: 48 calories per serving; 1 gm. protein; 9 gm. carbohydrate; 1.3 gm. fat; 4.5 mg. cholesterol; 0 fiber; 23.5 mg. sodium

Percent of calories from protein: 6%; from carbohydrates: 70%; from fat: 24%

Exchange values: less than ½ bread; less than ½ fat

The Easiest Apple Cranberry Crisp

This dessert has no added fat and is very popular with the kids, who love the crisp cereal topping.

Vegetable oil cooking spray

6 cups peeled, cored, and sliced apples

1/2 cup whole fresh cranberries, washed and chopped (by hand or in the food processor)

1/2 to 3/4 cup packed brown sugar

1 teaspoon ground cinnamon

Dash of nutmeg (I prefer freshly ground nutmeg)

KIDS LOVE THIS

Cereal topping:

2 cups low-fat granola, Mueslix® Honey Bunches of Oats® or a similar low-fat cereal

2 tablespoons honey

Preheat oven to 350°. Spray a flat 2-quart baking dish with cooking spray. Mix the fruit, sugar, and spices thoroughly. Pour into the prepared baking dish. Stir the cereal and honey together well, and sprinkle over the apple mixture. Bake for 30 to 40 minutes or until the fruit is tender but not mushy. Serve warm or cold, plain or with frozen vanilla yogurt.

Preparation time: 15 minutes. Cooking time: 30 to 40 minutes. Yield: 6 to 8 servings

Nutrition analysis for 6 servings: 288 calories per serving; 2.5 gm. protein; 70.5 gm. carbohydrate; 2 gm. fat; 0 cholesterol; 4 gm. fiber; 49.5 mg. sodium

Percent of calories from protein: 3%; from carbohydrates: 91%; from fat: 6%

Exchange values: 1½ fruit; ½ fat

Holiday Harvest Cake

I invented this recipe when I was trying to make a new dessert for Thanksgiving. I was pleased to find that the mincemeat adds moistness but not a heavy taste. That first cake was so successful that I now stock up on mincemeat during the holidays so I can make it year-round.

1 1/2 cups stirred all-purpose flour

1 cup stirred whole wheat flour

2 teaspoons baking soda

1 teaspoon baking powder

1/4 teaspoon salt (optional)

1/2 to 2/3 cup granulated sugar

1 teaspoon vanilla extract

1/2 teaspoon rum extract

3 tablespoons mild-tasting honey

1 whole large egg

2 large egg whites

2 tablespoons canola oil or low-in-saturated-fat vegetable oil

3/4 cup prepared mincemeat

3/4 cup unsweetened applesauce

1 cup skim buttermilk

Sherry glaze:

1 tablespoon light butter

1/2 to 3/4 cup powdered sugar

1 tablespoon cream sherry

Preheat oven to 350°. Grease and flour a 12-cup one-piece Bundt™ pan or tube pan. Sift the dry ingredients together in a large bowl. Set aside. Beat the vanilla, rum extract, honey, eggs, oil, mincemeat, and applesauce together in another bowl. Stir the liquid ingredients into the dry ingredients alternating with the buttermilk. Pour the batter into the prepared pan. Bake for 40 to 50 minutes or until a cake tester comes out clean. Cool, remove from pan, and drizzle with Sherry Glaze.

To make the glaze, melt the butter in a small saucepan. Stir in the powdered sugar and cream sherry until the desired consistency is reached. Let cool slightly, and drizzle over the cake.

Preparation time: 15 minutes. Cooking time: 40 to 50 minutes. Yield: 14 servings

Nutrition analysis with glaze: 276 calories per serving; 4 gm. protein; 57 gm. carbohydrate; 3.5 gm. fat; 16 mg. cholesterol; 2 gm. fiber; 365 mg. sodium

Percent of calories from protein: 6%; from carbohydrates: 83%; from fat: 11%

Exchange values: 1½ fruit; 1 bread; ½ fat

Kahlua Chocolate Cake

This recipe makes a rich, decadent-tasting cake with less fat and cholesterol than you would expect. Serve it on those special occasions when you want to serve an attractive and delicious chocolate dessert.

Cocoa powder for dusting

2 cups sifted all-purpose flour

1 1/2 teaspoons baking soda

2 teaspoons double-acting baking powder

1/4 teaspoon nutmeg

1/4 teaspoon salt

9 level tablespoons unsweetened cocoa powder

1 1/4 cups granulated sugar

1-ounce square unsweetened baking chocolate

1/2 cup canola oil or low-in-saturated-fat vegetable oil

1 1/2 cups skim buttermilk

1/4 cup honey

1/4 cup Kahlua or coffee liqueur

2 teaspoons vanilla extract

1 large whole egg

4 large egg whites

Mocha glaze:

1 tablespoon unsweetened cocoa powder

1 tablespoon plus 1 teaspoon water

3 tablespoons powdered sugar

2 teaspoons Kahlua or coffee liqueur

Preheat oven to 350°. Grease a 12-cup Bundt pan and dust it with cocoa powder. Sift the flour, baking soda, and baking powder together. Stir in the nutmeg, salt, cocoa powder, and sugar. Set aside. Melt the chocolate square and vegetable oil together in

Kahlua Chocolate Cake (continued)

the microwave on high for 1 to 2 minutes, or in a double boiler. Stir the chocolate and vegetable oil, and set aside. In a large bowl, beat the buttermilk, honey, Kahlua, vanilla, and eggs together well. Slowly stir in the dry ingredients. Beat in the melted chocolate/oil mixture for 30 seconds. Pour into the prepared pan, and bake for 50 to 60 minutes. Let cool, then remove from pan.

To make the Mocha Glaze, combine the cocoa powder, water, and powdered sugar in a small saucepan. Bring the glaze to a boil over medium heat, stirring constantly. Remove from the heat, stir in the Kahlua, and continue stirring until everything is dissolved. Cool slightly, then brush on the cake. Or if you prefer a slightly thicker glaze, cool the glaze until it's slightly thicker, then drizzle over the cake.

Preparation time: 15 minutes. Cooking time: 50 to 60 minutes. Yield: 14 pieces

Nutrition analysis: 274 calories per serving; 4.6 gm. protein; 43 gm. carbohydrate; 10 gm. fat; 16 mg. cholesterol; 0.5 gm. fiber; 225 mg. sodium

Percent of calories from protein: 7%; from carbohydrates: 61%; from fat: 32%

Exchange values: 1 bread; 2 fat

Lorna's Easy Blueberry Pie

Many people don't like to make pies because the dough doesn't always cooperate. Lorna's no-roll crust solves the problem— the crust is pressed into the pan instead of rolled out.

No-roll crust:

Vegetable oil cooking spray

1/4 cup canola oil or low-in-saturated-fat vegetable oil

1 tablespoon honey

2 tablespoons skim milk

1/3 to 1/2 teaspoon salt

1 cup stirred unbleached, all-purpose flour

Filling:

1 pint fresh blueberries, rinsed and dried

Streusel topping:

1/3 cup sugar

2 tablespoons all-purpose flour

Dash of salt

1 tablespoon honey

Preheat oven to 375°. Spray a 9-inch glass pie pan with cooking spray. Beat the oil, honey, skim milk, and salt together in a medium bowl. Stir in the flour, and continue stirring until everything is moist. Press the dough together, and place in the prepared pie pan. Pat the dough out with your fingertips until it covers the bottom of the pan and two-thirds of the way up the side. Make sure all cracks in the dough are pressed together. Fill the crust with the blueberries. (If the blueberries are very juicy, stir in 1 to 2 teaspoons of flour.)

Mix the streusel ingredients together with a fork until everything is moist and granular. Sprinkle the streusel over the berries. Press the pie dough down along the sides

Desserts and Other Delights

Lorna's Easy Blueberry Pie (continued)

until it is even with the blueberries, not higher. Bake for 30 to 35 minutes or until the crust is a caramel color and the blueberries are bubbling. Cool before serving.

Preparation time: 10 minutes. Cooking time: 30 to 35 minutes. Yield: 6 to 8 servings

Nutrition analysis: 245 calories per serving; 2 gm. protein; 39.5 gm. carbohydrate; 9.5 gm. fat; 0 cholesterol; 1.5 gm. fiber; 184 mg. sodium

Percent of calories from protein: 3%; from carbohydrates: 63%; from fat: 34%

Exchange values: ½ fruit; 1 bread; 2 fat

Patty's Prune Cake

This is a recipe that my friend Patty shared with me one day while we were watching the kids play volleyball. The prunes keep it moist and sweet and the spices give it an interesting flavor.

2 tablespoons canola oil or low-in-saturated-fat vegetable oil

2/3 to 3/4 cup granulated sugar

1 whole large egg

2 large egg whites

1/3 cup Solo® prune plum filling (Lekvar) (sold in a can with the canned pie fillings. This product can be used as a natural baking fat substitute.)

2/3 cup sour low-fat or skim milk*

1 teaspoon vanilla extract

1 1/3 cup stirred all-purpose flour

1/2 teaspoon baking powder

1/2 teaspoon baking soda

1/4 teaspoon salt

1/2 teaspoon ground cinnamon

1/4 teaspoon ground nutmeg

1/4 teaspoon ground allspice

Preheat oven to 350°. Grease an 8-inch round cake pan. Using an electric beater, beat the liquid ingredients and prune plum filling together in a medium bowl on high for 1 minute or until completely mixed. Set aside. Stir the dry ingredients together thoroughly. Stir the dry ingredients into the liquid ingredients. Beat on high for 1 minute. Pour into the prepared pan, and bake for 30 to 35 minutes or until a cake tester comes out clean.

*Note: To make sour milk, stir a teaspoon of vinegar into the milk. Warm it in the microwave on medium for 2 minutes or let it stand at room temperature for 1 hour. Stir before using.

Patty's Prune Cake (continued)

Preparation time: 10 minutes. Cooking time: 30 to 35 minutes. Yield: 6 servings

Nutrition analysis: 282 calories per serving; 5 gm. protein; 53 gm. carbohydrate; 6 gm. fat; 36.5 mg. cholesterol; 1 gm. fiber; 239 mg. sodium

Percent of calories from protein: 7%; from carbohydrates: 74%; from fat: 19%

Exchange values: ½ fruit; 1½ bread; ½ meat; 1 fat

Chip's Wacky Cake

I don't know who invented the original wacky cake, but my friend Chip taught me how to make it in college. I taught my children how to make this healthier version, and they have enjoyed making it ever since. It's a fun rainy day project for kids, and there is practically nothing to clean up.

Vegetable oil cooking spray

1 1/2 cups unsifted all-purpose flour

3 rounded tablespoons unsweetened cocoa powder

1 teaspoon baking soda

1/4 teaspoon salt

3/4 cup granulated sugar

2 1/2 tablespoons canola oil or low-in-saturated-fat vegetable oil

2 teaspoons plain red or white vinegar

1 teaspoon vanilla extract

1 cup cold water

4 tablespoons chocolate syrup

Powdered sugar (optional)

KIDS LOVE THIS

Preheat oven to 350°. Spray an 8-inch square pan with cooking spray. Put a flour sifter in the pan. Place the flour, cocoa, and baking soda into the sifter, and sift into the pan. Stir in the salt and sugar with a fork until the cocoa and sugar are evenly distributed. Make three holes in the flour/sugar mixture. Pour the oil into one hole. Pour the vinegar into the second hole and the vanilla into the third. Mix the water and chocolate syrup together, and pour that over the ingredients in the pan. Mix thoroughly with a fork, taking care that you get into the corners and bottom of the pan. Bake for 30 to 35 minutes or until a cake tester comes out clean. Let cool, and dust with powdered sugar if desired.

Preparation time: 10 minutes. Cooking time: 30 to 35 minutes. Yield: 9 servings

Nutrition analysis: 205 calories per serving; 4 gm. protein; 36 gm. carbohydrate; 5.5 gm. fat; 0 cholesterol; 0.5 gm. fiber; 167 mg. sodium

Percent of calories from protein: 8%; from carbohydrates: 69%; from fat: 23%

Exchange values: 1 bread; 1 fat

Desserts and Other Delights

English Biscuit Cookies

This is a basic rolled cookie recipe that tastes a little like an English biscuit. It produces a firm cookie dough that is easy to handle and cut. Have the kids help you roll out the dough and use the cookie cutter.

Vegetable oil cooking spray

2 tablespoons margarine or light butter, melted

2 tablespoons light cream cheese, softened

2 tablespoons canola oil or low-in-saturated-fat vegetable oil

3 tablespoons honey

1 large egg

2 teaspoons vanilla extract (1/4 teaspoon almond flavoring can be added for a slight taste of almond)

1/4 cup granulated sugar

2 cups unsifted but stirred unbleached, all-purpose flour

1/2 teaspoon baking powder

1/4 teaspoon baking soda

KIDS LOVE THIS

Preheat the oven to 375°. Spray a cookie sheet with cooking spray. In a large bowl, mix the margarine and cream cheese together until creamy. Add the oil, honey, egg, vanilla, and sugar, and mix thoroughly. Set aside. Stir the flour, baking powder, and baking soda together with a fork. Stir the dry ingredients into the liquid ingredients until a firm dough forms. Place a large piece of waxed paper on the counter. Sprinkle the waxed paper with flour, and roll out the dough until it's about ¼ inch thick. Cut out your favorite shapes with a cookie cutter, and place them on the prepared cookie sheet. Bake for 7 to 8 minutes or until golden on the bottom. Remove from the cookie sheet immediately.

Preparation time: 15 minutes. Cooking time: 7 to 8 minutes. Yield: 40 2-inch round cookies

Nutrition analysis: 44.5 calories per serving; 0.5 gm. protein; 7 gm. carbohydrate; 1.5 gm. fat; 6 mg. cholesterol; 0 fiber; 23 mg. sodium

Percent of calories from protein: 6%; from carbohydrates: 62%; from fat: 32%

Exchange values: ½ bread; ½ fat

Frozen Grapes

My neighbor Barb introduced me to this delightful dessert, which is good as a snack or hors d'oeuvre. The easy yet elegant, attractive, and delicious dish immediately became one of my favorites.

1 large bunch of ripe red or green seedless grapes

Wash and dry the grapes. Cut the grapes into small bunches of 3 or 4 grapes per stem. Place them in a single layer on a cookie sheet. Freeze the grapes for 3 to 4 hours or until hard. Take them out of the freezer, and serve them in an attractive serving dish. Frozen grapes are good as a dessert, as a snack (children love them), or as an appetizer with a glass of wine. As the grapes are exposed to the warmer room-temperature air, they take on a pretty, frosted look. But don't let the grapes thaw completely, as they turn mushy after being frozen.

KIDS LOVE THIS

Preparation time: 5 minutes. Freezing time: 4 hours. Yield: 4 servings

Nutrition analysis: 147 calories per serving; 1.5 gm. protein; 34 gm. carbohydrate; 0.5 gm. fat; 0 cholesterol; 3 gm. fiber; 4 mg. sodium

Percent of calories from protein: 4%; from carbohydrates: 93%; from fat: 3%

Exchange values: 2½ fruit

Desserts and Other Delights

Honey Spice Cake

This caramel-colored snack cake gets its moistness from honey and its flavor from a wonderful combination of spices.

Vegetable oil cooking spray

1/2 cup plus 2 tablespoons honey

1/4 cup to 1/3 cup packed brown sugar

1/4 cup canola oil or low-in-saturated-fat vegetable oil

1 teaspoon vanilla extract

1 whole large egg

2 large egg whites

1 cup skim milk

1/4 cup nonfat plain yogurt

1 tablespoon Butter Buds, natural dehydrated butter

1 cup sifted unbleached all-purpose flour

1 cup sifted whole wheat flour

1 teaspoon baking soda

1 teaspoon baking powder

1/4 teaspoon ground cloves

1/4 teaspoon ground mace

1 teaspoon ground cinnamon

1/4 teaspoon salt

1/2 cup raisins (optional)

KIDS LOVE THIS

Preheat oven to 350°. Spray a 9-inch square pan with cooking spray. Beat the liquid ingredients and Butter Buds together in a large bowl. Set aside. Sift both flours, baking soda, baking powder, spices, and salt together. Stir the dry ingredients into the liquid ingredients until everything is mixed well. Stir in the raisins. Pour the batter into the prepared pan. Bake for 40 to 50 minutes or until a cake tester comes out clean.

Preparation time: 15 minutes. Cooking time: 40 to 50 minutes. Yield: 9 servings

Nutrition analysis: 288 calories per serving; 5 gm. protein; 51.6 gm. carbohydrate; 7 gm. fat; 24 mg. cholesterol; 1 gm. fiber; 230 mg. sodium

Percent of calories from protein: 7%; from carbohydrates: 71%; from fat: 22%

Exchange values: 1½ bread; 1½ fat

Desserts and Other Delights

New England Baked Apples

We go apple picking every year, so I'm always trying to find new ways to cook apples. Baking has always been one of my favorite methods because the apples don't have to be peeled, which saves a lot of time. This recipe is popular because the flavors appeal to everyone.

Vegetable oil cooking spray

3 tablespoons lemon juice

1 tablespoon melted light butter

1 tablespoon Butter Buds, natural dehydrated butter

2 tablespoons pure maple syrup

3 tablespoons packed brown sugar

1/4 teaspoon rum flavor (optional)

Dash of ground cinnamon

Dash of ground nutmeg (I prefer freshly ground nutmeg)

4 medium-large firm red apples

2 to 4 tablespoons or more apple cider or apple juice

Preheat oven to 350°. Spray a 9-inch glass pie plate with cooking spray. Mix the lemon juice, melted butter, Butter Buds, maple syrup, brown sugar, rum flavor, cinnamon, and nutmeg thoroughly. Very carefully core the apples, being careful not to pierce the bottom of the apples. Fill each apple with the syrup mixture. If there is any mixture left, mix it with the apple cider, and spoon it into the bottom of the pie plate. If there isn't enough liquid to cover the bottom of the pie plate, add a few tablespoons of apple cider. Bake uncovered for 30 to 50 minutes, adding more cider if the juices evaporate too much. Hard, crisp apples take more time to bake than the softer variety. When the apples are easily pierced with a fork, remove from the oven. Let sit 5 minutes. Carefully place the apples into dessert bowls, and spoon the juices from the bottom of the pie plate over the apples. These baked apples can be served plain or with vanilla nonfat yogurt. They are great as a dessert, snack, or breakfast treat.

Preparation time: 10 minutes. Baking time: 30 to 50 minutes. Yield: 4 servings

Nutrition analysis: 174 calories per serving; 0.5 gm. protein; 41.5 gm. carbohydrate; 2.5 gm. fat; 5 mg. cholesterol; 3 gm. fiber; 34 mg. sodium

Percent of calories from protein: 1%; from carbohydrates: 88%; from fat: 11%

Exchange values: 1½ fruit; ½ fat

Sherried Fruit Crisp

I invented this recipe years ago and it quickly became a favorite.

Vegetable oil cooking spray

6 cups peeled, cored, and sliced apples, pears, or peaches

1/4 cup sweet sherry

2 tablespoons packed brown sugar

1 tablespoon unbleached all-purpose flour

1 teaspoon ground cinnamon

Crisp Topping:

2/3 cup unbleached all-purpose flour

1 teaspoon ground cinnamon

1/2 cup packed brown sugar

1 tablespoon honey

2 tablespoons canola oil or low-in-saturated-fat vegetable oil.

Preheat oven to 350°. Spray a 2-quart shallow baking dish with cooking spray. Pour in the sliced fruit, and stir in the sherry. In a small bowl, mix the sugar, flour, and cinnamon together. Stir into the fruit mixture. Make the crisp topping by mixing all the topping ingredients together until crumbly. Sprinkle the topping over the fruit mixture. Bake for 30 to 35 minutes or until the fruit is tender but not mushy. Serve warm or cool, plain or topped with nonfat frozen vanilla yogurt.

Preparation time: 10 minutes. Cooking time: 30 to 35 minutes. Yield: 6 to 8 servings

Nutrition analysis for 8 servings: 200 calories per serving; 1 gm. protein; 40 gm. carbohydrate; 4 gm. fat; 0 cholesterol; 2 gm. fiber; 6 mg. sodium

Percent of calories from protein: 2%; from carbohydrates: 28%; from fat: 16%

Exchange values: 1 fruit; ½ bread; ½ fat

Tofruity Shake

I'm not very fond of tofu, but, because of its health benefits, I looked for a way to incorporate it in my diet. This fruit shake's deliciously sweet and fruity taste hides the taste of the tofu. It uses strawberries, but peaches and nectarines are equally tasty. Be creative and use your favorite fruit or berry.

1/3 cup or 3 ounces drained, soft, cold tofu

4 hulled, large strawberries, fresh or frozen

1/2 medium-sized banana

1/4 cup cold skim milk

1/2 cup cold, nonfat strawberry yogurt

1 tablespoon honey, or to taste

Put all the ingredients in a large blender. Blend on high for 1 minute or until completely smooth and creamy. Serve cold in a tall glass.

Preparation time: a few minutes. Yield: 1 serving (1¾ to 2 cups)

Nutrition analysis: 266 calories per serving; 14 gm. protein; 45.5 gm. carbohydrate; 4.5 gm. fat; 1 mg. cholesterol; 3 gm. fiber; 90 mg. sodium

Percent of calories from protein: 20%; from carbohydrates: 65%; from fat: 15%

Exchange values: 1 fruit; ½ bread; 1 meat

Piña Colada Shake

Enjoy a touch of the islands for breakfast or a snack.

1/2 cup cold nonfat plain or pineapple yogurt

1/4 cup cold orange or pineapple juice

1 cup cold fresh pineapple chunks or well-drained, naturally-sweetened canned pineapple

1/4 to 1/2 teaspoon coconut extract (optional)

1 tablespoon oat bran

Honey to taste

Combine all the ingredients in a large blender or food processor, and blend until smooth. Pour into a tall glass, and serve immediately.

Preparation time: 5 minutes. Yield: 1½ cups or 1 to 2 servings

Nutrition analysis for 1 serving: 249 calories per serving; 8.7 gm. protein; 54.5 gm. carbohydrate; 1.5 gm. fat; 2 mg. cholesterol; 3 gm. fiber; 91 mg. sodium

Percent of calories from protein: 13%; from carbohydrates: 82%; from fat: 5%

Exchange values: ½ milk; 1½ fruit

Sunshine Shake

I don't like the taste of carrot juice alone, but I found that combining carrot juice, orange juice, and bananas makes a delicious shake that's filled with heart-healthy antioxidants. This makes a wonderful breakfast-on-the-go drink or a delicious snack.

1 cup cold fresh orange juice

1/2 cup cold carrot juice*

1 small ripe banana, peeled

Combine all the ingredients in a large blender or food processor, and blend until smooth. Pour into a tall glass, and serve immediately.

Preparation time: 5 minutes. Yield: 2 servings

Nutrition analysis: 133 calories per serving; 2 gm. protein; 32 gm. carbohydrate; 0.5 gm. fat; 0 cholesterol; 3.4 gm. fiber; 19.6 mg. sodium

Percent of calories from protein: 6%; from carbohydrates: 90%; from fat: 4%

Exchange values: 1 vegetable; 2 fruit

*If you don't have carrot juice, just add an additional ½ cup of orange juice or your favorite fruit juice.

Banana Strawberry Shake

1 small ripe banana, peeled and sliced

4 to 6 cold strawberries, washed, dried, stemmed, and sliced

1/2 cup cold nonfat plain yogurt (strawberry or banana yogurt can also be used)

1/2 cup cold skim milk

1 tablespoon honey, or to taste

Dash of vanilla extract (optional)

Put all the ingredients in a large blender or food processor, and blend until smooth. Pour into a tall glass, and serve immediately.

Preparation time: a few minutes. Yield: about 1½ cups

Nutrition analysis: 352 calories per serving; 11.5 gm. protein; 79 gm. carbohydrate; 1.5 gm. fat; 5.5 mg. cholesterol; 5 gm. fiber; 130 mg. sodium

Percent of calories from protein: 12%; from carbohydrates: 84%; from fat: 3%

Exchange values: 2½ milk; 2 fruit

Select Bibliography

I have compiled a list of my favorite well-written and easily understood books and newsletters about nutrition and health for those of you who would like further information on the subject.

Books

Brody, Jane E. *Jane Brody's Good Food Book.* New York: Bantam Books, 1987.

Brody, Jane E. *Jane Brody's Nutrition Book.* New York: Bantam Books, 1988.

Clark, Nancy. *Sports Nutrition Guidebook.* Champaign, Illinois: Human Kinetics, 1990.

Connor, Sonja L., and William E. Connor. *The New American Diet.* New York: Simon and Schuster, 1986.

Dunne, Lavon J. *Nutrition Almanac.* New York: McGraw-Hill Publishing Company, 1990.

Goldbeck, Nikki, and David Goldbeck. *Nikki and David Goldbeck's American Wholefoods Cuisine.* New York: New American Library, 1983.

Kowalski, Robert E. *Cholesterol and Children.* New York: Harper and Row, 1988.

Kronhausen, Eberhard, and Phyllis Kronhausen. *Formula for Life.* New York: William Morrow and Company, 1989.

Herbert, Victor, and Genell J. Subak-Sharpe, eds. *The Mount Sinai School of Medicine Complete Book of Nutrition.* New York: St. Martin's Press, 1990.

Hausman, Patricia, and Judith Benn Hurley. *The Healing Foods.* New York: Dell Publishing, 1989.

Hausman, Patricia. *The Right Dose.* New York: Ballantine Books, 1990.

Margen, Sheldon, and the Editors of the University of California at Berkeley Wellness Letter. *The Wellness Encyclopedia of Food and Nutrition.* New York: Rebus, 1992.

Ornish, Dean. *Stress, Diet, and Your Heart.* New York: New American Library, 1984.

Simone, Charles B. *Cancer and Nutrition.* New York: McGraw Hill Book Company, 1983.

Newsletters

Center for Science in the Public Interest. *Nutrition Action Health Letters.* Washington D.C.: CSPI.

Editors of the University of California at Berkeley's Wellness Letter. *The University of California at Berkeley Wellness Letter.* New York: Health Letter Associates.

Environmental Nutrition, *The Newsletter of Diet, Nutrition and Health.* New York: Environmental Nutrition Inc.

Harvard Heart Letter. Boston: Harvard Medical School Health Publications Group.

Harvard Women's Health Watch. Boston: Harvard Medical School Health Publications Group.

Tufts University Diet and Nutrition Letters. Boston: Tufts Diet and Nutrition Letters.

Index

Cindy's crumb, 226-227
holiday harvest, 233-234
honey spice, 244-245
calcium, xx
California Grilled Fish, 212
California Turkey Burgers, 199
calorie consumption, xv
cancer, xv
Cancun Rice Salad, 76-77
Candied Carrots, 114
Cape Cod Shrimp, 15
carbohydrates, complex, xvi-xviii
cardiovascular disease, vii
carrot
    and potato soup, cream of, 64
    ginger soup, zesty, 57
    purée, parsnips and, 129
Carrots and Parsnips, 115
carrots,
    candied, 114
    Dijon glazed, 112
    nutrients in, 3
casserole, chick-pea, 99
catfish, baked, 211
cauliflower curry soup, Ruth's, 65
cheese
    and onion spread, Martha's, 21
    mousse, cranberry, 225
    spread, chutney, 17
cheese, macaroni and, 151
cherries, nutrients in, 3
Chick-Pea Casserole, 99
chick-pea soup, fabulous, 56
chick-peas and rice, Spanish, 103
Chicken Meatballs, 16
Chicken Melba, 187-188
Chicken Stir-Fry, 189-190
Chicken Stroganoff à la Vicki, 195
chicken
    dinner, all-in-one, 193-194
    fingers, Susan's, 206
    salad, grilled, 79
    sandwich, southwestern, 45
chicken,
    baked chile, 185
    curried, 186
    Dijon honey, 207

east Indian, 196-197
green taco, 192
grilled maple, 191
krispy baked, 200
lemon yogurt, 201
pretzeled, 203
roasted pepper, 198
salsa, 204
sea island, 205
chili, Mrs. Bowers' quick and easy, 171
Chip's Wacky Cake, 241
chips,
    sweet potato, 116
    tortilla, 28
chive salad dressing, creamy, 90
Chocolate Marshmallow Cookies, 231
chocolate cake, Kahlua, 235-236
cholesterol, vii, ix-xi, xii
chowder, chunky corn, 53
Chowdery Fish Stew, 213
Chunky Corn Chowder, 53
Chutney Cheese Spread, 17
Cindy's Crumb Cake, 226-227
Continental Vegetable Soup, 60
cookies,
    chocolate marshmallow, 231
    English biscuit, 242
cooking tips, 9-12
corn chowder, chunky, 53
corn pudding bread, creamy, 37
corn pudding, Dutch baked, 137
corn salad, black bean and, 75
crab, jiminy, 20
Cranapple Orange Bread, 34-35
Cranberry Cheese Mousse, 225
Cranberry Crisp, 228
cranberry crisp, easiest apple, 232
Cream of Carrot and Potato Soup, 64
Cream of Pumpkin Soup, 67
Cream of Zucchini Soup, 61
Creamy Chive Salad Dressing, 90
Creamy Corn Pudding Bread, 37
Creamy Green Pasta Sauce, 141
creamy salad dressing, sweet, 92
Creamy Spicy Tomato Sauce on Pasta, 161
creme, pear, 230

Index